MALCOLM X

As They Knew Him

Also by David Gallen:

Malcolm X: The FBI File
Introduction by Spike Lee
Commentary by Clayborne Carson
Edited by David Gallen

MALCOLM X

As They Knew Him

David Gallen

Carroll & Graf Publishers, Inc.
New York

Collection copyright © 1992 by David Gallen
Part I and Chronology copyright © 1992 by David Gallen and
Peter Skutches

The permissions listed on page 6 constitutes an extension of this
copyright page.

First Carroll & Graf edition 1992
Second hardcover printing 1992
Third paperback printing 1992

Carroll & Graf Publishers, Inc.
260 Fifth Avenue
New York, NY 10001

Library of Congress Cataloging-in-Publication Data

Gallen, David.
    Malcolm X: as they knew him / by David Gallen.—1st Carroll & Graf ed.
        p.   cm.
    Includes bibliographical references and index.
    ISBN 0-88184-851-4 : $21.95. — ISBN 0-88184-850-6 : $11.95
    1. X, Malcolm, 1925–1965. I. Title.
BP 223.Z8L5734   1992
320.5'4'092—dc20
[B]   92-6436
                                                                              CIP

Manufactured in the United States of America

Dedication

For Richard and Jill Gallen,
the only parents I ever wanted.

Acknowledgments

I would like to thank everybody who agreed to share their memories of Malcolm X with me, particularly James Farmer, Professor Kathryn Gibson, Peter Goldman, the late Alex Haley, Robert Haggins, Benjamin Karim, Charles Kenyatta, William Kunstler, Claude Lewis, Dick Schaap, Mike Wallace, and Alice Windom; all of whom were extremely generous with their time and spirit.

I also wish to thank Clayborne Carson, Professor of History at Stanford University, and his research team for the extensive data used to produce the chronology for this book.

I am, however, most grateful to Peter Skutches, who seems to be able to do just about anything.

To all of the above I offer my sincere gratitude. Your contributions have greatly improved the quality of this book.

—David Gallen

Permissions

The publisher gratefully acknowledges permission to reprint from the following:

The Estate of James Baldwin, for "Martin and Malcolm" (*Esquire,* April 1972).

Beacon Press, for the June 1963 interview between Dr. Kenneth B. Clark and Malcolm X, which initially appeared in *The Negro Protest* (Beacon Press, 1963).

Pierre Berton, for his television interview with Malcolm X (January 19, 1965).

Alex Haley, for his essay "Alex Haley Remembers" (*Essence,* November 1983).

Illinois University Press, for excerpts from *The Death and Life of Malcolm X* by Peter Goldman (Illinois University Press, 1973).

Maria Laurino, for her essay "Who Were the Killers?" which originally appeared in the *Village Voice* (February 26, 1985).

Claude Lewis, for his December 1964 interview with Malcolm X.

McGraw Hill Publishing Company, Inc., for excerpts from *Soul on Ice* by Eldridge Cleaver (McGraw Hill, 1968).

Playboy Enterprises, Inc., for the interview between Alex Haley and Malcolm X (*Playboy,* May 1963).

Sarah and Joe Rainey, for the interview between Joe Rainey and Malcolm X on WDAS Radio, Philadelphia (March 8, 1964).

WBAI Radio, for the interview between Richard Elman and Malcolm X (May 1962).

William Morris Agency, Inc., on behalf of the Estate of Robert Penn Warren, for the essay "Malcolm X: Mission and Meaning" by Robert Penn Warren, which originally appeared in *Yale Review* (December 1966); and for the interview between Robert Penn Warren and Malcolm X, which appeared initially in *Who Speaks for the Negro?* by Robert Penn Warren (Random House, 1965).

Contents

I

As They Knew Him
Oral Remembrances of Malcolm X
by David Gallen and Peter Skutches

II

Getting It On the Record
Conversations With Malcolm X

MALCOLM X

As They Knew Him

CHRONOLOGY

May 10, 1919	Earl Little, a Baptist preacher from Georgia, marries Louise Norton in Montreal. Soon after they set up residence in Philadelphia, Pennsylvania.
1922 or 1923	Earl and Louise move with their three small children to Omaha, Nebraska.
December 1924	According to *The Autobiography of Malcolm X*, a party of hooded Ku Klux Klansmen warns Louise, then pregnant with Malcolm, to get her family out of town, as her husband is stirring up trouble in the black community with his UNIA (Universal Negro Improvement Association) "back to Africa" preachings.
May 19, 1925	Malcolm Little is born at University Hospital in Omaha.
December 1926	The Little family moves to Milwaukee, Wisconsin.
January 1928– December 1929	Earl Little buys a house in Lansing, Michigan, where he continues to preach. On November 7 the Littles' home is set afire and burns to the ground; the family escapes unharmed. The next month Earl

Little builds a new home on the outskirts of East Lansing, Michigan.

August 1930

In Detroit, Michigan, the followers of W.D. Fard, an itinerant peddler and preacher known as "The Prophet," establish the first Temple of Islam.

September 28, 1931

Earl Little is run over by a streetcar and dies; rumor holds that he was murdered by the Black Legion, a local white supremacist group.

January 9, 1939

Louise Little suffers a complete nervous breakdown; she is declared legally insane and formally committed to the State Mental Hospital at Kalamazoo, where she remains for twenty-six years.

Spring 1939

Malcolm tells his favorite teacher that he wants to become a lawyer; he is told that "that's no realistic goal for a nigger."

August 1939

A social worker recommends that Malcolm be placed in a juvenile home; Judge John McClellan concurs.

May 1940–
February 1941

Malcolm is placed in various foster homes in the Lansing area.

February 1941

Moves to Boston; lives with his sister Ella.

1941–42

Holds a variety of jobs—among them shoe shining, dishwashing, and soda jerking—and works off and on for the New Haven Railroad; becomes involved with Boston's underworld fringe.

December 1942	Moves back to Michigan for about four months.
March 1943	Moves to New York City; again works for the New Haven Railroad.
October 25, 1943	U.S. Army finds Malcolm mentally disqualified for military service; he is classified 4F.
1943–44	Malcolm works intermittently on the railroad; known on the streets as Big Red, he also pushes dope, plays the numbers, peddles bootleg whiskey, and hustles. Under the stage name of Jack Carlton he works as a bar entertainer at a New York nightclub, The Lobster Pond, in July 1944. In October he returns to Boston for two months or so.
January 1945	Returns to Michigan after a holiday stint at a New York nightclub; works briefly as a busboy at the Mayfair Ballroom in East Lansing (he later claimed he danced there under the stage name of Rhythm Red) and as a waiter in a local night spot called Coral Gables.
August 1945	Moves back to New York; lives in Harlem.
December 1945	Embarks on Christmas season stealing binge in Boston with his

friend Bea and her sister Joyce Caragulian, Francis "Sonny" Brown, Kora Marderosian, and Malcolm Jarvis.

January 12, 1946   Attempts to reclaim a stolen watch he left for repair at a Boston jewelry store and is arrested; indicted for carrying firearms, larceny, and breaking and entering.

February 27, 1946   Begins serving prison term at Charlestown Prison, where he initiates his own reading program in the prison library.

January 10, 1947   Transferred to Concord Reformatory for fifteen months; during this time he is converted by a fellow inmate to the NOI (Nation of Islam) teachings of the Honorable Elijah Muhammad.

1948–52   Transferred to Norfolk Prison Colony in March 1948 and gains access to an excellent library; transferred back to Charlestown Prison two years later, on March 23, 1950, where he serves the balance of his sentence.

August 7, 1952   Paroled from state prison.

August 8, 1952   Travels to Detroit; in Inkster, Michigan, gets job as a furniture salesman in a store managed by his brother Wilfred.

August 31, 1952   Travels to Chicago, Illinois, with members of Detroit Temple No. 1

to hear the Honorable Elijah
Muhammad speak.

September 1952   Receives his *X* from the NOI. And
thus becomes Malcolm X.

January 1953   Leaves the furniture store for an
assembly line job at the Ford Motor
Company's Lincoln-Mercury
Division, which he leaves for the
Gar Wood factory in Detroit.

June 1953–
June 1954   Quits Gar Wood when named the
assistant minister at Detroit Temple
No. 1. Becomes first minister of
Boston Temple No. 11 in the winter
of 1953, then in March 1954 acting
minister of Philadelphia Temple No.
12; in June 1954 becomes minister
of New York Temple No. 7.

1956   Betty Sanders joins New York
Temple No. 7; she is renamed Betty
X.

April 14, 1957   NOI member Hinton Johnson is
beaten by New York police and
jailed; outside the 123rd Street
police station, where a contingent
of Muslims from Temple No. 7 has
gathered, Malcolm demands that
Johnson be taken to hospital.

January 1958   Telephones Betty Sanders with a
marriage proposal from a gas
station in Detroit on January 12;
she says yes. They are married two
days later by a justice of the peace
in Lansing. On January 19 the

	newlyweds drive back to New York and take up residence in East Elmhurst, Queens.
November 1958	A daughter, the first child of Betty and Malcolm, is born; she is named Attallah.
July 1959	A three-week tour as Elijah Muhammad's ambassador takes Malcolm to Egypt, Mecca, Iran, Syria, and Ghana.
July 13–17, 1959	On *News Beat* WNDT-TV Channel 13, New York, airs "The Hate That Hate Produced," a five-part report by Mike Wallace; it features Malcolm X, among others, and brings the Black Muslim movement to the attention of the general American public.
March 3, 1960	On the New York WMCA radio program *Pro and Con* William Kunstler interviews Malcolm and the Reverend William H. James on the topic "Is Black Supremacy the Answer?"
December 25, 1960	A second daughter, Qubilah, is born to Malcolm and Betty.
October 16, 1961	Malcolm appears on the NBC television program *Open Mind* with Morroe Berger, Kenneth B. Clark, Richard Haley and Constance B. Motley; the moderator is Eric P. Goldman, and the topic is "Where Is the American Negro Headed?"

1961	Participates in a one-hour dialogue with James Farmer, head of CORE (Congress of Racial Equality), on the *Barry Gray Show* on WMCA radio in New York.
April 27, 1962	NOI member Ronald Stokes is killed by police gunfire in Los Angeles mosque, and six other Muslims are wounded; the next day Malcolm is dispatched to Los Angeles by Elijah Muhammad. The following week Malcolm discusses the incident on New York's WBAI radio with Richard Elman.
December 1962	Rumors of adultery and six illegitimate children fathered by Elijah Muhammad cause numerous Muslims to leave Chicago Mosque No. 2; Malcolm speaks with three of Muhammad's former secretaries, all of whom have children by him.
1962	Ilyasah, a third daughter, is born to Betty and Malcolm.
May 1963	The *Playboy* interview, "a candid conversation with the militant major-domo of the black muslims," is published in the monthly magazine. Around the same time Malcolm is interviewed on television by James Baldwin.
June 1963	Interviewed on television by Kenneth B. Clark.
August 28, 1963	Attends the civil rights March on Washington as an observer;

comments that he can't understand why Negroes should become so excited about a demonstration "run by whites in front of a statue of a president who has been dead for a hundred years and who didn't like us when he was alive."

November 10, 1963	Delivers his most influential speech up to this time, "A Message to the Grass Roots," at the Northern Negro Grass Roots Leadership Conference in Detroit.
November 22, 1963	President John F. Kennedy is assassinated in Dallas, Texas.
December 1, 1963	At an NOI rally in New York Malcolm states that Kennedy "never foresaw that the chickens would come home to roost so soon," despite a directive from Elijah Muhammad that no Muslim minister comment on the assassination.
December 4, 1963	Suspended from his ministry by Elijah Muhammad for ninety days for his remark on the death of the president.
January 15, 1964	Visits Cassius Clay (Muhammad Ali) for a week's vacation at his fight camp in Miami, Florida; their friendship becomes increasingly strained thereafter.
March 8, 1964	Announces his break with Elijah Muhammad and the NOI as well as

his intent to organize a "black nationalist party" to heighten the political consciousness of Afro-Americans.

March 9, 1964	Interviewed by Joe Durso of the New York WNDT-TV Channel 13 news program *The World at Ten*.
March 10, 1964	Tells *Ebony* magazine that the Black Muslim leaders have "got to kill me. They can't afford to let me live. . . . I know where the bodies are buried. And if they press me, I'll exhume some."
March 10, 1964	The NOI sends Malcolm a certified letter requesting that he return all NOI property, including the house in East Elmhurst.
March 12, 1964	At the Park Sheraton Hotel in New York Malcolm holds a press conference to announce the formation of the MMI (Muslim Mosque, Incorporated).
March 20, 1964	Appears on Joe Rainey's phone-in radio show, *Listening Post*, broadcast out of Philadelphia, Pennsylvania, on station WDAS.
March 26, 1964	Meets Martin Luther King, Jr., face to face, for the first and only time, after a King news conference in the U.S. Capitol.
April 8, 1964	The NOI files eviction proceedings against Malcolm.

April 13– May 21, 1964	Malcolm travels abroad; under the name of Malik El-Shabazz, he flies first to Frankfurt, then on to Cairo and Jedda.
April 20, 1964	Writes of his pilgrimage to Mecca in a letter: states that many white people he met during the pilgrimage displayed a spirit of unity and brotherhood that provided him a new, positive insight into race relations; in Islam, he now feels, lies the power to overcome racial antagonism and to obliterate it from the heart of white America.
April 21–30, 1964	Honored as a guest of the state by Saudi Arabia's Prince Faisal.
April 30– May 6, 1964	Flies to Beirut to speak at Sudanese Cultural Center, then back to Cairo; travels by rail to Alexandria, where he boards airplane to Nigeria.
May 6–10, 1964	Appears on various Nigerian radio and television programs; speaks at the University of Ibadan.
May 10–17, 1964	Tours and lectures in Ghana; addresses the Ghanian parliament on May 14 and on May 15 has audience with President Kwame Nkrumah, which Malcolm describes as his highest honor not only in Ghana but in all of Africa.
May 17–19, 1964	Flies to Monrovia, Liberia, then to Dakar, Senegal, and from there to

Morocco; spends his thirty-ninth birthday in Algiers.

May 21, 1964	Returns to New York.
June 9, 1964	Interviewed on *The Mike Wallace News Program.*
June 28, 1964	Announces the formation of the OAAU (Organization of Afro-American Unity), which will be committed to doing ''whatever is necessary to bring the Negro struggle from the level of civil rights to the level of human rights.''
July 9–November 24, 1964	Travels abroad; flies to Cairo via London under the name of Malik El-Shabazz.
July 17, 1964	Attends African Summit Conference as representative of the OAAU; appeals to the delegates of the thirty-four African nations to bring the cause of the twenty-two million black people in the United States before the United Nations.
September 1, 1964	In New York, Civil Court Judge Maurice Wahl issues order that Malcolm X must vacate residence in East Elmhurst by January 31, 1965.
September 12, 1964	''I'm Talking To You, White Man: An Autobiography by Malcolm X'' is printed in the *Saturday Evening Post.*

September– November 1964	Malcolm tours Africa: by mid October he has visited eleven countries, talked with eleven heads of state, and addressed most of their parliaments; for another five weeks he will continue his tour "to better acquaint himself with the problems facing the continent," as he says in a speech in Lagos.
November 24, 1964	Returns to New York.
November 30, 1964	Flies to London for an Oxford Union debate on December 3; he speaks for the motion that "extremism in the defense of liberty is no vice, moderation in the pursuit of justice is no virtue."
December 1964	Requests interview with Claude Lewis, then of the *New York Post*, to get something "on the record."
1964	A fourth daughter, Gamilah, is born.
January 19, 1965	Interviewed by Pierre Berton on his television show in Toronto, Canada.
February 5, 1965	Flies to London, where he addresses the First Congress of the Council of African Organizations on February 8.
February 9, 1965	Flies to Paris, but is refused entry by French government officials; returns to London and on February 13 flies back to New York.

February 14, 1965 | Malcolm's house in East Elmhurst is firebombed in the early morning hours.

Malcolm flies to Detroit to deliver an address at the First Annual Dignity Projection and Scholarship Award ceremony sponsored by the Afro-American Broadcasting and Recording Company at the Ford Auditorium; it is Malcolm's last major speech.

February 18, 1965 | Malcolm's family is evicted.

February 20, 1965 | In a telephone conversation with Alex Haley Malcolm says that "the more I keep thinking about this thing, the things that have been happening lately, I'm not at all sure it's the Muslims. I know what they can do, and what they can't, and they can't do some of the stuff recently going on. . . . The more I keep thinking about what happened to me in France, I think I'm going to quit saying it's the Muslims."

After an OAAU business meeting in the evening, Malcolm refuses his friend Earl Grant's invitation to spend the night at his apartment: "You have a family," says Malcolm. "I don't want anyone hurt on my account. I always knew it would end like this."

February 21, 1965 | At 3:10 P.M., just after he has begun to address an OAAU rally at the

Audubon Ballroom, Malcolm is shot several times; a black male later identified as Talmadge Hayer (a.k.a. Thomas Hagan) is arrested. Malcolm is pronounced DOA at Vanderbilt Clinic, Columbia-Presbyterian Hospital.

February 22, 1965   Elijah Muhammad denies that he or the NOI had anything to do with the slaying of Malcolm X.

February 27, 1965   Malcolm's body is moved from the Unity Funeral Home in Harlem to Bishop Alvin S. Child's Faith Temple Church of God in Christ at 1763 Amsterdam Avenue for the funeral services, which are presided over by playwright-actor Ossie Davis; approximately fifteen hundred people attend the services, five hundred of them outside the church itself. Early in the afternoon Malcolm is buried at Ferncliff Cemetery, Hartsdale.

March 11, 1965   A grand jury indicts Talmadge Hayer (22), Norman 3X Butler (26), and Thomas 15X Johnson (29) for the murder of Malcolm X.

November 5, 1965   *The New York Times* heralds the publication of *The Autobiography of Malcolm X*, written with Alex Haley, as "an eloquent statement."

1965   Betty Shabazz gives birth to twin daughters, Malaak and Malikah.

January 12, 1966   The trial for the murder of Malcolm
                    X opens.

March 2, 1966   Hayer testifies that he and three
                    accomplices were hired to kill
                    Malcolm X; he states that neither
                    Butler nor Johnson was implicated
                    in the slaying.

March 11, 1966   Hayer, Butler, and Johnson are
                    convicted of murder in the first
                    degree.

April 14, 1966   New York Supreme Court Judge
                    Charles Marks sentences all three
                    defendants to life imprisonment.

I

As They Knew Him

Oral Remembrances of Malcolm X

by David Gallen and Peter Skutches

As They Knew Him

Just after 3:00 P.M. on February 21, 1965, a mild midwinter Sunday in Harlem, Malcolm X had stepped up to the podium in the Audubon Ballroom to address a public rally when his customary greeting, *"Assalaam alaikum,"* was interrupted first by an outburst from the back of the audience, apparently a heated argument between two men, and then, several seconds later, not fifteen feet away from the stage, by several blasts of gunfire. Malcolm X fell. He was dead.

That particular Sunday Kathy Gibson, who rarely missed an opportunity to hear Malcolm X speak, failed to make it to the Audubon. She had been at a party late the night before, and she recalls that her teenaged nephew Calvin had "taken the Amsterdam Avenue bus uptown from his church on 147th Street and had seen the commotion outside the Audubon, and he came to my house immediately and he said, 'Malcolm has been assassinated.' God, I jumped out of my bed; I screamed and I was really just beside myself. I called my girlfriend Leola who used to attend with me, and the next week I wore a black dress every single day. That was my way of mourning him."

Malcolm's personal photographer, Robert Haggins, remembers being "late getting to the meeting that Sunday. When I finally got there, I was going up those long stairs at the Audubon Ballroom and Malcolm was on a stretcher coming down, and when he got close to me I could see his mouth was opened, his eyes were open, and I knew that he was dead."

Up in Providence, Rhode Island, C. Eric Lincoln, a professor and author of *The Black Muslims in America,* was lecturing at Brown University that afternoon. A few days before he had asked Malcolm to come to Brown to speak to a group of undergraduates the next Tuesday, and Malcolm had said, " 'I tell you, Professor Lincoln, I may be dead on Tuesday.' I said, 'Come on, Malcolm, cut the bullshit; come on up and talk to these kids,' and he said, 'You know I'll come, but I want you to hear me: I may be dead on Tuesday.' Then I realized that he was serious, so I said,

'Malcolm, if that is true, why don't you go to the police? And he said, and I quote, 'They already know it. But, okay, tell your kids that I'll be up there on Tuesday if I am alive.' Then Sunday—that was Thursday—on Sunday I was lecturing at a big podium and in the middle of my lecture someone handed me a note that said Malcolm X had been assassinated."

"I was at home in New Jersey," recalls journalist Claude Lewis, "and a flash came on television. My wife came running in and she started yelling, 'Malcolm! They've shot Malcolm!' I said, 'You are kidding.' 'No,' she said: 'He hasn't died yet; they haven't announced if he has died yet.' I thought, God! I've got to get to somebody. I asked if Betty [Shabazz] was all right, and she told me there had been no mention of Betty. I had a sick feeling that he was going to die and within an hour he was dead. So, I thought, this is the end of the best part of the movement."

For African-American historian John Henrik Clarke, the assassination of Malcolm X extinguished "the brightest light we had produced in the twentieth century, and our movement was set back a generation." That movement had to a large extent been defined by Malcolm's words—words that exalted the blackness of African-Americans and raised their consciousness not just to their civil rights but to their human rights as well.

In 1965 Ralph Wiley was thirteen years old and growing up in the Mississippi River Delta. To the teenaged Wiley, Malcolm X was a name only, his death merely "a news item," but Malcolm was eventually to become for Wiley "pure rhetoric." In that rhetoric, sportswriter Wiley says today, lay his salvation: "The rhetoric is my relationship to him. I have no personal memories of him; I have no personal feelings about his conduct. What I have is the fact that he saved my mental life."

Assassins' bullets silenced the man. The words, however, had already been spoken. Another generation of African-Americans has been born since that mild February Sunday afternoon in 1965, and Malcolm's words now speak to them, vitally, of their pride and dignity and power and beauty. Malcolm's words still hold their fire, perhaps because he was, as Benjamin Karim, formerly Malcolm's trusted assistant Benjamin Goodman, describes him, "a man ahead of his time." In Karim's view of Malcolm X, "people around him didn't understand the magnitude of what he was trying to do. He was too advanced for us, or his thinking was; we weren't ready for him. Perhaps now we are, but not then."

From the beginning of his public career in 1953 up to its untimely end in 1965 Malcolm X consistently addressed the plight of his people; he spoke, as he repeatedly said, for twenty-two million black Americans. He spoke with sincerity, he spoke with passion. He had the gift of the griot, and he seems often to have spoken with the voice of the prophet. "He was a prophetic figure," says Peter Goldman, author of *The Death and Life of Malcolm X,* "but I don't mean that to be taken too literally. He wasn't Nostradamus; he wasn't predicting events. He conveyed a sense of the direction in which events would flow and I think a lot of what he taught us has come true. Which isn't necessarily happy for us."

The words of Malcolm X contribute richly to the oral tradition of African-American history. In the words of people who knew Malcolm intimately or met him professionally, of people whose lives were dramatically touched or radically altered by him, the significance of Malcolm X to that history continues to grow.

Early in 1961 a demonstration protesting the assassination of the Congolese prime minister Patrice Lumumba attracted thousands of Harlem blacks to the United Nations. It also drew harsh criticism from the national black leadership. Eager to learn the Black Muslim position on the demonstration, three of its organizers— Rosa Guy, Abby Lincoln, and Maya Angelou—arranged to meet Malcolm X two days later at his temple restaurant in Harlem.

Writer and professor of American studies Maya Angelou recalls her first impression of the minister of New York Temple No. 7: "Malcolm was very young, very handsome, very dignified, very contained, very much his own man. He was very gracious to us, very courteous. We came into the restaurant," she continues. "He stood. He had some men with him. He excused them and invited us to sit at the table with him. He held a chair for the woman who was sitting next to him and we sat and had tea, bean pie—it was about 11:00 in the morning—and he listened to us. We were very excited because we had expected maybe fifty people to come downtown at our request and instead thousands of people had come down from Harlem and rushed into the United Nations and upset the General Assembly and screamed, and then we went to the Belgian Embassy and Consulate and surrounded it and so forth; so we were very excited about our success. Malcolm listened to us talk, and then he told us that *The New York Times* had already phoned to find out his response and he had said that no, he did not think it was communists who had initiated the demonstration, that black people did not need communists to tell them they were unhappy or ill treated, that they found support in African connections. And he encouraged us to continue, but he said that the Muslims would not join us because Muslims do not march in that way, but that he would not put us down either, that none of the NOI would put us down. He said that privately he was proud of women who supported him and stood up with courage. He just said all the right things, and we were really impressed with his dignity, intelligence, and good looks."

Dignity, intelligence, nobility, graciousness, warmth, courage, compassion, fearlessness, sincerity, cunning, imagination, charisma: such qualities of mind and character today stand first in the memories of those who knew Malcolm X. During his lifetime they constituted the strength of character that so readily inspired security, confidence, pride, and devotion in his admirers.

Not only was Malcolm "someone who held you in awe" to CUNY professor Kathryn Gibson, but also "it was like you knew you had a big brother at home who could knock down anybody who messed with you; he was the protector." Ralph Wiley, who knew Malcolm only through his words, found in him a surrogate father. He observes that Malcolm "like all of us, was a greatly flawed man, no doubt; how could he not be. No doubt he died horribly, and there will always be a debate about whether he was ridiculous or violent. All I know is that without him I doubt very seriously that I would be able to do the things that I do today. So I can't complain. It's like having a father who's a tough disciplinarian or a Saturday night drinker or something; he is still your father, no matter what. I don't think that's too much of a stretch either, I really don't, because I consider myself a well-rounded man and I never knew my father."

Journalist and sportscaster Dick Schaap remembers Malcolm's imposing presence: "I don't remember how tall he was, but you had the feeling he was six foot five or six. He towered. I remember him walking like a king. And acting like a king." John Henrik

Clarke remarks too that "in another time and place he could have been a king, could have made a nation and could have destroyed one." For many, like Kathryn Gibson and the people she knew, in New York Malcolm was "just the king."

Malcolm has also been compared to prophets, and to saints and martyrs. To James Small, bodyguard to Malcolm's sister Ella Collins, he was "the next thing to God"; and civil rights attorney William Kunstler points out that when "an internal memo from J. Edgar Hoover said we have to prevent at all costs the rising of a black messiah," the FBI chief could well have been thinking of Malcolm X.

The man can get lost in the metaphors, but, as university professor Michael Thelwell observes, Malcolm's own ministry made him just that—"a living metaphor." The message of Elijah Muhammad to the Lost-Found Nation of Islam was "couched in starkly fundamentalist terms," Thelwell explains, "in extremes and stark contrasts—black versus white; sin versus righteousness; utter depravity versus pure holiness. The Messenger [Elijah Muhammad] was sent to reclaim and uplift the black race, which was lost in moral darkness and abysmal degradation." As incomplete or historically inaccurate as this vision of the black race in America may have been, "in a fundamentalist logic," Thelwell points out, "the degradation and depravity had to be extreme— total, really—so that the redemption, which required an unnatural discipline, sacrifice, and total obedience, could appear all the more glorious and miraculous. Which is why Malcolm, as the living evidence of the fulfillment of this promise—the complete transformation and remaking of the black nation—had to be shown as emerging out of a previous condition of unrelieved depravity." Prior to Malcolm's conversion to Islam he was not, Thelwell asserts, "the moral monster of Muslim legend. That was dramatic emphasis. Because, if in the Messenger all things are possible and if the message could redeem and reform this monster of depravity into a disciplined, clean-living, exemplary respecter of self, God, and people, what could it not do for the entire race? Malcolm redeemed was the word incarnate, the message made flesh, the living metaphor and exemplar of the redemption of an entire race."

Still, "the fact," according to John Henrik Clarke, "that he had come up from the lower depths and worked his way out of the mire, that he'd been a crook, he'd been a pimp, he'd been a procurer of women and abuser of women, and he sat down and thought his way out of it," cannot be overlooked; to do so would be to ignore the makings of Malcolm's especial character.

Cartoonist Elombe Braath, who worked in the early 1960s for the radical black New York tabloid *Citizen-Call,* notes that "people go from those who demonize Malcolm—his enemies—to those people who do just the opposite; they try to make a myth, they mythologize and idealize him. Malcolm was a man, a human being, just like the rest of us." Braath, however, would further argue that "Malcolm X was a great man, but in order to become great like him what you've got to do is go through all the mistakes he made, and that's crazy."

Of course, Malcolm's errors alone did not make him great, but his successes cannot be divorced from the experience that shaped the man behind the ministry, image, myth, or metaphor. *The Autobiography of Malcolm X,* written with Alex Haley and published in 1965, after Malcolm's death, recounts much of that experience and introduces us to the man. Alex Haley, who had interviewed Malcolm in depth for both *Reader's Digest* and *Playboy* before collaborating with him on the autobiography, knew the man. Over a period of two years, in more than fifty interviews, Haley had the opportunity to observe the Malcolm of the tabloid headlines outside the public arena, outside the sound booths of radio stations and beyond the hot glare of the lamps in television studios, away from the podium and the microphone. In Haley's recollection of that time lie glimpses of another Malcolm, the Malcolm inside the metaphors.

Throughout the period of his collaboration with Alex Haley, Malcolm's days left him little time for himself. Nor did his nights; Haley remembers "how he would stay up so late night after night, how he would go out and try to help recruit somebody who was teetering—some Christian black, a Baptist or Catholic or Methodist, who was teetering on the edge of leaving their church to come to the Nation of Islam. Malcolm would go visit these people late at night—I know I said late; I'm not talking eleven or twelve but, you know, eight thirty, nine o'clock—and he would tell me often about how he had done that. This would, of course, be on the nights he was not with me. It's just one example that he really cared about the individuals he was talking to, trying to guide them to the light of Islam, and he would speak of them in such a warm way."

On the nights Malcolm did spend with Haley at his house on Grove Street in New York's Greenwich Village he would often arrive tired and harried, perhaps overextended, tense. Haley's friend and researcher, George Sims, might also be there: "We'd grown up together in Henning, Tennessee, our hometown," Haley reminisces. "George had always been a heavy reader—as a kid he used to read the labels on tin cans." Libby's, Heinz, and Campbell eventually gave way to *Othello, Hamlet,* and *Macbeth;* George became a Shakespeare buff. "Well, nobody knew it," Haley continues, "certainly I didn't know it and George didn't know it, but so was Malcolm. One night he just kind of dropped something like 'Didn't Shakespeare say it?'—whatever it was—and George, well, he rose to that like a trout to a fly and said something like Shakespeare also said whatever. And George and Malcolm were suddenly almost like bonded in their love for Shakespeare. After that almost every night that Malcolm would come down to my place— sometimes he'd had a day that just left him angry as he could be, and he was uptight and he was mad—he and George would get into something about Shakespeare or some of the other people way back in literature and that would temper Malcolm. His anger would kind of go away and he would become more . . . I guess, more malleable, from an interviewer's point of view. And after he had talked long enough, I would say, you know, 'Look, fellas, we got to talk about Mr. Malcolm here,' and then I would start questioning him. But that little session they would have at the outset of Malcolm's arrival each evening was most helpful; it just kind of cleared the air, eased what might otherwise have been a lot of tension."

Haley also recalls a particular evening in November of 1962 or 1963 when Malcolm was indeed feeling some of the burden of his days. "I happened to come upon the fact that the next day was his eldest daughter Attallah's birthday," says Haley, "and I just knew Malcolm, as busy as he was and as guilty as he was about not spending much time with his family and what not—he just felt awful about that, and he practically revered his wife, Sister Betty, and she just went on taking care of things at home while he was away—I just knew he'd forgot. So that afternoon before the day I knew was the birthday for Attallah I just went uptown and I bought a large brown doll with all kinds of little frou-frou around her frock, with ruffles and frills and so forth, and I put it into a closet. And Malcolm came that night and we had our regular interview, and when he was getting ready to leave, I just sort of quietly said—I just went to the closet and I said—'You know, Brother Malcolm, I was just happening to be looking at my notes and I noticed that tomorrow is the birthday for Attallah, and I know as busy as you are you just simply haven't had time to stop and pick her up something. I knew you'd want to, so I got this for you,' and then I handed him the doll. That was as close as I ever saw Malcolm to tears, as he took the doll. He didn't say much of anything, but I knew he was deeply moved. And then he went on out." (Incidentally, Attallah is also Haley's godchild, and she still has the doll.)

Invariably, though, no matter how busy or preoccupied or frazzled Malcolm might be by the time he got to Grove Street, which was usually about nine o'clock at night, Haley notes that "he would instantly pick up the phone and call his wife; he would sort of review the day with her and say little pleasantries to her and ask about the children. And then he would stay with me until about 11:30, something of that nature, when again he would call his wife and tell her that he was on the way to traveling home in the blue Oldsmobile."

Whether Malcolm was driving downtown in his blue Oldsmobile or traveling on the west coast of Africa, his family, it would seem, never strayed far from his mind. Maya Angelou speaks of late nights in Ghana in May 1964, quiet times at the end of busy days when Malcolm would sit with her and her friends Julian Mayfield and Alice Windom, "and he would have tea—he would be gracious too, not putting us down for having brandy and ginger—and he would talk at length about Betty and about the children. He really was a family man. In other circumstances, if racism and other kinds of cruelties were not operating against him, he would have been the typical family man, having the job and looking after the wife and children and, being a religious man, being in a church or a temple, whatever. That is really who Malcolm was, I think."

"He was very loving toward his family; that stood out the most with me," affirms James Booker, formerly a staff reporter for New York's *Amsterdam News*, "that he was a very gentle family man who loved his children and his wife."

Malcolm's concern for his family also stands out in James Small's memories of Malcolm's brother Wilfred and his sister Ella. "Malcolm's family," he says, "didn't view him as a big shot. They loved him and remembered him liking to sit around home eating big bowls of ice cream or telling jokes rather than giving lectures at podiums, at which he was brilliant. The world sees the side of him at a podium; they don't see the side of him worrying about his home and his family, but that was more of the real man than the one who had to go out and give lectures—that was work, only an aspect of his life."

Malcolm's close friend and former assistant Benjamin Karim worked with Malcolm for eight years. He stood behind Malcolm at the podium, but away from the podium, "away from the public," the Malcolm that Karim remembers with warmth and laughter "was very humorous. He would tell jokes; he would sit down and eat banana splits after banana splits and he would discuss things just like you and I would, so that you saw the human side of the man as opposed to the idol that the public made of him."

John Henrik Clarke too remembers a less public Malcolm— and again a man with a penchant for ice cream. "There is a restaurant still in existence called 22 *West;* we would meet in the back of 22 *West* and all Malcolm would have was one cup of coffee, although he might sometimes sneak in three if we were having a long conversation. He rarely ate away from home, and there he ate his traditional one meal a day. I learned from his wife that sometimes in the one meal at home he had a tendency to overdo it because he loved ice cream and his daughters indulged him, and so did she."

At that one meal a day, even before the ice cream, Malcolm rarely lacked appetite. "On Sundays sometimes he would invite us [the assistant ministers] over to his house. It was almost like a family, very close," recalls Benjamin Karim, and "we would have about eight or nine appetizers, like Muslims have, and by the time you finished the appetizers, really, you were about full. But Malcolm, Malcolm would take—he could eat!—Malcolm would take an egg, a deviled egg, and I mean he'd take one bite and it was gone! And he always drank a quart of milk with every meal." On one of those Sundays, as Karim tells it, "we were all sitting around the table and Betty came in, and she had an attitude—yeah, I mean she was cool, Betty's very cool; you know, she had an attitude. So she walked in and she brought the glass and his quart of milk and she set it on the table, and she turned around and walked away. And Malcolm never looked around, and when she was about to cross the threshold into the next room, he said, 'Pour it,' you know, and she turned around and she poured it, but it was . . . it was . . ." It was "a little while after they were married," adds Karim. It is surmised that she did pour it for him and not on him.

On April 14, 1957, Nation of Islam member Hinton Johnson was praying in a Harlem street. When a police officer from the 123rd Street station ordered him to move on, Johnson refused. The policeman began beating him, hitting him on the head, and then placed him under arrest. "In the meantime," as Benjamin Karim recounts the incident that introduced him to Malcolm X and the NOI, "some lady there in Harlem ran down to the mosque and told Malcolm that one of his followers had been struck in the head by a policeman and taken to jail. Malcolm and a small group of Muslims went to the precinct to have this man taken to the hospital. The police officer denied the man was there. So Malcolm left and came back with a much larger group of people—matter of fact, hundreds of people—and finally they did take Johnson to the hospital where he was operated on by Doctor Matthews, a neurosurgeon. But thousands and thousands of people had gathered in front of that hospital, Sydenham Hospital, in Harlem. In the meanwhile groups of Muslims were encircling police officers, and Malcolm told the police commissioner that if Johnson died he wouldn't be responsible for what would happen to those police officers that were encircled by all those Muslims. Fortunately, Doctor Matthews came out and told Malcolm that the man would live."

The Hinton Johnson incident brought Malcolm wider public attention in Harlem, and the following Sunday Harlemites flocked to hear Brother Minister Malcolm speak at Temple No. 7. Benjamin Karim was among them. "I heard him one time," says Karim, "and from that Sunday in 1957 until February 21, 1965, I was with him."

Malcolm's sermon that Sunday altered Karim's life. And his diet. "Malcolm spoke about pork," Karim recalls, "spoke a lecture on the swine, and let me tell you something, that night I was invited to dinner with a friend of mine and he had pigs' feet—this was after Malcolm had finished speaking—which I used to eat because I was raised that way, but to show you how subliminal things are, things that you think are gone, I put a little piece of it in my mouth and it almost burned. I sat at that table—I had never had any problems eating pork—and I couldn't spit it out in front of these people—we were raised together—but I couldn't swallow it either, so I made an excuse to go to the bathroom and I spit it out and after that I vomited all over the place. I came back and told them I was sick and I didn't want anything to eat. That was the last time I have eaten any pork—that was 1957!—and I tell you Malcolm just had an effect on people that was astounding."

Certainly, Malcolm's effect on Charles Kenyatta was dramatic. In 1952 or 1953 they were working together at a construction site in Detroit. At the time Malcolm was also teaching at Detroit Temple No. 1, and he invited Kenyatta to attend one Sunday. So "I went to the mosque that Sunday and listened to him teach Islam, and then," says Kenyatta surprisingly, "I went back home and lost my family." Malcolm had evidently delivered another of his vehement lectures on the swine, and Kenyatta had indeed listened. "I had been to Windsor, Ontario, as people from Detroit go over to Windsor to buy food, and I had bought a bunch of pork chops and a lot of swine, and when I went back home I threw it all out." He then lost his family, Kenyatta explains, "because my wife by that time kind of thought I had lost my mind. . . . No one could teach about the swine like Malcolm could."

The responses of both Karim and Kenyatta to Malcolm's lectures on the swine attest vividly to the possible impact of Malcolm's oratory. The already powerful effect of Malcolm's rhetorical style was heightened further by his physical stature. Malcolm at the podium stood tall; he seemed, in the words of Kathryn Gibson, a "very giant," and "he was so commanding" the first time she heard him speak that she listened "enthralled." She remembers particularly his "very direct look" and the "down-to-earth, unstilted manner" in which he spoke, a simple but forceful manner that especially appealed to her as a young person. "It was at the time when hundreds of kids were involved in boycotts in the South," she recalls, "and they were being hit by police and hosed down, and the dogs were set on them, and it just seemed like a terrible thing to do. I was young myself, and it just seemed like nobody was defending these kids. And I remember Malcolm using the analogy of a snake: if a snake bites your child, you don't go out looking for that snake; you go out looking for any snake that you can see, because any snake has the same potential as the snake that bit your child. I remember him saying that, and it really stuck with me."

In the early 1960s poet and professor Sonia Sanchez was working in Harlem with New York CORE. For the most part she accepted the media image of Malcolm as a brash, obstructive racist either to be dismissed or feared—until she actually heard him speak, and he was "saying out loud what African-Americans had been saying all along behind closed doors, but he was willing to say it out loud, and in that way he was willing to release blacks from the fear that had enveloped them for so many years, because there he was saying it on TV and all over the streets of Harlem." After that, says Sanchez, "things began to change for me. I began to go to my friends saying Malcolm said this and Malcolm said that. And they said, 'But, Sonia, you know Malcolm is a racist; how can you talk like that about him?' But the point is, you know how sometimes you are in the house and the sunlight comes in and you rush to pull down the shade, but before you pull down the shade the light comes in anyway; that's what had happened to me, standing on that island there on Seventh Avenue: the light had come in. And I began to listen to everything that he was saying. You had to hear him and see him to be moved; you couldn't hear Malcolm and not be moved. You had to be in a crowd of people when he spoke; there was such electricity."

Kathryn Gibson felt something like that electricity pass through Malcolm's audiences at the Audubon. Malcolm, she recalls, "could speak for hours and I never saw him use a note. And he never lost track of his point, even though people would jump up and yell—it was like the Baptist church, if you know the Baptist churches; there is this thing in our community, in our church, where you respond to the preacher, and as he is speaking you say, 'yes' or 'make it plain' or 'teach'—you talk back—and people did that constantly and Malcolm never lost track. It just sort of kept on pumping him and kept him going. He was so very dynamic. I don't know anyone who equals him, I really don't."

"The exciting time was to see him with a crowd; the students just loved him," says Alice Windom of Malcolm's visit to Ghana in May 1964. Huge crowds had gathered wherever Malcolm agreed to speak, but none larger or more receptive than the assemblage of enthusiastic students at the University of Ghana in Legon. There, evidently, the chemistry was perfect: "He was theirs and they were his," says Windom. "They fell in love with each other." The Ghanaian students may well have felt the hold of what Windom describes as Malcolm's "compelling, strong personality. He was photogenic, and that never hurt anybody," she continues, "and a spellbinding orator and a person of tremendous integrity and very devoted to the liberation of the African people."

That tremendous integrity and Malcolm's devotion to the plight of his people as well as his commanding stature, his proud stance, and his formidable oratorical skills inextricably fused the man with the message: "It wasn't just the message, it was the *messenger and* the message," avers Kathryn Gibson. The messenger, in Windom's phrase "spectacular and spellbinding," captured the imagination and held the attention of his audiences from Lagon to London to Los Angeles. Benjamin Karim also speaks of people, "thousands of people," who gathered at outdoor rallies to hear Malcolm X. Their concentration intense, they would "stare so long—and this is the truth—that evidently, the liquid on the eyeball must have dried up, and they would begin to blink their eyelids very rapidly, as though they were waking up from some sort of a hypnotic spell," but in a moment they would again appear to be mesmerized. "He had the ability to hold the minds of thousands of people," says Karim, "even in the rain; I have seen thousands of people stand in the rain and listen to Malcolm, and nobody would leave."

In Ghana, at Temple No. 7 or the Audubon in Harlem, at the Oxford Union, at Harvard and Howard, at outdoor rallies and in the streets—like Robert Haggins, they were ready for him.

Robert Haggins, in 1960 a staff photographer and reporter for the New York *Citizen-Call,* arrived early at the restaurant on 116th Street and Lenox Avenue for his interview with Malcolm X. He had been sitting there maybe five minutes when, as Haggins tells it, "this tall gentleman with a briefcase came in. His entourage following him, he came over to my table and said, 'Are you Mr. Haggins? I'm Malcolm X.' I said, 'Fine,' and pulled out my pad. 'What is your last name?' I said. And he said, 'That's it, X.' And I said, 'How did you get a name like X? X must be an initial. What is the whole name, what is the rest?' He said, 'You want me to give you my slave name?' 'Slave name?' I said. And he said, 'Yes. I dropped my slave name. That name was Malcolm Little, but I don't carry a slave name anymore. I carry X. I carry X because I don't know my real last name.' Then we got into an exchange, one that was going to change my life forever. We started talking about how we got our names and how ridiculous it was for me to carry the name of Haggins or any other English or Irish name when I was not ethnically either and how people were bought and slaved like cattle and their names changed to reflect who owned them. I had never had anybody awaken me like that before in my life. . . . Malcolm X was, I think, the realization of everything that was recessed in my mind. I was ready for Malcolm. I didn't know it at first, but I was."

Malcolm too was ready. In the restaurant, mosque, ballroom, street, or lecture hall, he rarely missed the opportunity to teach. And like the best teachers he was equally willing and always eager to learn. "He was the fastest learner of anybody I've ever known," states John Henrik Clarke, who was "his history man—if you want something on history, you turn to me—and once he had read it and analyzed it, he knew more than I knew about it." Malcolm's passion for learning is reflected in what Benjamin Karim perceives as three of the things Malcolm loved most: "truth, knowledge, I mean knowledge just for its own sake, and teaching"—and according to Karim, "the thing that he hated most was ignorance."

Ignorance, certainly, was not tolerated by Malcolm at Temple No. 7. Karim, like all the assistant ministers, soon found himself attending a public speaking class in which "he gave us assignments that, believe it or not, would make a Harvard student put his books down and leave. We had to read *The New York Times* daily or the old *Tribune,* either one of those papers, and the London *Times* and *The Peking Review,* which was published in China; then there was a newspaper out of Indonesia and many papers from other countries. We would read them along with our *Time* magazine and *Newsweek,* and we watched the news, and with all this we studied geography too. And history, the history of the events in the news and how it led to a particular thing that was going on at the moment. Malcolm was more of a teacher than he was the man the public thought he was."

"He was always very witty," says Karim, "and he always had an answer for questions; it may not have been the answer that you were looking for, but most times he would answer, and sometimes he would answer in a way that you would have to figure out what he meant by that." For an instance Karim offers Malcolm's answer to a question a Muslim brother once asked Karim. " 'What is the strongest urge in a human being?' he asked me. So I thought a minute and I said perhaps the urge to reproduce himself, the sex urge; but I also said that I would ask Brother Minister—we never called him Malcolm, we always called him Brother Minister or Brother Minister Malcolm—and when I asked him, do you know what he told me? He said the strongest urge in a human being is the urge to eat. He said to take a man's food from him for a week, then bring in the most beautiful woman you can find and strip her, and then bring in a plate of lamb chops and peas and mashed potatoes and set it in front of him—and then see which one he takes a piece of first. I soon saw the picture."

Any occasion or encounter might prompt a lesson from Malcolm. "We were going to Bridgeport one night," Karim recalls, "and this man came up, obviously a person who begs for money to buy something to drink, you know, wine or something—I think we were on St. Nicholas Avenue or Seventh Avenue—and he said, 'Mr. X, could you give me fifty cents so I could get a bowl of bean soup?' Because at that time fifty cents could buy a big bowl of bean soup and a big piece of corn bread, and that's a meal, or an even bigger bottle of wine. So he gave the guy fifty cents, right? So we were sitting in the car—we don't support wine habits, we don't give people money to buy alcohol, wine, or drugs and all that—and everybody was quiet, and Brother Minister gave a smile 'cause he knew this man didn't want anything to eat. So we're driving down Seventh Avenue, and nobody's talking, nobody's saying, 'Brother Minister, why did you give the man the fifty cents? You know the man is not going to buy any food with that money.' Nobody said anything. Then all of a sudden he said, after about twenty blocks on our way to Bridgeport, 'I know what you're thinking,' and we said, 'No, Brother Minister, no, we're not thinking anything,' and he said, 'Yes, you are.' He said, 'I don't know if that man is really hungry, if he really wants something to eat or something to drink, but had I not given him the fifty cents, it would have been on my conscience that perhaps the man was hungry, and I couldn't allow a person to be hungry if I could afford to feed that person.' And he started teaching us about charity, and he went right on down to nature, about the ants and how the female ant will regurgitate her food just to feed another ant. He taught us about charity all the way to Bridgeport, Connecticut."

Alex Haley also recalls riding with Malcolm through the streets of Harlem. On West 136th Street, "all of a sudden, he slammed on the brakes. The car screeched, jerked to a stop. I was sure somebody had hit us. By the time I got my wits together Malcolm was out on the driver's side and he was standing like an avenging devil; there were three young men who had been shooting craps, and he was just staring them down. He said, 'Other people are in their pajamas studying you and your people, learning more about them. That [the Countee Cullen Library, which houses the Schomburg Collection] is the greatest repository of information about the black man in existence, and what are you doing? The best you can do is to be out here down on your knees shooting craps against the door.' They were young men—nineteen, twenty, twenty-one, that age range—and just about anyone else who would have dared to interrupt them so rudely would certainly have had some severe physical problems, I would suspect. But not

Malcolm, because of his charisma, because of the power of his image. Those young men went slinking away because it was Malcolm who talked to them like that. And I have often thought of that; I have often thought about how young black people talk, you know, this or that about Malcolm. But you don't hear much about the deep, fervent thing he had about young black people who had educated themselves."

In the black youth of America—in their freshness of thought, in their energy and anger, in new ideas unencumbered by an old slave mentality—Malcolm saw hope for all black Americans. "The black college student," Malcolm told Benjamin Karim, "will be very instrumental in the liberation of black people in this country." Psychologist Kenneth B. Clark remembers a meeting he had arranged with Malcolm for students at the Lincoln School, and "when we got there he had the reporters and interviewers put aside. He spoke with the young students, and he said, 'You know I put students ahead of everything and everybody.' And he did."

Education, in Malcolm's view, bridged the river to liberation, and he urged young African-Americans to learn. Although he had no "formal Ph.D.," notes Sonia Sanchez, "he had a Ph.D. in Malcolmism, he had a Ph.D. in Americanism, in what had gone wrong with this country, and he brought it to you. And for the first time many of us began to look at ourselves again, and to say hold it, it's possible to get an education and not sell your soul. It's possible to work at a job and not demean yourself, it's possible to walk upright like a human being. And, you see, what people don't really understand about what Malcolm taught me—I don't really know what he taught other people—he taught me that I could really be human myself and I didn't have to hate anyone to do that. He touched the core so thoroughly that you could walk upright, and therefore you knew who you were and you just said to people, 'I'm coming among you as an equal,' with no need to put anyone down. And that is probably the most important lesson to be learned from his life. He taught me, and I'm sure a number of others, that you are indeed worthy of being on this planet earth."

Malcolm X had no Ph.D.; nonetheless, he readily matched, and often trammeled, the wits of students and professors alike on numerous American college campuses, for the most part in the

South and Northeast, in the early 1960s. Malcolm's addresses to
college audiences aroused indignation, hostility, enthusiasm, rage;
his debates stirred controversy. Indifference fled. From the outset, at Boston University in 1960, to Malcolm's memorable defense of extremism in the pursuit of human freedoms four years
later, in December 1964, at Oxford University, an appearance by
Malcolm X on any campus became an event.

In 1960 C. Eric Lincoln was working on a graduate degree in
theology and preparing to research his dissertation on the black
Muslims; he was also enrolled in a human relations seminar that
included both students and faculty not only from Boston University but also from Harvard and MIT. Some of the participants in
the seminar, aware that black Islam forebade its ministers to
speak before any audience in which whites were present, challenged Lincoln to contact Malcolm and convince him to attend a
meeting of the seminar as a guest lecturer. To everyone's surprise,
the national leader of the NOI, the Honorable Elijah Muhammad, granted Malcolm the permission he needed.

Malcolm arrived at Boston University on a Thursday afternoon. Lincoln describes the occasion: "The place was packed with
as many professors as graduate students from all three institutions [Boston University, Harvard, and MIT]. Malcolm arrived
with an autoguard headed by Louis Farrakhan, who was then
minister of Elijah Muhammad's Temple No. 11 in Boston and a
protégé of Malcolm X. There were also perhaps fifteen members
of the FOI [Fruit of Islam, the paramilitary arm of the NOI] from
the local temple. Malcolm X showed up on schedule, and there
was a very audible gasp from the people who were waiting to hear
him; to the best of my knowledge, I was the only black person
present. Once all these men had come in and taken their positions around the room to guard the speaker, I introduced Malcolm X. I believe he introduced Minister Farrakhan as the head
of Temple No. 11 and then began to lecture on black Islam. It was
an extremely interesting lecture. Malcolm talked the party line
and did it with verve. He spoke part of the time in Arabic and
showed that he had a good command of French, and the people
were all sort of flabbergasted. There was also the whole physical
presence of the Fruit; I recall that when the group walked in the
professor next to me—he was from MIT—said to me, 'My god,

Eric, every one of them has on a Brooks Brothers suit!' So Malcolm made a great impression on the crowd that day. The next week I got a call from a professor at Harvard asking if I could get Malcolm X to come and speak over there. He went to Harvard and afterwards said to me, 'Thank you for giving me the opportunity to speak to all those blue-eyed Willies. Now can you give me the opportunity to speak to some black people?' So I sent him to Clark College in Atlanta, my home base; he lectured at Clark and then went on to lecture at Morehouse, and that is what launched Malcolm lecturing on the college scene."

Robert Haggins, who had recently become Malcolm's official photographer, accompanied him on his first trip to Harvard in 1961. He rode to Cambridge with Malcolm in the blue Oldsmobile. The FOI followed, conspicuously. So as not to "attract too much attention—thirty cars, one behind the other, going through the streets—or to cause alarm," as Haggins tells it, "we split up into smaller groups, like five cars, and let other cars go between so we would be staggered, so we wouldn't look like a parade. And we arrived at Harvard. They were very courteous, very polite. They had prepared a huge dinner for Malcolm, but Muslims only eat one meal a day, and Malcolm told them, 'I've eaten for the day; I only eat one meal a day, so I can't have anything to eat, but I will have ice cream and coffee.' And they said, 'Would you like some milk in your coffee?' And he said, 'Yes, that's the only thing I like integrated.' "

Haggins also describes some of Malcolm's dinner table conversation with various Harvard University department heads. The head of the biology department, for instance, asked Malcolm, " 'Mr. X, tell me, you don't really believe that one race of people is superior to another race of people, do you?' And Malcolm said, 'Of course not, but you teach that all the time.' And he said, 'No, I don't.' And Malcolm said, 'You do. You teach that, your books teach that. All of the biology books that I have looked at break people down into classifications; either they are dominant or recessive. Now, if you look at the dominant characteristics, you will find brown eyes, black hair, dark skin; those are dominant characteristics. You look at the recessive side and you'll see blue eyes, blond hair, fair skin. So what you are teaching black children is that they are superior human beings. You've been telling them that for years, but they don't believe you. All I've done is come and point out to them, if they don't believe what I'm saying, to believe what you white professors are saying. I just want black people to know where we come from and we shouldn't be ashamed of how we look. We are the dominant race of people.'

"Then he talked about history," Haggins continues, "and he said, 'You've lied about history. You've lied to us, and one of the biggest lies that you've told us is about all those white discoverers, like Christopher Columbus.' " Haggins vigorously espouses Malcolm's view of Columbus as a man lost both actually and morally. No brave voyager who discovered a new world, Columbus, Haggins points out, never even landed on American soil; he did, however, murder more than half the populations of both Puerto Rico and Trinidad, says Haggins, and then brought slavery to the islands from Africa. Haggins recalls Malcolm saying, " 'Take Christopher Columbus: here's a man who discovered absolutely nothing. He got lost, he didn't know where he was. He was floundering around in a boat and he didn't know where the boat was going. He was looking for India and made a mistake. He thought that he had discovered India and called those people Indians, after the word *indigo,* a Latin word which means blue-black. The original Indians were blue-black, the blackest people on earth, Indians. Then Columbus landed on this island, San Salvador, and told the people, "I have discovered you in the name of the Queen of Spain," which is the most ridiculous thing I've ever heard. How can you discover a human being? Somebody's about to have dinner and you intrude, and he says to you—he's polite enough to say—"Look, come in and partake of my meal. Sit down and share what we have; it's not much, but we'll share it with you." And then you stand up and say, "I discover you! You are now discovered, you are Indian." They must have looked at each other wondering, like, where did this fool come from.' Malcolm told that story at Harvard, and they laughed. Then they looked at each other and said, 'He's right. That makes sense.' "

In 1962, at the invitation of the civil rights group Project Awareness, Malcolm visited Howard University in Washington D.C. to debate the future of the black community in America with integrationist Bayard Rustin. Malcolm at that time stood firmly in the forefront of Elijah Muhammad's black Muslim nationalist, separatist ranks. Media coverage of the upcoming debate, especially of Malcolm's appearance, had generated considerable excitement on the campus; it had also aroused a lot of curiosity, and some disdain. Michael Thelwell, then a student at Howard and a participant in Project Awareness, recalls that "a number of not particularly distinguished faculty who were approached to moderate the debate and invited to have dinner with the speakers had declined because they wouldn't 'dignify' Malcolm with their presence. Which we found to be extremely odd. At that time the attitude among my friends who organized the event was one of curiosity about Malcolm; we only knew what the media was reporting about him. But in terms of an intellectual commitment, a political commitment, we were all convinced that the only practical solution, the only alternative, for black people was integration—changing the country's situation so as to include black people on all levels of society: political, cultural, and above all, economic—and that anything else couldn't work. And that Bayard Rustin was the most articulate and militant spokesman for this position."

Whoever may have declined their invitations to that dinner had little effect on its success. At Howard as at Harvard Malcolm politely refused his meal. "He didn't eat anything; he just sat there really kind of alert and drank endless cups of coffee," recalls Thelwell. "But the thing is, even though there were about twenty-five people gathered in this little dining room to have dinner with him and Bayard Rustin, who was an eminent national figure, it was Malcolm's extraordinary charisma, the magnetism of the guy—or perhaps it was because the press had created such a demagogue out of this guy—that kept everybody's eyes turning to him every time he very graciously answered any question directed to him or very graciously avoided any question he didn't feel like answering, but in a very skillful and disarming manner. He completely dominated the occasion; he had a way of looking at people very calmly before he'd answer a question, and you'd see the person who'd raised the question look back at him and be mesmerized as he smiled . . . I mean, people had a very strange response. He was simply one of the most impressive presences and naturally charismatic figures I'd ever seen. There was a certain kind of integrity; his presence suggested a certain kind of

control, an intense purposefulness, a dignity, and an independence of mind that was quite unusual in black men then. A
pride."

Later that evening, at the debate, the twenty-five hundred people who packed the Crampton Auditorium at Howard University
responded thunderously to that presence. The stature of "a very
tall, wiry, handsome guy" stands out in Thelwell's memory of that
night. "When Malcolm strolled to the microphone for the first
time there was a radiant intensity—he may have stood in a spot-
light, I don't know, but radiant was certainly the impression I got
—and then he started his delivery. He spoke of our origins and
then said that he came to us in the name of all that is eternal, the
black man—that before you are an American you're black, before
you were a Republican you were black, before you were a Democrat you were black—and it was just extraordinary. The audience
just erupted, and it continued through the whole course of that
debate. Whether or not Malcolm won that debate doesn't matter;
the fact is that emotionally and intellectually he was in total control. It wasn't necessarily just the function of rhetoric or the ele-
gance of poetry in the delivery, it was the message. And you have
to understand that here's an audience at Howard University—at
that time, as it is perhaps now, an institution that saw itself as a
means of ascension for young black people into the American
dream, the mainstream, a school that prepared southern black
students to be what the school imagined was acceptable to white
America. That integration, as I now reflect on it, was the aim of
the vast majority of the upwardly mobile Howard University students, and yet that whole place erupted viscerally, powerfully,
with a shout. It wasn't an intellectual experience purely; it was a
very primal, emotional thing. I've never really seen a crowd respond quite that way, especially a crowd I'd have predicted to
respond just the opposite way."

As Thelwell reflects further upon that evening at Howard, he
attempts to identify what qualities other than Malcolm's "incredible magnetism" might account for the astounding effect he had
on his audience. Thelwell believes that, for one thing, Malcolm
"was able to be totally and fearlessly honest because, unlike Bayard Rustin and other civil rights leaders, he had no intellectual
and political obligations to a set of allies or to any constituency in

the liberal establishment. Rustin had to constrain his remarks, had to couch them in terms that were acceptable to his white allies—I mean, it was a kind of self-censorship; it limited what he said, limited his analysis of the black situation to a certain mainstream, orthodox, accepted version of reality. Malcolm didn't have to do that. Malcolm had no obligation to any liberal orthodoxy. His constituency was black, the Nation of Islam, so he could speak the truth in terms as blunt as possible or necessary and not worry about anybody being offended, not worry about support, and this made him extraordinarily attractive to young black people because finally here was somebody who didn't have to kowtow to anybody. He spoke exactly what the goddamn truth was as he saw it. And that is very different from somebody appealing for tolerance, somebody appealing for acceptance. Malcolm said, 'What the hell are you talking about? The American white man is the worst killer the world has ever seen. Who brought the Africans here? Who killed the red man? Who dropped the bomb on Hiroshima? What are you talking about?' The other thing he had which most people don't know about is a remarkable gentleness and tenderness for black people—a real compassion. Not compassion, but a real love and a real solidarity, a real sensitivity to black people. He held a genuine concern for us, and people recognized it immediately. When Malcolm X said brother or sister, or any of those terms of kinship and mutual responsibility, he meant it."

In any debate Malcolm X was a formidable opponent, as James Farmer, the founding director of the Congress of Racial Equality (CORE), well knows. In his autobiography, *Lay Bare the Heart,* Farmer recounts one of Malcolm's most memorable single blows in a public debate. In response to Malcolm's insistent demand that blacks call themselves blacks because they were blacks before they were Americans, Malcolm's adversary—a black but not, in this instance, Farmer—repeatedly stated that he called himself first of all an American. When Malcolm then asked why, his adversary, now shouting, replied that he had been born here, in America. "Malcolm smiled," writes Farmer, "and spoke softly: 'Now, brother, if a cat has kittens in the oven, does that make them biscuits?' "

With some circumspection, then, Farmer agreed to debate Malcolm at Cornell University in 1962 on the condition, as he relates it, "that Malcolm speak first and I speak second so that Malcolm would rebut first and I would rebut last. I didn't want him to blow me away with one of his great one-liners, as he did Rustin. Malcolm accepted that until almost the last minute when he wired the people at Cornell and said that 'the Honorable Elijah Muhammad teaches us only to attack when attacked; so I must speak last or no debate!' So they asked me if I would debate him speaking last. I told them yes, provided that Malcolm agreed to an open-ended cross discussion between the two of us, after his rebuttal, with the moderator staying out of it; and he agreed to that."

Farmer, of course, had devised a strategy, which was "to make Malcolm's speech for him." Stealing Malcolm's fire, Farmer enumerated in his opening speech the many crimes against them that blacks had endured throughout history. After vividly presenting the plight of twenty-two million black Americans, he offered CORE's nonviolent direct action solution. Before turning the platform over to Malcolm, however, Farmer asked that Malcolm speak no further of the disease—its symptoms were clear, the diagnosis certain—but to put forward his solution, his cure. "That's where he was very weak," Farmer points out. "When he was called upon to give a program or plan, he began to quote the dogma of Elijah Muhammad, calling for land or a black state or demanding the government give us money which it owed us for reparations to purchase an island someplace. He was very weak on that, so I wanted him to spend his time wandering around in that jungle. He didn't want to do that because he knew that was his weak point and I was going to eat him alive on it. So when he stood up he was at first thrown off balance because he couldn't give his usual speech, because I had given it already. He fumbled with the microphone, with the gooseneck; there was nothing wrong with it. Then he began, saying, 'I have a lot of respect for Brother James; he's the only top leader of so-called Negroes who has the guts to face me in a debate on a public platform, and I respect him for that,' and he talked in that vein for two or three minutes, and obviously he was fishing around for a speech, and he was flustered, and then the speech came together and it was vintage Malcolm. The ideas came together in his mind and he roared, not attacking me but attacking this idiocy of nonviolence,

'Someone slaps you on one cheek and you're going to turn the other? What kind of nonsense is that?' He said, 'You've seen it on TV! You've seen those firehoses rolling black women down the street! The skirts flying! You've seen the police dogs turned loose on little black children, biting their flesh and tearing their clothes!' And then he roared again, 'Don't let those dogs bite those children! Kill the damn dogs!' Everybody in the audience rose to their feet in applause. He had the audience then, and most of them were white. Not many speakers could throw a speech out a window like that and start from scratch and come through the way he did. He came through like a champion, which he was."

A young, blond coed from a college in New England boarded a plane to New York; she was obviously upset. Just a few hours earlier Malcolm X had spoken at the college. He had drawn parallels between the racism of white slavemasters, the "white devils" who so cruelly victimized blacks in the South before the Civil War, and their sexism in the treatment of women—white women, their wives, mothers, sisters, daughters—whose gentility, it was purported, divorced them from their female sexuality and therefore justified the sexual use, and abuse, of black women by the white male oppressor. The plantation had thus bred in white America a deplorable moral history that included the hatred, rejection, and denial not only of the African slave but also of white southern womanhood. After the lecture Malcolm had flown back to New York.

The coed must have boarded the first flight that followed Malcolm's to New York. On her arrival she took a cab to Harlem. She found the Muslim restaurant on Lenox Avenue, where, as it happened, Malcolm was sitting with Benjamin Karim and some other members of his staff. Still noticeably disturbed, the young woman approached Malcolm. She spoke with a white southern accent; her clothes spoke money, and her demeanor shouted white breeding, privilege, background. Confronting Malcolm, she demanded to know if he truly believed there were no good white people. When Malcolm replied by telling her he believed only in people's deeds, not their words, she asked him what then she could do. "Nothing," he informed her.

"Nothing." Of any of the statements Malcolm may have made to his own regret, this one comes first to Alex Haley's mind. "All he had said was 'nothing,'" says Haley, "but he worried about it; he played it back and wished it had been played differently."

According to Benjamin Karim, it would have been played differently, had Malcolm been alone when the young, blond, white college student approached him. Karim feels that Malcolm had to answer as he did because he had to "satisfy us wicked people around him who at that time didn't believe there were any white people anywhere that were any good. I think that he would have been more amiable if we hadn't been there; he had a softness that could be touched." Karim had, after all, witnessed Malcolm's amiability with college students, both white and black. He remembers how, when Malcolm had finished one of his lectures, the students, mostly white, "just crowded around him, I mean just like bees around honey in August. Malcolm was a very amiable person, he was really a very likable person. He had a very sincere admiration for college students, whether they were white or black —I could see that in him—I guess, because of his respect for knowledge and the fact that he believed that the younger students wouldn't grow up as racist as their parents. We grew up in a society as racist as its law, but Malcolm had some faith that the younger white college students would grow up different."

Malcolm's rebuff of the white college coed who sought him out in a Harlem restaurant reached the pages of *Life* magazine. Political activist Yuri Kuchiama had read the article in *Life;* she remembered it on September 16, 1963, the day she spotted Malcolm X at the center of a crowd of black people in the Brooklyn criminal courthouse. "I had thought, gee, that takes a lot of nerve," says Kuchiama about the coed, "and I could see why Malcolm was upset and said there's nothing you can do for me, you should just work in your own community. I didn't want to make the same mistake," she continues, "but I did want to meet him. I stood on the outer rim of the group around him, and I kept moving in closer, and I could see that he was looking and noticed this Asian woman was coming in closer and closer, and then I went right up to him and said—I know it sounds so stupid—'Can I shake your hand?' He looked at me very quizzically and sternly, then he showed that fantastic smile of his and put out his hand,

and asked, 'For what?' I got a little bit scared and just sort of blurted out, 'I just wanted to congratulate you on all you're doing for your people.' He looked at me distrustingly. 'I don't know what you mean,' he said, and I said, 'I admire all you do, but I don't agree with everything you say.' Malcolm asked, 'What don't you agree with?' I said, 'Your feelings about integration,' and he said, 'I can't give you a two-minute dissertation on my feelings toward integration. Why don't you come to my office and we'll discuss it.' I couldn't believe it. 'Make an appointment with my secretary,' he said."

As it turned out, Yuri Kuchiama did not see Malcolm again until the following year, on June 4, when Malcolm attended a reception at her apartment in Harlem for the Hiroshima-Nagasaki Peace Study Mission. Malcolm also spoke on that occasion, and "the one person in the United States the Mission most wanted to meet" that day disappointed no one—neither the Mission nor Kuchiama herself. Prior to that Kuchiama had been personally "sort of disappointed," because Malcolm had not replied to several letters she had written him, but "when he came to my apartment that day," she recalls, "the first thing he said was that he knew I had written to him several times, and although he hadn't responded to my letters, he did appreciate them, but he had lost my address and he had been traveling. He then promised that 'from here onward, if I ever go anywhere again, I'll write to you.' And I couldn't believe it! He kept his word. He knew thousands of people, and I got twelve postcards from eleven countries from him. I hope I never lose them; I hope to pass them on to my kids. I will always treasure them."

A white college coed followed Malcolm to Harlem. He offered her only nothing. He did not allow her to see the Malcolm who surprised Yuri Kuchiama, the Malcolm who, to her, was "very warm, very sincere, and genuine and humble."

The coed burst into tears. She ran out of the Muslim restaurant, out onto Lenox Avenue, and disappeared in a taxicab. Malcolm X may have convinced her that he indeed believed there were no good white people, that he viewed her as useless and held her at best in contempt. Chances are, he had. To his own regret.

* * *

"Blue-eyed Willies" he called them, the students at Harvard University. Malcolm nevertheless returned to Harvard several times and each time found his audience receptive, stimulating, eager—and even, Benjamin Karim tells us, a reason for hope.

Too, white men were denounced by Malcolm as "white devils." He fervently preached that all white peoples, Jews and Gentiles alike, their babies and women and children, would be struck down by the almighty hand of Allah. The time of Armageddon had begun, Malcolm declaimed, and his pulpit rhetoric spared only the faithful among the black Muslims. Still, blue-eyed sportscaster Dick Schaap particularly remembers an afternoon he spent with Malcolm. "Malcolm was looking to move out of the Hotel Theresa," Schaap recalls. "He had his offices, I think, on the mezzanine or the second floor, and he was looking to move, and I went with him, looking at various places where he enjoyed the game of haggling with all the Jewish merchants as to what rent he would pay. It was a game; he knew it was a game and he was enjoying it—he was having fun doing it."

Apparently, Malcolm did not always conform to his pulpit image. Schaap observes that, as with "many activists of the time, Malcolm's rhetoric and his personal beliefs were not exactly the same thing. He preached one way and he preached hatred, but one-to-one he did not hate people until they showed whether they deserved to be hated or not. I found the same thing true of Harry Edwards, who was a leader of the revolt of black athletes against the white establishment. Harry's rhetoric was all 'kill whitey' and 'burn the stadiums' and all that, and then he'd say, 'Let's go have a drink.' And I think Malcolm was similar. Malcolm didn't hate people because of their color, Malcolm hated the injustices he had seen."

Journalist Claude Lewis was introduced to the minister of Muslim Mosque No. 7 at a New York radio station in 1962. Malcolm's public image had not led Lewis to expect the man he met. "Malcolm was the first to offer his seat to a white woman who came into the studio," Lewis recalls, "which surprised me, because that wasn't his image. He was so polite and friendly and warm and kind of engaging; that's what stood out, and it made me want to know the real Malcolm X as opposed to his image."

By 1962 the image was fierce, and the black nationalist rhetoric inflammatory. It augured violence, it advertised intolerance, it mongered racist hatred. Malcolm's words were quoted in the daily press and broadcast on the radio. His image was repeatedly being cast on television screens across America. Malcolm X was news.

The media lent Malcolm's compelling voice further force. "It's 1991, and we've now heard all the shocking rhetoric it's possible to hear," notes author and journalist Peter Goldman, but "in Malcolm's day a guy standing up on television saying white folks are the devil and are going to suffer the wrath of Allah, and it's going to be bad; saying that your cities will burn, and that black people do not or may not want the company of white people and that we reject you, that we want power over our own communities and we don't want integration or, as Malcolm put it, 'coffee with a cracker'; saying that black people have a worth and pride and history of their own—I mean, that was radical stuff then. It was revolutionary."

The fact that Malcolm failed to "produce a twelve-point program for the salvation of black America" Goldman finds far less significant than Malcolm's "great force as a teacher, as a consciousness-raiser, at a time when that was a very critical role." Not only television but also radio and the press helped Malcolm realize more fully the power of that role. "He was very public relations conscious, very sophisticated about the modern media and how to use it," says Goldman, who is currently working on a book about political consultants, and adds, "They could learn a few things from Malcolm about creating media events."

Schaap too comments on Malcolm's skill at "manipulating the press. He charmed the press and provided it with material; he was exciting. He probably never had the following that he liked to imply he had, but most political leaders don't have the following they imply they have. He was good at dealing with the press and good at using the press." Although "Malcolm tried to call it as hard and as straight as he could with the press in terms of his philosophy and outlook," says former newspaperman James Booker, "he did know how to play his loaded words and get in his emotional comments so they would get good mileage in the right places."

Malcolm clearly recognized the power of the press, television, and radio. Indeed, Robert Haggins recalls a conversation in which Malcolm identified the news media as "the most powerful entity on earth. And I asked him how," says Haggins, "and he answered that the media has the power to make the innocent guilty and to make the guilty innocent; and that's power. Because they control the minds of the masses. And it's easy to do, once you understand how the media works, he said. You see, with the media you are very selective about what information you give people—you don't have to lie to them, you just have to be selective about what you tell them—because human beings gather information and they form opinions based on the information you have given them."

However masterfully Malcolm may have used the news media, he was, Haggins believes, at the same time misused—or misrepresented—by them. Referring to a photograph in a German publication, Haggins says, "That's Malcolm, with his family; it's a side of Malcolm that most people never saw. Let me tell you a story about that. You know that Malcolm sometimes, during his deliveries, would get so worked up and get so emotionally charged and angry—I think it's normal for any human being in the position of being black in white America to be angry—and he would be so angry that sometimes he would ball his fists and do like that [Haggins raises a clenched fist]; and the press would wait for that and take those pictures, and they would be the only pictures that would get published. I did the same thing, and Malcolm called me aside and said, 'I can get those pictures any day of the week, a dime a dozen. I don't like those pictures. I am not a monster, and I want you to show me as a human being.' That is why now, after twenty-five years, everybody wants to see my photographs; newspapers and magazines, everybody."

The balled fist or pointed finger, the raised arm; the indignation and the anger; the rhetoric; the fire, irony, and conviction; the grimace, the snarl: the image. The media collaborated with Malcolm in making that image, and the image in turn made news. According to Alex Haley, it also made Malcolm uneasy. Haley explains: "I think that Malcolm was embarrassed, genuinely embarrassed, by a lot of his prominence in the media. I know he was discomfited by it, because—I didn't know this until later—his prominence in the media was what some others in the movement were using to undermine him with Mr. Elijah Muhammad. You know, things were said, so I later heard and learned. They were saying things to Mr. Muhammad, like saying that Malcolm seemed to be wanting to take over the organization [the NOI], that his picture was in the papers more than the leader's was. And this was very, very true. It was also true that it was Malcolm's job; he was the one who spoke for the organization, who represented the organization. He took on the interviews and all kinds of things that hardly anyone else within the organization would have been able to take on, or do, I would imagine—certainly not in the way he did—but it was, as I said, discomfiting him. He was frustrated by the fact that he was expected to be the vibrant, vocal spokesman and that it was causing him to be cut down, defiled even, chewed away, by those who were envious or jealous of his prominence. So he had a lot of bitterness about this thing of being out there in the public eye as much as he was."

Malcolm twice appeared with PBS newsman Joe Durso on the WNDT-TV interview program *The World at Ten*, which in the 1960s often featured significant figures in the civil rights movement. Already familiar with Malcolm's public image, Durso had expected "somebody who was more—I'm not sure what word to use—not more active, not more dynamic. Perhaps more extreme, but that's not the right word either. More militant, I guess, or more flamboyant. And I think the name added a mystique, it had a certain impact: Malcolm X. It was a very memorable name, so I expected someone with a little more fire perhaps." Instead, Durso was struck by Malcolm's conservative manner and appearance: "He was dressed in a business suit—as I remember, a pinstripe suit—and he looked for all the world like a businessman or a person who might make news behind the scenes but not like somebody who was out front and visible and fiery. He was much more low-key than I had expected." For Durso, "low-key" also describes Malcolm's style in the PBS interviews: "He was very forthright. He didn't make fiery speeches; he responded to questions and he made his points compellingly, in a dialogue. I guess I expected more of a platform speaker, somebody who was very militant. He was more cerebral than physical. He reasoned. He was almost like a college professor." Malcolm may have adopted this style, Durso suggests, because PBS was "considered the home of intellectual programming in those days" and Malcolm probably "understood the audience that he was reaching was more interested in dialogue than in his more flamboyant theatrics." Durso's suggestion that Malcolm understood his audiences, their predispositions as well as their expectations was in general true, so it would appear; he also evidently understood the effect and value of inconsistency. Malcolm's behavior often failed to conform to his image, and often confounded his observers.

Attorney William Kunstler first interviewed Malcolm on WMCA radio in 1960. Before that, though, they had "met on a number of occasions and got to be, relatively speaking, friends." Kunstler speaks relatively because "at the time Malcolm was talking a lot about white devils—this was before he came back from Mecca—and it would have been impossible, I think, for any white person to get too close to him during that period of his life." One interview with Malcolm that Kunstler will never forget, however, was neither broadcast on the radio nor conducted by him. Kunstler tells the story: "My first wife had become quite friendly with Malcolm and he did many favors for her, including one which I've always remembered. He agreed to sit for an interview by a paraplegic reporter from *The Patent Trader,* which is an up-county Westchester newspaper with probably no black readers at all, and he sat for four hours doing an interview with a man who could only take down what Malcolm said by typing with the big toe of one foot on a typewriter. It was apparently an excruciating ordeal for Malcolm, but he sat for this white reporter, whose constituency could be only all white, and was as kind and considerate as anyone could be in such an interview, and I've always remembered that. It was a side of Malcolm that no one really knows about, and it was indicative that the man really had enormous compassion and was willing to give up four hours to a reporter whose column really meant nothing to him one way or the other."

Malcolm's image did not capture many sides of the man. It simplified the man; it could not contain him.

The NOI could not contain Malcolm either. On March 8, 1964, *The New York Times* ran an article announcing "Malcolm X Splits With Muhammad," and reporting Malcolm's plans to establish a black nationalist party and to cooperate with other local civil rights actions in order to heighten the political consciousness of African Americans. The announcement cannot have come entirely to the NOI leader's surprise. Three months earlier, on December 4, 1963, Elijah Muhammad had suspended Malcolm from his ministry, supposedly for ninety days, because at an NOI rally on December 1, contrary to a directive from Muhammad that no Muslim minister discuss the recent assassination of President Kennedy, Malcolm had replied to a question from the floor that Kennedy "never foresaw that the chickens would come home to roost so soon."

Benjamin Karim remembers it this way: "Mr. Muhammad had issued an edict, I guess you could say, that no minister should speak out against the dead president, because black people loved President Kennedy so much and it could turn the black community against the Muslims. Mr. Muhammad was supposed to speak in New York City on December 1, 1963, at Manhattan Center. He canceled it, perhaps because of Kennedy's assassination, and Malcolm asked him if he could speak in his place, which he allowed him to do. The title of his speech, which was the only written speech I've ever known Malcolm to speak from—I had the written speech at one time and I let somebody have it, but hopefully I can get it back—was 'God's Judgment on America.' It wasn't 'The Chickens Coming Home to Roost.' But a lady stood up in the audience and asked Malcolm what did he think of Kennedy's assassination, and he made that statement that it was a sign of it's chickens coming home to roost."

Malcolm's statement was of course widely reported in the press, and to many Americans, both black and white, it seemed exultant. The statement is ambiguous, but in Dick Schaap's opinion, "it was not a very smart thing to say. Only I don't think he meant it in the way people interpreted it, I don't think he was exactly gloating over it. I think he was being realistic—that the atmosphere of violence had produced more violence." What Malcolm meant, according to Karim, was that "the chickens coming home to roost was simply the culmination of American history; it had culminated in the act of a citizen of this country assassinating his own president."

After the rally "John Ali went back to Chicago," says Karim, "and told Mr. Muhammad that Malcolm had spoke out against the dead president, and they suspended him. I was in the temple when this happened. We were told that if Malcolm comes back to give him a job in the restaurant washing dishes, and I went and told him what had taken place. Plus," Karim adds, "he knew that he wasn't going to be able to get back in. I think that's the point at which he actually made up his mind to leave."

Although dedicated to his ministry and to the leadership of Elijah Muhammad, Malcolm had been frustrated by the apolitical stance of the NOI for some time prior to the suspension, according to Benjamin Karim. Karim cites the Ronald Stokes incident as a case in point. Stokes died of gunshot wounds on April 27, 1962, when the Muslim mosque in Los Angeles was fired upon by police; six other Muslims were also wounded. The next day Malcolm was dispatched to California by Elijah Muhammad. "When he went out there," says Karim, "he told these Muslims that they should retaliate in kind. The police commissioner in L.A. called Mr. Muhammad and told him to bring Malcolm out of California because he was about to cause some bloodshed. That's what it really got down to; he had actually gone out there to have the Muslims retaliate against the police for that incident. Mr. Muhammad went along with the police commissioner. Malcolm became very disillusioned, but he never went against Mr. Muhammad or did an opposite thing from what he was told to do. That was just one of the things."

Karim mentions two other things that thwarted Malcolm's emerging political consciousness. "We were never active in any kind of civil rights movement. And we didn't even vote. As Malcolm became more worldly he saw that we were becoming smaller and smaller and not moving in the direction that the whole world was moving. And I believe that all these negatives that were happening within the Nation of Islam—always very vocal, but no movement—had much to do with him leaving."

In Karim's view, then, Malcolm's eventual split with Muhammad was effected by his own ambitions as well as by pressures from within the ranks of the NOI. Karim offers the following analogy: "It's like a baby, like when a baby outgrows his mother's womb and forces push him into a higher world. I think there were forces, so to speak, that were pushing Malcolm on, along with the exterior forces of those corrupt [NOI] officials."

That forces inside the NOI conspired to oust Malcolm from his ministry, and indeed from the Nation of Islam itself, is echoed by other voices. Malcolm had begun his career as a Muslim minister in 1953. "Until Malcolm came on the scene," Charles Kenyatta says of the Nation of Islam, "you could have put all their following in a station wagon and still have some room left. The teaching of Islam was never geared to reach from the back streets to the universities. It was strictly what we could call a back street religion."

In 1963 the back street religion was a national phenomenon; so was Malcolm X. In eleven years he had risen through the ranks of the NOI to become by far the most dynamic of the Muslim ministers and certainly the most visible both in the Nation and in the national media. Malcolm's popularity easily rivaled Elijah Muhammad's own. As Claude Lewis sees him, "Malcolm had developed into such a dominant figure in the eyes of the blacks that he had superseded Elijah Muhammad. People liked Elijah Muhammad because he brought us Malcolm X. But when Malcolm spoke, people really listened, and I think that disturbed people in the Nation at that time and it certainly pushed Elijah Muhammad into the background."

Malcolm's prominence in the media and his high regard among American blacks outside the Nation as well as in it increasingly irritated the NOI officials in Elijah Muhammad's Chicago headquarters, in the opinion of Benjamin Karim. They had more than face to lose. Karim explains: "Mr. Muhammad had an illness—bronchitis—and many of the officials around him thought that he was going to die; and if he had died, Malcolm would have inherited that position as the leader of the Nation of Islam. At that time Muslims had built quite a few businesses—very lucrative ones—and had even bought a jet, a jet plane. There was a lot of money floating around and a lot of people were spending money in areas where it shouldn't have been spent, and Malcolm spoke out against it. And they knew that if Mr. Muhammad had passed on, they would not have their positions anymore, because they were the first people that Malcolm would have gotten rid of. I think that had more to do with it—economics—and they had gotten greedy. They were living a lifestyle they had never lived before and had money, the kind of money they'd never dreamed that they would have had before."

Nor did Elijah Muhammad himself escape Malcolm's moral scrutiny. Malcolm was visiting the NOI headquarters in Chicago, according to Karim, when "one of Mr. Muhammad's sons, W. D. Muhammad, who is well known today, Wallace D. Muhammad, had taken Malcolm aside and told him—matter of fact, Dick Gregory did too, in Chicago; he and Dick Gregory were very close, they had a very close friendship—but W. D. Muhammad had told Malcolm that these secretaries had these children, had been pregnant. He said they were children of Mr. Muhammad and that they were afraid that the newspaper would get a hold of it and in so doing they could almost destroy the Nation of Islam, because we thought that Mr. Muhammad was infallible. Really, seriously, you can't imagine; you know, like Hirohito—the same as the Japanese thought of Hirohito is how we thought of Mr. Muhammad. So what Malcolm did was to call a gathering of all the ministers, and he told them what had happened and that they should take stories out of the Bible that showed an imperfection in a holy man—like Noah, you know, after the flood, he got drunk. . . . So you're planting these seeds of imperfection about these holy men [in the minds of the Muslim brothers and sisters, Malcolm told us], so when the paper hits, the imperfections of the prophets that have already been implanted in their minds will absorb the shock that the newspapers come out with. It would have caused shock waves throughout the Nation of Islam."

By December 1963 Malcolm was uncomfortably enmeshed in the internal politics of the NOI. He had his enemies inside the NOI ranks, and his ill-timed comment on Kennedy may indeed, as some believe, have provided them with the very pretext they needed to suspend, and in effect disempower, Malcolm X. Elombe Braath describes a cartoon he himself drew around that time. It shows "Malcolm, who has written on the blackboard, like a hundred times, 'JFK was not a devil.' He is holding his wrist, wringing it, and Elijah Muhammad is sitting at a table with his son-in-law Raymond leaning over and whispering in his ear. It was sort of a conspiracy. And Malcolm had got suspended."

And silenced. For ninety days. "One thing I used to remind him of," says Charles Kenyatta, "is that for twelve years you have been teaching these men how to love Elijah Muhammad and I said in ninety days they haven't changed their mind that easy, and I was right, because they too were part of the plot."

About two weeks before the official announcement in *The New York Times* of Malcolm's break with Elijah Muhammad, the *Amsterdam News* printed an article by James Booker that suggested tensions inside the NOI might be widening the rift between the suspended minister of Mosque No. 7 and the leader of the black Muslims. The article did not please Malcolm or the NOI. Booker recounts that "Malcolm had told me or implied there was friction between him and Elijah Muhammad, and I had heard from others close to him about the nature of the problems, and no one had told me this was off the record. After I wrote an item which hinted at these problems, this friction, Malcolm caught a lot of flak from within the [black Muslim] movement and he came up to the office to deny that he had said it, and he came up with about five of his guys. And while he was going into the editor's office, which was on the same floor as mine, five of his guys just stood around me. They shook up the office, they were like storm troopers. Malcolm just stormed past me. Everybody on the staff knew what it was about. I was a little nervous, but I knew that what I had written I had gotten directly. And for Malcolm to now deny it because of internal problems, that was not my concern. My editor did not make me retract it, and in fact, as conditions developed, two weeks later he had his official split with the movement. The next time he saw me he just gave me this wry smile."

After ninety days of silence Malcolm announced his split with Elijah Muhammad; from the outset it was probably inevitable. Like Benjamin Karim, Peter Goldman thinks that when Malcolm was first informed of his suspension from the NOI, "he knew that he would not be going back. I think he had sources, and he had an understanding of the way their procedures worked. I was working for *Newsweek,*" Goldman continues, "and it was right in the thick of the massive Kennedy coverage. We were doing a short item on Malcolm's remark about the chickens coming home to roost and his suspension, and I called him—in this case not for an extended interview but just for, in effect, one quote—and I thought we'd be on the phone for a couple of minutes. He understood that kind of thing; he was used to TV guys wanting sound bytes, so normally it would have been a quick, businesslike phone call—in effect, him saying here's your quote, and I would say thanks and then good luck, and good-bye. In this case he kept the conversation going and asked me what I thought, which he had never done before, and he never did it afterwards; so that's not a bad indicator. I'm not sure that vulnerability is the word, but he seemed to have a contingent sense of his own life at that moment, I think."

For three months Malcolm stood outside the Nation of Islam. His suspension stripped him of his ministry. It shut him out of the Muslim community in Harlem that he had led and cut him off from the brothers and sisters whose lives he had touched and changed, like that of Benjamin Karim. "We ate only once a day," Karim relates, "and believe it or not, a lot of people don't bathe every day, but that was insisted upon. Our diet changed; where we ate white bread we were told to eat wheat bread, what a lot of people now call health food. Movies were cut out. Parties were cut out. We had a juke box that only played jazz and Middle Eastern music or music from Africa—no blues, perhaps because a lot of blues is sad and a lot is talking about my woman left me or I caught somebody with her, or something like that." According to Karim, suspension meant for Malcolm, as for any member of the mosque, that "you are not supposed to speak to any Muslim, in fact. If you were suspended, say, for instance, for taking someone's watch, you would probably be given a year out. That's really like a year in prison, because not many people speak your language now that you have learned to live a certain lifestyle, and to take you out of that lifestyle and put you back in the public so you can no longer associate with Muslims is hell. And it's hard for somebody outside the community to really understand that that was a punishment." Nonetheless, whatever pain the suspension may have caused Malcolm, "when he first left, split, he didn't," Karim points out, "say anything against Mr. Muhammad."

Robert Haggins emphasizes too that Malcolm "never really attacked Elijah Muhammad as such; he always respected him because he was his first real teacher. And he taught Malcolm that he was a black man, that he was an African and had every right to be proud of his heritage and every right to understand and to learn the truth and to look at the truth of religion and to look at the truth of history." What Malcolm was taught as Muslim doctrine, according to C. Eric Lincoln, "could be summed up and often was summed up by Elijah as, quote, 'to tell you the truth about the white man and to tell you the truth about yourself. Only when you know these two truths can you ever be free and can you ever obtain justice or equality.'"

C. Eric Lincoln also recalls an exchange between Malcolm and the late journalist Louis Lomax at the Muslim restaurant in Harlem. "In the course of this conversation Lomax, who wrote the book on the Muslims called *When the Word Is Given,* said to Malcolm, he said, 'Look, Malcolm, why don't you stop all that Mr. Muhammad shit? Why don't you start your own movement and lead your own movement? You got the brains,' and so on and so forth. And Malcolm leaped up from the table as if he had been stuck with a hat pin—I had never seen a man so furious—as if he was going to attack Lomax on the spot, but we were all friends, and he said, 'Lou Lomax, don't you *ever* say that to me again. Mr. Muhammad is responsible for everything that I am today. He brought me from nowhere to where I am and as long as I live I will be loyal to him, and I don't want to hear that anymore!'"

On March 11, 1964, three days after Malcolm severed his ties with the NOI, he issued a public telegram in which he acknowledged Elijah Muhammad as his "leader and teacher" and gave him "full credit for what I know and who I am."

Then he continued.

Peter Goldman views Malcolm's departure from the NOI as part of a continuum, a process of politicization, that had started years before. "The Nation of Islam is a very cloistered group," explains Goldman, "or was, as Malcolm found it and as he left it, and to a great degree still is. Its politics was a kind of anti-politics, a psychic withdrawal from the white world. Its metaphor was 'give us four or five states, give us some land of our own,' but its reality was a kind of psychic withdrawal from the community. Meanwhile, the civil rights movement was coming to life in the South and Malcolm was viewing it from the North with a kind of split vision. It was irresistible in terms of black people fighting for justice in society. On the other hand, it did not relate to the lives of black people in the northern ghetto, and he realized both these things. He wanted to be, as I said before, part of his time. And to be part of his time, he was going through a process of politicization, taking the Nation public, putting on these great rallies, being on the air a lot, being in the papers a lot—I think, not for self-aggrandizement; I'm sure he enjoyed the attention, but I don't think that that was his motive. I think his motive was to make the Nation relevant to the world. So I think a metamorphosis had begun. He got involved too in the internal politics of the Nation, which led to his exile. At that point, though, I think he was probably ready to be exiled. I think it was a continuum that started years before. It wasn't simply breaking with Elijah Muhammad; it was a process."

In the process Malcolm lost one of his most valued friends.

According to Alex Haley, between 1962 and 1964, when he and Malcolm were working together on the autobiography, besides "Mr. Muhammad, whom Malcolm revered, absolutely adulated," there were "two other people he highly respected. One of them was a young fellow who had been a folk singer or a popular singer [Gene Louis Walcott], and he had become a member of the Nation of Islam and was very popular and highly liked. Malcolm called him 'my little brother,' and they were most fond of each other. And this young man was Louis Farrakhan, as he is known today, and I think that is what he was termed then, although he was probably called Louis X or had a number of Xes—I don't know how many—but that is one person Malcolm was really close to. And he was very proud of being the big brother, so to speak, of little brother Farrakhan. And similarly, there was another young fellow who got to know Malcolm and vice versa, and they just had a marvelous attachment to each other, and that was the young Cassius Clay."

"It was Malcolm," as Charles Kenyatta tells it, "who was most responsible for him [Clay] wanting to become a member of the NOI. He had a brother in there by the name of Rudy. Rudy had been a member, but Muhammad Ali had not been. So Muhammad Ali—I mean Cassius, as he was called at that time—used to come to the mosques at different places, whatever city he would be in, and Malcolm might be there too, and like many others, he was so attracted to Malcolm's teaching that when he would come to the mosque, he would always sit up front."

In January 1964, six weeks into his suspension, Malcolm spent some time with Cassius Clay at his training camp in Miami, Florida, where Clay was preparing for the world heavyweight boxing championship match with Sonny Liston the next month. Malcolm was there again in February, when Clay won the title. Despite the silence imposed upon him by the NOI, Malcolm had continued to serve Clay as his spiritual advisor, and Haley remembers that "Cassius wasn't going to have it without Malcolm being there, and Malcolm was there. Malcolm called me before the fight and said it was sure to be one of the greatest upsets in modern times, or something like that. And afterwards he called me back, and you could hear all this whooping and hollering going on in the background of the dressing room. Malcolm could not have been higher in his life than when he and Cassius Clay were so close as they were. And then they fell out. When Malcolm was ejected from the Nation of Islam, Cassius Clay stayed with the Messenger, Mr. Muhammad."

Clay's friend James Brown, then the star running back for the Cleveland Browns, was also in Florida that February. Because Malcolm had been suspended by the NOI for his statement regarding the Kennedy assassination, James Brown believes, "Malcolm decided, I guess, that he was going to form his own group. And he was there, in Miami, basically to see if Ali would be a part of his group. Everybody was avoiding Malcolm at the time, because he wasn't in good standing with the Nation, and of course he wasn't in good standing with America, so he was more or less by himself, and I used to go visit with him and we used to talk. Then, the night of the fight, the night he won, after Ali won, we all went to this little black motel. Ali went with me into the back room; he left Malcolm and the other people in the front room, and Ali talked for about two hours about Elijah Muhammad and the powers of Elijah Muhammad, and that he wasn't going to go with Malcolm because the power was with the little man—a man of little physical stature, but he was a brilliant man, and he, Ali, was his follower and from that night on he would not really deal with Malcolm.

"When he came out of the room, Malcolm said to me, 'Jim, don't you think that now that Ali is the heavyweight champion of the world, he should stop bragging as much as he used to?' I agreed with him, because I felt that now Ali was in the driver's

seat and he did not have to talk the way he did before. So that was
the only conversation that Malcolm, Ali, and I had after Ali had
come out of the back room and joined everybody else. The essence of the situation was that Ali said that he would no longer
deal with Malcolm. That part of it bothered me, because I knew
Malcolm had been the one who recruited him into the Nation of
Islam."

It was soon after the Liston fight that Cassius Clay changed his
name to Muhammad Ali. He remained loyal to the NOI and the
leadership of the little man with the powers, Elijah Muhammad.
On March 12, 1964, at a press conference in New York, Malcolm
announced the formation of the Muslim Mosque, Incorporated.
If he was upset or hurt by the disaffection of Ali, "this is something I never heard him say," says Charles Kenyatta, "but I know
that it affected him to a degree, because, at the time, and as a
matter of fact, Ali was supposed to go with us when the split
came."

On May 17, 1964, in Accra, near the end of an exhilarating
African tour, Malcolm by chance encountered Muhammad Ali,
who was also touring Africa; accompanying Ali was Herbert
Muhammad, Elijah's son. Malcolm shared some of the pain in
that moment with Alex Haley. "I know," states Haley, "that one
of Malcolm's most down experiences in his life was subsequent to
when he went on a trip to Mecca. He was coming back, I think,
too happy, and he was in some airport in one of the African
countries. He was walking through the airport; he turned left, and
then saw that there was Muhammad Ali—he had changed his
name now—and they came towards each other and their eyes
met, and Malcolm saw Muhammad Ali look away from him and
walk past him without speaking, and that just ripped Malcolm up
and down. I don't think he ever got over the hurt of that."

In the spring of 1964, from April 13 to May 21, Malcolm toured
the Middle East and Africa. He flew first to Cairo, then to Jedda,
and made a pilgrimage to Mecca. He sent Dick Schaap a postcard. "It said, 'Greetings from Mecca'" and described the holy
city as "'the fountain of truth, love, peace, and brotherhood.'"
(Schaap mentions by the way that the *Herald-Tribune* printed
Malcolm's message "the day after he was shot, and unfortunately,

the original of the postcard vanished in the composing room that day; so all I've got is a photostat.")

Alex Haley also received a postcard from Mecca. In "fine handwriting," says Haley, Malcolm wrote that he had " 'eaten from the same plate with fellow Muslims whose eyes were bluer than blue, whose hair was blond, blonder than blond, whose skin was whiter than white.' " Malcolm then added, " 'And we were all the same.' " Haley finds in this message from Mecca a sign of profound change in Malcolm: "I don't think anything I ever saw or heard connected with him gave me the feeling or impact that that did of how much he had changed, because that would not have been the Malcolm I had known earlier. There is no way he ever would have written or thought or felt that earlier. So he was changing very much."

"I had gotten two postcards from him," recounts James Farmer, "from Mecca, on his two separate trips there. He went to Mecca and then left Mecca and went elsewhere, the Third World, and then returned to Mecca. At a later date I asked him if those postcards had indicated a change in his thinking, and he asked if I could refresh his memory as to what he had said in the cards. I told him the first card had said: 'Dear Brother James, I am now in Mecca, the most beautiful and sacred city in the world, where I have witnessed pilgrims of all colors'—and he had underscored all colors—'worshipping Allah in perfect peace and harmony and brotherhood such as I have never seen in the States.' Second card, and it was signed with his new name, the name he had accepted over there—Malik El-Shabazz: 'Here I am, back in Mecca. I am still traveling, trying to broaden my mind, for I've seen too much of the damage narrow-mindedness can make of things, and when I return home to America, I will devote what energies I have to repairing the damage.' When I asked him if that indicated a change in his thinking, he said that yes, as a matter of fact, it did. 'I have some explaining to do,' he said, 'I was not so lucky as you were. I had very little formal education, eight grades. I am self-educated. I read for myself; mostly in prison I read the dictionary backwards,' and he said, 'consequently I believed everything the Honorable Elijah Muhammad told us, and the Honorable Elijah Muhammad told us that Islam was a black man's religion—exclusively—and that the blue-eyed devils could not get close to

Mecca, that they would be killed if they tried to enter that sacred city. In Mecca I saw blue-eyed blonds worshipping Allah just as I was, kneeling right beside me, so obviously the Honorable Elijah Muhammad had lied.'

"Malcolm had to do a lot of rethinking then," Farmer continues. "He was an honest man. He didn't try to adjust the facts to fit what he had been saying, he tried to adjust what he had been saying to fit the facts. He said then, 'When I was in Accra, Ghana, I met with the Algerian ambassador to Ghana, and he asked me what my program was, and I proceeded to tell him my plan and programs for my black brothers and sisters. He said, "Well, Brother Malcolm, that leaves me out, doesn't it?" I asked what he meant; he said, "I'm your Mohammedan brother, but I'm not your black brother. Racially, I'm Caucasian." ' And Malcolm said that shook him up even more for some reason and he really had to sit down and do some thinking. And reexamine, search his soul, ask himself where the process had led him. He said, 'Well, I have come to the conclusion, Brother James, that anybody who will fight along with us—not for us, but with us—is my brother, and that goes for your three guys, too'—Schwerner, Goodman, and Chaney; those were the three who were killed in Mississippi, and he knew very well that two of those were my staff members and that two of them, Schwerner and Goodman, were Jewish. So this was quite a concession for Malcolm X to be making. I asked him why his speeches at Harlem Square Saturday afternoons had not reflected that so far, that change in direction, and he said, 'Brother James, you must be enough of a politician to understand that if a leader makes a sudden right angle turn, he turns alone.' "

Benjamin Karim too was struck by the change in Malcolm, because, like Malcolm, he had been "taught there were no white people who were Muslims, no Caucasians. We were also taught that Caucasians could not enter the city of Mecca. So we really had something unique, just unique for black people. Not only that, but our Islam was different than that the rest of the Muslims had in the world. But when Malcolm made the pilgrimage to Mecca—the hajj—when the hajj is made, there are millions of people from all over the world, every color, every shade in the world—and during that pilgrimage he did not see any signs of any kind of racism, any kind of color prejudice, or any notion of it, or any consciousness of anybody conscious of his or her own color. The Mufti—the Grand Mufti, I believe, of Jordan—with blond hair and blue eyes! So he was really shocked into reality, and that shock woke Malcolm up that humanity is one." Karim does note, however, that "everybody is not ready for the same truth."

Perhaps Malcolm himself was not ready for that truth five years before, in July 1959, when he visited Mecca for the first time, or perhaps he was in no position to acknowledge it. He was traveling then as Elijah Muhammad's ambassador. "He had been to the Middle East before," Peter Goldman points out. "He had gone over there for Elijah Muhammad. He was quite aware that there were white Muslims. He would deny it, I mean, he would flat out deny it, as a matter of politics, when he was in the NOI." C. Eric Lincoln also remarks that when Malcolm had traveled to the Middle East before, he had gone "as the emissary of Elijah Muhammad, and he always wore the blinders of being the most faithful follower of Elijah Muhammad, so what he saw he saw through those eyes. But it is possible that on that last trip the blinders were off, or at least partially." Change has its degrees. "I do not believe," Lincoln states further, "that Malcolm was suddenly and completely metamorphosed with his break with Elijah Muhammad; I think that would have taken time."

Lincoln observes too that "people who look for changes see them." They also interpret them. John Henrik Clarke views Malcolm as a man who had been constantly undergoing change long before the events in "the last few years of his life. People think," says Clarke, perhaps referring to a letter from Malcolm about his experience in Mecca that was printed in *The New York Times,* "that when Malcolm went to Mecca and wrote that card back saying he observed whites and browns and all different colors praying together, they think that meant his change toward integration, but that was an observation and not an analysis, and people have done Malcolm a terrible injustice by misinterpreting that." What may have seemed like a very abrupt change was, Clarke repeats, "not a change at all, it was an observation."

Or it may have been an ambiguity. Malcolm was quite familiar with ambiguities, according to Peter Goldman: "Probably as long as I had known him, he was feeling ambiguities. He just couldn't admit them, ambiguities about the world. It was not quite so—no pun intended—it was not so black and white as the doctrines of the Lost-Found Nation of Islam made it seem. I think he had already come to understand that whites were not literally the devil. I think he continued to believe, probably till the day he died, that you can search the history of white people for angelic deeds and not find a whole lot of them. I think in his sort of mercurial last year—*mercurial*'s the wrong word, *protean* is probably better—he was going through changes at great velocity, and I think as he was learning more about the world he was, I think, growing himself. I mean, I think his move toward 'orthodox' Islam —I'm not sure there is such a thing as orthodox in Islam, but I mean the way Islam is practiced in the Middle East—I think it deepened his religious understanding and also deepened his human understanding. He was no longer a man of certainties, and I think that once that falls away, a guy of his intelligence flowers."

A month after his pilgrimage to Mecca Malcolm visited Ghana. Among the African-American expatriates in residence there Malcolm again met Maya Angelou. She recalls that "the trip was a real eye-opener for Malcolm on so many levels." Angelou had always respected and appreciated Malcolm, "but my appreciation increased really noticeably after he said, 'I have always said whites were blue-eyed devils, but I have been to Mecca and I have seen whites with blue eyes with whom I felt a brotherhood, and so I can no longer say this—that all whites are evil.' It took a lot of courage to say that—an amazing amount of courage. It took an incredible amount of insight, first, to give up what one had said for years and years and say, 'Just wait a minute, let me relook at this, let me rethink, respeak this,' but he had the courage to do so and the insight to do so, and then the courage to say so, which just humbled me. He had no loyalty to misconceptions. He was intelligent and courageous enough to admit when a position no longer held true, and that's amazing. Very few people have that; most people would rather like to say what they say they believe in and then repeat themselves instead of saying, 'I'm not in love with the position, I'm in love with the search for truth'—and that was Malcolm."

Alice Windom had been living in Ghana since the autumn of 1962. She had met Malcolm only once before, in 1960 or 1961, in

Chicago, at the NOI temple, where he had spoken and demonstrated his "spectacular and spellbinding" oratorical skills. In Africa Malcolm was equally exciting with a crowd, but Windom and other of the African-American residents in Accra also had the opportunity to see him and speak with him in more leisurely circumstances. "He seemed very relaxed," says Windom, and "we felt we got to know him there. He was a very sensitive and very wise person."

Windom reflects upon that spring when Malcolm was in Africa. "He had been in Ghana for a week, May 10 to 17. That week was just filled with high points, everything was a highlight—the speeches, the time we would sit in the hotel talking, when Malcolm wasn't too tired. Usually, we were all smoking, and he wasn't, and he would talk about the bad effect of smoking on your health and advise us that we ought to stop, not in any holier-than-thou way, but just to say that if you were going to be around for the struggle, you needed to take care of your health and smoking was bad for you. Those were the quiet times, and also when we would be in a restaurant or hotel, chatting. . . .

"We talked about what was going on in the States, what his plans for political activity were when he returned to the U.S., what those of us who were African residents could do to cooperate with his new organization—the OAAU [Organization of Afro-American Unity]. He said that when he got back to the U.S., he intended to organize people to work on racial problems in the U.S., and we would be his cooperating or coordinating agency in Africa. One of the things he was doing in Africa was eliciting support to bring charges against the U.S. for racism with the United Nations. Malcolm had been chafing to get into the political life of the U.S.; that was one of the differences he had with the NOI. The prohibition that the NOI had placed on Malcolm's political involvement was the only specific aspect he mentioned about being happy that he was no longer a member of the NOI. I didn't get the impression he was glad to be out of the Nation. I doubt that he was, because it meant he had to go out and build a new organization."

In July 1964 Malcolm returned to Africa as the representative of the OAAU for the African Summit Conference in Cairo, at which he appealed to the delegates of the thirty-four African nations to bring the cause of the twenty-two million African Americans in the United States before the United Nations. After the second summit conference in August Malcolm extended his stay in Africa well into November; he visited a third of its countries, talked with their heads of state, addressed their parliaments. In Ethiopia he ran into Alice Windom.

"The only time I saw Malcolm after he left Accra [in May]," Windom recalls, "was in Ethiopia later on that same year. I had gone with Julian [Mayfield] and Maya [Angelou] to Cairo, hoping to meet Malcolm there, and I had found him gone. I went on to Ethiopia to work for the United Nations, and the second or third day I was there he walked into the hotel dining room. He was traveling in East Africa. He was interested in seeing Emperor Haile Selassie and he was not successful in doing that; the Emperor was a client of the U.S. and really did not want to meet with Malcolm for that reason. He told me about the other heads of state that he had met in East Africa and he felt he had had a successful trip there, but again Ghana probably was the high point because of the presence of the large African-American community there. The Ghanaians were also progressive politically because of Kwame Nkrumah's leadership and the groundwork he had laid to educate people about the whole racial situation everywhere in the world; everybody was ready for Malcolm there."

More than Malcolm's understanding of Islam had changed when he returned to New York that May from his tour of the Middle East and Africa, although his experience in Mecca was of course, in Charles Kenyatta's words, "the big story, and the reporters kept asking, 'Did you see them?' And Malcolm said, 'Yes, I saw them. They had blond hair and blue eyes,' and it developed that their religion was different. So this is what caused a big stir." Another change—less dramatic perhaps, but one noticed immediately by Kenyatta—was that "he and I were the first to start growing beards. He had started when he was over there, and he came back and I had a beard, so we were both laughing about it. In Islam, at that time, black Muslims had skinny heads, clean faces, and they started to say he and I were losing our minds." What the black Muslims were saying had more to do with hope than hyperbole: "Because," says Kenyatta, "that was one of the things that

Elijah Muhammad—due to the fact that Malcolm had a number of mental breakdowns in his family, that was one of the things that they were relying upon, that Malcolm would eventually go crazy."

There was also another story that May, according to Kenyatta. "I think I'm one of the only ones—in fact, I know I'm one of the only ones—that detected his hurt. And he was going to be, if you could understand how the Nation of Islam was when a member was put out of the mosque. Oh, I've seen older men cry and weep, because they didn't want to go back into what they called the grave; and Malcolm was no different. And the whole crux of the story, I believe, is that ten or fifteen minutes before he was assassinated, if Elijah Muhammad had asked him to come back, he would have come back." Rather than working through the recently formed MMI or founding the OAAU, Malcolm, Kenyatta says, "would have preferred to stay [with the NOI]. No question about it, that I do know."

Malcolm's independence from the NOI meant, as Alice Windom has observed, "he had to go out and build a new organization." Similarly, Alex Haley notes that "he had to create some organization of his own because the power base was gone. His power base had been the Nation of Islam." To use television journalist Mike Wallace's terms, he had lost his constituency. Wallace remembers "feeling at the time that this is a man in transition, this is a man who is evolving, this is a man who deserves a wider constituency. And I remember feeling how sad it was that he was unable to find that constituency and the money and whatever else is needed to get launched. As a reporter—obviously, I'm just a reporter—but in my heart I felt that he had a great deal to offer and I was sad that he wasn't finding the support in the community."

The black community, however, was already divided. "Determined [as Malcolm was] to start his own organization," in Claude Lewis's opinion, for him or "for anybody to step away from the original leader and come up with his own program, and to offer a new ideal, a new playing ground" required more than intelligence, will, charisma, or rhetoric. It required staff, financing, strategy, community support. Malcolm had entered a field already crowded with players—among them his one friend in the civil rights leadership, James Farmer, director of CORE. The public, Lewis continues, "had grown used to people like Roy Wilkins [of the NAACP] and like the head of the Urban League, Whitney Young, whom Malcolm referred to as 'Whitey' Young—he would pretend to slip in his language." And, of course, like the eloquent president of the Southern Christian Leadership Conference, Dr. Martin Luther King, Jr. (After the split with Elijah Muhammad, Lewis notes, Malcolm "began to say kinder things about Martin Luther King, Jr., because he used to laugh at King. King got the peace prize, but we've got the problem, he would say." The sally James Farmer particularly remembers came "after King's speech in the March on Washington, which I missed—I was in jail at the time—and Malcolm said [of King's dream] that it was a nightmare, only he's too dumb to know it.") As Mike Wallace points out: "There were so many leaders, there were so many voices. I mean, think back to that time. I mean, there were so many black voices out there and talking and established and it was a very jealous group, one vying with the other for attention, constituency, support, money."

On March 12, 1964, when Malcolm had announced at a press conference the formation of his militant black nationalist organization, the Muslim Mosque, Incorporated, he had stated emphatically that he would use his personal resources not "to fight other Negro leaders or organizations" but to "find a common approach, a common solution, to a common problem." Malcolm had spoken earlier that day with C. Eric Lincoln, who recounts the conversation. "Malcolm was [going to be] on the news at about 11:00 that morning and I asked him what he was going to do, and he said, 'I really don't know, Professor; I haven't made up my mind, but I'll tell you what I am not going to do: I am not going to start a movement in the competition of the Honorable Elijah Muhammad. I could never do that.' He said he might start some kind of school for black people to learn how to become Muslims, and I guess what he meant by that, although he didn't say so, was orthodox Muslims. He made it clear to me that he wasn't going to start a community movement and that he hadn't thought through what he was going to do."

Up to that time Malcolm had needed neither his own organization nor a plan. Professor Lincoln thinks it a "truthful hypothesis to conclude that because Malcolm was so completely reliant on Muhammad, it was never necessary to work out a plan for the future." He also suspects that "when Malcolm and Elijah came to a parting of ways, it was a sudden, cataclysmic event in the lives of both people. If Malcolm had had any intention of leading a group from that point on, he was caught without having had a chance to give it any kind of thought. One would suppose that had Malcolm survived he would have had the time to do that because he had spent all of his time, as [Louis] Lomax correctly said, telling us what Mr. Muhammad had said." Mike Wallace has a similar thought: "I felt that Malcolm had yet to realize himself on his own. I used to say back then in discussing him that he was playing Bishop Fulton Sheen to Elijah's pope."

"A new Malcolm," though, was in the making; so Peter Goldman feels. Struggling to define both a new role and a new politics for himself, he was, Goldman asserts, "in effect recreating himself yet again, not for the first time in his life, and he didn't have long enough to do it. He was like a guy suddenly out there in the sunlight and blinking in the bright sun and sort of sorting out ideas in literal and psychic motion for the rest of his life, and there wasn't time to make it whole. When he did come out, he was sort of arguing a very conventional line—I hate to say conventional; it was probably akin to the early black power ideology. It was black control of the politics and the economy of the ghetto, blacks controlling places where they were. That was probably routine stuff even then, but it flowered with the black power movement a couple years after Malcolm's death. But as he traveled abroad other elements came into his thinking, both religious and political, and I think he was still trying to sort all of them out. And he had a lot of contending voices at home, a lot of factions within his group and a lot of outside people all wanting a piece of him, essentially. So would he have ever found what he was looking for? I'm not sure, but he sure didn't have a chance to try."

On June 28, 1964, six weeks after Malcolm's return to New York from Africa, he announced the formation of the Organization of Afro-American Unity. "It was formed in my living room," remembers John Henrik Clarke. "I was the one who got the constitution from the Organization of African Unity in order to model our constitution after it. Malcolm's joy was that we could

match up [our constitution with the African one]; we could find
parallels between the African situation and the African-American
situation—that plus a whole lot of other things we agreed with
that had nothing to do with religion, because we agreed with the
basic struggle. We agreed on self-reliance, about what people
would have to do, and that an ethnic community was really a
small nation and that you need everything within that community
that goes into a small nation, including a person who would take
care of the labor, the defense, employment, morality, spirituality
—no matter what religion you follow, you need one person whose
main concern is the spirituality of the community." In essence,
though, the OAAU was designed to alter the perception of the
African-American struggle for freedom as a domestic issue by
placing it on the international level of human rights. "Malcolm
saw the African-American situation," Clarke says, "and he saw
civil rights really as a part of human rights, and he wanted to
internationalize it." It was a program, if not a plan.

Although Malcolm may have not yet formulated a concrete
plan, a pursuable strategy, for the struggle of blacks in America,
he was nevertheless, Peter Goldman thinks, "trying a number of
things. He was trying to make a human case against the United
States at the U.N., charging systematic violation of human rights.
That was getting nowhere; there were too many U.S. client states
who gave him attention but not much more. He had committees
of well-meaning people working on various aspects of various
programs; none of it ever happened. That was not his thing, and I
don't think it's important to, not quite relevant to, judge him
solely by that measure." For Goldman, the measure of Malcolm's
greatness lies in his power as a teacher, in his ability to raise the
consciousness of his people to their race and to history. Goldman
sees Malcolm "moving beyond a kind of victim psychology. The
Nation of Islam was a kind of codification of a victim psychology,
and I think Malcolm was trying to move beyond that—and in very
different ways from what Martin Luther King was doing. For all
the vast differences between them, they had a similar objective,
which was to get people in motion to seize history so as not to be
its objects but to be its subjects, to grab control of history."

Malcolm strove to change history. "He was the cutting edge of
the black struggle," in William Kunstler's view, and he was fight-

ing a war. "There really is no concrete plan," says Kunstler. "This is a civil war, essentially, waged in many corners of this country, and it's a war that is in many ways a highly psychological one. It is a war that changed black people's awareness of themselves—the terribly low self-image, which was created by whites in a racist attempt to keep blacks in a subservient slave or neo-slave capacity, and a corollary feeling of white superiority over blacks." Attitudes have changed, but "until those things are eradicated—which will take generations, or even centuries," Kunstler thinks—Malcolm's war goes on.

Another generation is hearing Malcolm's words. "Because he spoke to separatism," Mike Wallace concludes, "because he spoke to nationalism, because he spoke to black pride. Because he was a superb speaker and in the national media capital . . . But the fact is," Wallace adds, "he was on his uppers, wasn't he? I mean, he didn't have money, he didn't have funds. He didn't have a big following. He had a devoted but small following."

Small though Malcolm's following was, Claude Lewis indicates that "a lot of blacks—Negroes, in those days—identified with Malcolm, but they were afraid to come out in the open. I suggested that I would like to sign up with him, and he said that you don't have to come out in the open, because the roots are the strongest part of the tree—only you don't see them." Malcolm's appeal, and contribution to the black movement in the 1960s, for Lewis, "was that he made blacks feel good about themselves and to feel more confidence; to appreciate their physical characteristics. I remember clearly in those days people trying to bleach their skin and straighten their hair. Malcolm said that was wrong, [that we should] love Mother Africa. Here was a guy who made black people feel good about their thick lips and their hair, which used to be called nappy, and he allowed them to have self-esteem and convinced them that they had power, they had authority, and that they were not minorities if you looked at it from a world perspective."

Malcolm was "dangerous," says Sonia Sanchez. He indeed roused the pride of black Americans, but he also stirred their minds and imaginations, and after his return from Mecca, Sanchez explains, we felt "his impact on the black intellectual class—the black middle class, the class of people who had other influences too—as he was in New York, which was the center of the new Black Renaissance. In the same fashion that [Marcus] Garvey finally guided some of the intellectuals to deal with him on some levels, [so] Malcolm did with us. Our poetry [echoed] this man, resounded with what he was saying. The point is, most of the intellectuals I knew at that time were followers of Malcolm, although they had not announced it (that's the key)—even the so-called middle-class blacks. He stirred their imaginations through his words to remove the restraints and constraints that they found themselves in; they were beginning to give money to him. Malcolm stirred the imaginations of all blacks, whether they admitted it or not. He stirred them to go back to their yearning of 'I want to be a lawyer, a doctor, an Indian chief—but I also want to have my dignity,' and he was saying it's possible. You had to have the experience after coming through this educational system that hounded you, that said, 'Yes, you have a degree, but you're inferior. Yes, you're a doctor, but you're still a nigger,' [and Malcolm said,] 'I can tell you how not to be a nigger in this country.' "

The messages of Malcolm X had always reached the streets, and the urban reality warranted his cries for freedom and dignity and justice. The northern ghettos echoed his calls for unity, for racial solidarity. In Harlem they rallied and demanded the human right to be "by any means necessary." Malcolm's people were city people. "The line that he adopted," notes Elombe Braath, was "more militant . . . more African nationalist and more revolutionary—you know, really more germane to black people in this country, particularly those in the urban areas. Malcolm, his people, the people who supported him, were in the cities. . . . And people took up that line, and all in the spirit of Malcolm X. And all through the years the more they've professed it, the more people have been out here [in the streets]. That goes for myself. I see Malcolm as representative of an era. . . .

"Malcolm represented that era."

"I'll tell you something else," Ralph Wiley says. "I had no idea of what he looked like until much later in life, his complexion, nothing—nothing did I know about how he looked until I was thirty years old. This is what I am saying about the pureness of the rhetoric: it was like a life preserver. I was slowly going down. I can't express to you the weight of the deaths, of the murders—not his but the people involved in the civil rights struggle. . . .

"Mr. Medgar Evers in Mississippi, Ms. Mary Louise, the three civil rights workers, Bobby Kennedy," Wiley counts them, "and probably most startling, Dr. [Martin Luther] King—that was right in Memphis. So there was a dullness of spirit, and I suppose I could have gone either way. In the context of my life I was not being informed; I was being formed, but not in the right way. I was either going to become a very bitter person or a very cowardly person, one or the other, until I read about this gentleman."

The gentleman was Malcolm X. "He came into my consciousness at such a time when I really could have been psychologically devastated," states Wiley, who had grown up "thinking that if you had any personal dignity, you were only going to be killed, and if you were black and accepted it, you were a second-class citizen. To me that's now nonsense, not necessarily because of what King said but by what Malcolm X said." Wiley had grown up in Memphis, and "what Dr. King was saying was inherently obvious to me, although white people may have been shocked that, well, black people are human and should be treated fairly and equally in a social sense, that to me was self-evident. But this other proposition, this proposition that I could also be a man, was very much in question."

Wiley had grown up too with demonstrations and reprisals, with racist incidents and iniquity, with death, murders, assassinations. But: "Here was a man who said, well, death doesn't matter —the Oxford Union debate [December 3, 1964; Malcolm defended the use of extremism in the pursuit of freedom]. He said that any time a government refuses to accept [the just demands of the people], then those people have a right to protect and try to uplift themselves by any means necessary. People take that now [to mean merely] 'oh, by any means necessary,' like that's what I do as a free-lancer, that's by any means necessary. I wish there was a way I could tell you, but . . .

"He allowed me to, through his own experiences he allowed me, to say, 'Hmmm, that is right. Of course, that's right—oh my goodness, I can do what I want to do. I don't have to accept certain behaviors imposed upon me. I don't have to bear the brunt of humanity.'"

"To me Malcolm X is pure rhetoric," Ralph Wiley says, and purely through that rhetoric, Malcolm X, he says, "saved my mental life."

William Kunstler, who served as special trial counselor to Dr. Martin Luther King, Jr., in the early 1960s, speaks of a telephone conversation between Malcolm and Dr. King on February 14, 1965: "There was sort of an agreement that they would meet in the future and work out a common strategy, not merge their two organizations—Malcolm then had the Organization of Afro-American Unity and Martin, of course, was the president of the Southern Christian Leadership Conference—but that they would work out a method to work together in some way. And I think that that quite possibly led to the bombing of Malcolm's house that evening in East Elmhurst and his assassination one week later."

Eventually Kunstler, a New York attorney, would find himself representing two of the co-defendants, Thomas 15X Johnson and Norman 3X Butler, who had been convicted, along with Thomas Hayer, of the murder of Malcolm X. At the trial in 1966 Hayer testified that he and four accomplices had indeed been hired to assassinate Malcolm; he had also tried to exonerate both Johnson and Butler. In Kunstler's reconstruction of the events in the Audubon Ballroom that Sunday afternoon in February, Johnson and Butler were not even there.

Kunstler narrates. "[Benjamin Goodman] warmed up the audience for the half hour before Malcolm came out at three o'clock. Goodman, who [now] has a Muslim name [Benjamin Karim] and lives in Richmond, I believe, was a member of the Nation of Islam's Fruit of Islam, which was essentially the security guard, and his job was to see whether any Fruit of Islam people were in that audience, because Malcolm had given orders that no one was to be searched—but the idea was, if they saw any FOI people, they would watch them. But they saw no one in there, and both Butler and Johnson were members of the Fruit of Islam in Manhattan, and so Goodman swears—and I have an affidavit from him—swears that they were not in the hall. And the D.A. never called him as a witness, even though he was facing the audience just as Malcolm gave his salaams and was shot. The incident about the hand in the pocket did occur, but it occurred between two men who were seated in the back. The idea was that one would stand up and scream, 'Nigger, what are you doing with your hand in my pocket?' and the other would throw a smoke bomb, and then everybody's eyes would turn to the back while Hayer and his two companions, who were sitting in the first and second rows, would rush up and assassinate Malcolm. So the incident happened, but it was not Butler and it was not Johnson. In any event, they would be in the back if that were true, because that shout came from the back of the room and not the front. Goodman didn't know Hayer from a hole in the ground, so he would never have recognized him."

Furthermore, Kunstler argues, "Butler and Johnson weren't picked up till a week later, Hayer was found at the scene. And how would Hayer have gotten together with them? Because Hayer was really not a New Yorker at all. He lived in Paterson, and he was a member of the Newark mosque. And he named the four people that went with him, whose Cadillac it was and where it was appointed, and how they cased the dance at the Audubon Ballroom the night before, and how they made all the arrangements to do the assassination and get back in the car and across the George Washington Bridge and over to Paterson again; and it was all a Jersey operation. [After the trial] Hayer named all of them and told where they lived, and that was not enough to get a new trial because nobody wanted a new trial except Butler and Johnson. The D.A. was satisfied, the judge was satisfied, Betty Shabazz was satisfied, and they wouldn't even have an evidentiary hearing to have Hayer come down and talk about this on the stand. So everyone wanted to wipe it out."

It is Kunstler's opinion that the crime against Malcolm "was committed by members of the Newark mosque, including Thomas Hayer, and it was undoubtedly the result of terrible, terrible hostility which was engendered by the FBI telling [both Malcolm and Elijah Muhammad] in anonymous letters that they were going to kill each other [and which] created this terrible, terrible tension that led these five men at the Newark mosque to eliminate Malcolm X; and even though they fired the guns, three of them, the FBI was the real hand on the trigger."

When the news broke that Malcolm X had been cut down by

assassins' bullets, Mike Wallace recalls feeling mostly "utter shock and dismay. But," Wallace notes, "he had predicted it. It was almost a death wish, I felt, because he went around saying these things about Elijah particularly and the black Muslim leadership in general, and the Nation of Islam was a tough crowd."

An interview with Malcolm that Wallace particularly remembers occurred when "we were over at 480 Lex and he came to my office and sat down with me—this would've been 1964, this was a few months before he was killed—and he was having trouble getting his OAAU together. He didn't have a large constituency, he didn't have funds. He was up against the Muslims, but he was also up against the SCLC and NAACP and he was trying to find his niche in that constellation of black organizations, and he said—I don't know how we got into it, but he began to tell me about Elijah being a lecher, and he told me the story of how he had spawned these children, sired these children, with a young woman who had served him as a secretary or aide, and I didn't believe him, and he said, 'I'll get them on the phone.' And he got them on the phone, and I listened, and it was quite apparent; and that's when I did the interview with him in which I said, 'This must be very dangerous for you,' and he said, 'Yes, I'm probably a dead man already.'"

One night, in his office at the New York Post, Claude Lewis received a telephone call from Malcolm. "He said, 'Can we talk?' I said, 'Sure, what's up?' and he said, 'I want to give you a story that I haven't given anyone else.' He began to tell me about Elijah Muhammad impregnating one of his young secretaries, and I said, 'Well, you weren't saying that in the past.' He said, 'Well, I found out and I have the people—the young woman and other people—who will speak about this.' This was three months before he was killed. I took it to the editors at the Post and they said, 'Well, we don't want to take it on the basis of a phone call,' which I didn't understand, so we never ran the story. Consequently it got out from other sources. I think that's the thing that really angered the Muslims. To them, he had dishonored a god by bringing Elijah Muhammad down to human levels on human terms. That was a fatal mistake." By discrediting Elijah Muhammad, Lewis believes, Malcolm hoped to enhance his own image and build his own organization, the OAAU. "What I think he forgot,"

Lewis adds, "was that he had trained, or at least he said he'd trained, many Muslims on how to kill. He forgot that they might turn the gun towards him, and that is probably what they did."

Robert Haggins also remarks that Malcolm "needed protection from the very people that he had trained"—and knew it. Certainly, says Haggins, "he was conscious that he was going to be killed. He told me this and he told other people the same thing; as a matter of fact, he went on the air and said so." He talked about it often and candidly with Claude Lewis, and said that "he expected to be killed. The unsettling thing for him was that he never knew when it was going to come—the next month or that year. He just didn't know [as] there was no real indication. He kept saying, 'I have a lot to get done, a lot of things to tie together, to bring together, because the movement will go on long after I am gone.' That was primary in his concern, that the ball not be dropped. He was going to stay in the fight."

Malcolm's fight had always been in America; but, then, by the summer of 1964 so was his fate. With no doubt Peter Goldman says, "Malcolm had very specific and very real fears and they were focused on the Nation of Islam. There are suggestions that he changed his mind in the last week and began to believe that there was some government agency that might be involved also. I've interviewed one of the assassins. If it was a government plot, he's unaware—but that's entirely possible. I don't believe that it was. Malcolm expressed his fear to people that he saw in Africa, again it had to do with the Nation of Islam. For a long time he postponed his return to the U.S. and was encouraged by friends he met over there to stay there, where he was safe. And they weren't thinking CIA, because he wouldn't have been safe from the CIA in Africa."

"Everyone was talking about Malcolm's impending death, and Malcolm was talking about it, in my apartment," James Farmer recalls. Malcolm had visited Farmer at his apartment shortly before the CORE director set off on his tour of Africa. They were also talking about it in Ghana, Farmer discovered, when he arrived in Accra near the end of January 1965. One conversation about Malcolm's death, however, did surprise—and disturb—Farmer. He was speaking with a "young lady" in his hotel dining room, and "the thing that surprised me was that she said Muslims

are not going to kill him. [She said] there was another group far
more dangerous than the Muslims that was after him, and they
were going to get him, but it would be blamed on the Muslims. I
asked her who this other group was, and she refused to say and
said if I quoted her or used her name—any of this—she would
deny she ever saw me. I pressed her on it, and she became almost
hysterical and began looking around to see who was overhearing
and finally she got up and left the table and walked out. And she
had called the date of his murder, his assassination, very close.
This was February 1, and she said he was going to be killed sometime between then and April 1." Twenty days after that conversation Malcolm was dead.

Farmer tried several times over the next few years to locate the
woman he had met in Ghana, and eventually he traced her to
New York. He spoke with her on the telephone, and when he
mentioned their conversation that evening at the hotel in Accra,
"she was quiet a moment. Then she said, 'I don't remember any
such conversation at all and I can't talk anymore. I've got a role in
an off-Broadway production, I'm acting now and gotta go to re-
hearsal, but call me back about the middle of next week, because
rehearsals will be over by Tuesday of next week.' I called her back
on Wednesday and her number had been changed to an unlisted
one. So she was still running scared."

But from whom? Farmer thinks "it was either of two groups or
both. The Mafia—the U.S. Mafia—because Malcolm was hurting
their drug trafficking business in Harlem with his street corner
meetings, his Harlem Square meetings, where he had large
crowds on Saturdays, and he was telling the young blacks to chase
the pushers out of Harlem—you know who they are, you know
the clothes they wear, the shoes they wear, the cars they drive, the
women who hang on their arms—chase 'em out! Now these pushers were black, but they were tied in with the mob downtown and
young guys were chasing them out of Harlem. And the other
possibility was the CIA, and their motives could have been two.
One, Malcolm was damaging the image of the U.S. abroad, especially in Third World countries. Two, Malcolm was internation-
alizing the race issue here by seeking to persuade—and making
progress toward persuading—African delegations of the United
Nations to bring the United States up on charges of violating the

U.N. human rights charter. So it could have been one or the other or both. They sometimes work together, as they did, you know, in their attempt to kill Castro."

For Robert Haggins, Malcolm's attempt to internationalize the African-American struggle for human rights accounts in part for the assassination. On his last tour of Africa, after the African Summit Conferences of July and August 1964, Malcolm visited, Haggins says, "thirty-three African countries and had commitments in his pocket from three African leaders. No one since has done that. Jesse Jackson made an attempt, but he couldn't do it. Malcolm X had three written commitments from African nations, and I believe that it was one of the reasons he was killed—because he had decided to take the United States of America to the U.N. and charge them with violation of human rights. The hell with civil rights, we are human beings first, let's get our human rights and then our civil rights will follow. Nobody was like Malcolm on that. He was all alone. He still is!"

"There were some crazy things going on then. You wouldn't believe it!" Benjamin Karim is talking about the random freakish incidents that were occurring those last edgy weeks before Malcolm's assassination. Like the night Karim called Malcolm's house and got a recording that the number he had dialed had been disconnected. He had in fact just left Malcolm; they had been to a meeting, and Karim was calling to make sure that Malcolm had gotten safely home. So, as Karim tells it, "we [the brothers] knew that something was wrong. So we got in, filled up about three cars—everybody was armed—and we drove across the Triborough Bridge like Pancho Villa, man, with rifles hanging out the car. We went to his house. When we got out there, he was home. We knocked on the door and he came out and we told him the operator had told us that his telephone had been disconnected. He said that somebody had called the telephone company and told them to disconnect this phone because he wouldn't be home for some time. Alright, in the meantime, there was a car that was parked down the street from his house. So we lined the street with these rifles, everybody had rifles, and this car began to move out very slowly, very carefully, and there was about twenty men out with rifles. So when the car got up to where we were, we put a roadblock there, and it was detectives, who were watching his house. But, you know, they just went on. I had to say that to say this: that we were with him, we were all together, and there was nothing that could cause us to break away from him, probably except his death. . . . He was our leader."

The gray winter days had held cause for alarm. There had been death threats, more than several of them. Malcolm would speak of them "rather matter-of-factly" with the collaborator on his autobiography, Alex Haley: "He would just say, 'Brother, I don't think I'm going to live to read this book in print.' " Haley remembers Malcolm describing "the time he had been in Los Angeles, and he was in a car with others and they came to some kind of tunnel. [That's when] they saw another car behind them, in which they knew were people who were enemies: They were all members of the Nation of Islam, but they were all anti-him. And as this other car drew closer—it seemed, like, in this tunnel—he had a cane; he, Malcolm, had a walking cane—and he slipped that cane out of the back window and worked it behind so that it looked like a rifle barrel. And the other car fell back rapidly, and they got away without difficulty."

A similar incident occurred in Boston the first or second week in February. "The word was out that the people from Farrakhan's temple were going to assassinate Malcolm," and Benjamin Karim had volunteered to go in Malcolm's place. "Because to me," says Karim, "it was an honor." Malcolm nevertheless attended the meeting at his sister Ella's house, as did Karim. When they left, "some of the Muslims from Farrakhan's temple—and Malcolm had put shoes on his [Farrakhan's] feet when he first went to Boston, and food in his mouth—so, when we left, this Lincoln came out from behind us. Well, we passed it, right, and saw it behind us. We had a shotgun because I had known in advance that they were going to try to assassinate Malcolm, before we even left New York. The only thing I didn't have was help. Malcolm's cousin was driving—his car was this old Cadillac—so when we drove into Callahan Tunnel, this Lincoln cut us off. I got out of the car, and a friend of mine—we were in Japan together—pulled the shotgun from the floor and pointed it out the window, but he didn't pull the trigger. So I told him to give it to me, because if he wasn't going to pull the trigger, then I would, and I really was, but he wouldn't let me have it. In the meantime Malcolm's cousin was backing this old, rackety Cadillac into the Lincoln, I mean, he was hitting that thing, right. But, anyway, they saw the shotgun and I think that's what drove them back into the car that they were driving and that at the same time Malcolm's cousin was tearing apart with that old Cadillac. So we drove on to the airport. We got out at the airport and came into Eastern Airlines. We were standing there with a loaded shotgun, and the police came up and arrested us. Nothing ever came of it, we went back to a trial and we were all dismissed." (Louis Farrakhan, by the way, was not in the Lincoln. "No, he was safe at home," says Karim, "eating bean pie.")

On February 19 Maya Angelou returned to America. She spoke to Malcolm on the phone that Friday, "and he was telling me about some people trying to shoot him in the Lincoln Tunnel, and said to me, 'Why don't you stay [in New York]?' and I said that I had to go to California, but that I would be back in about a month, once I got my American legs back again, and on that following Sunday he was killed."

Active in the movement and headed for Mississippi, former Howard University student Michael Thelwell ran into Malcolm at the Newark Airport sometime around February 19 (Thelwell's memory places it two days before the assassination). William Kunstler, lawyer in the movement, was traveling with Thelwell. "Malcolm said he was going to Harvard," as Thelwell recalls their exchange. "He said he was going to Boston and that was why he was in the airport. But, for one thing, he needed a shave." Thelwell noticed, for another thing, that Malcolm looked "extremely worn down, and a little untidy. A little untidy, and even distraught, and that was the first and only time I had seen him looking that way, and so both Bill Kunstler and I were shocked. He had always been impeccably turned out—nothing elaborate, nothing flashy, but well groomed, perfectly groomed, and that contributed to the sense of control that you got from him—like here is somebody who is supremely controlled, supremely confident. And that had always been the case. And he mentioned something about people being after him and that he was in grave danger, and he was very clearly under considerable stress. And that was totally against the image that I had of him, certainly against the way I was used to seeing him. Bill Kunstler and I tried to reassure him, but it was just very sobering, kind of disconcerting, since I'd never seen him this way—worried, distraught."

Alex Haley spoke for the last time with Malcolm on Saturday evening, February 20. "His home had been bombed. He called, and it was the first time in all our acquaintance that I did not understand, I did not recognize, his voice when he called. You know how you know the voices of people you know, but he sounded like someone that was under a deep, heavy cold, and now I'm pretty sure it was stress to some degree. And he tried to make something jocular of it, he said something like 'You know, nobody would lend me a penny. Nobody would make me a loan in a bank. Nobody would write any insurance on me.' And he said that his house had been bombed—I knew that—and he said that he had nowhere for his children, his wife and children, to go. And he adored, I couldn't overestimate how much he adored, his wife and children, and how guilty he had felt that he wasn't doing the things he should, that he wasn't able materially to give them the things that he would have liked to. When he called me this day, he said that his home had been bombed and he had to get some place for his family to live. And then in this heavy, heavy, strained voice or tone or manner he asked if I would go to the publisher, if I would go back to Ken McCormick and ask him if it was possible that Doubleday might advance, I think it was, twenty thousand dollars, so he could get a home, and that was when he said, 'You know, nobody, no bank, would make me a loan.' And nobody would write insurance on him. I told him I would do the best I could, and he just said, you know, 'I'd appreciate it if you would do that.' And that was the last time I spoke with Malcolm, because the next day he was shot to death in the Audubon Ballroom."

Outside the Audubon Ballroom the next day, James Farmer was astonished to learn, "there was only one uniformed policeman, [since] Malcolm had given that interview to *The New York Times,* which was published a couple of days before, [and said] he was going to be killed because he knew too much, and at the Audubon Ballroom he was going to tell what he knew and who was going to kill him for knowing it." In fact, according to Peter Goldman, the police had been asked to take their guard detail off

the sidewalk in front of the Audubon as well as across the street—
by "a person speaking in Malcolm's name [who] was one of his
closest . . . aides, I guess, is the proper word—if it was possible
to speak in Malcolm's name. Why is difficult to know. The police
had knowledge that an assassination attempt was close; I don't
think they knew the day and the time, but they knew events were
in motion." Goldman's sources told him, too, that someone
speaking in Malcolm's name also instructed the brothers on guard
duty to leave their guns at home and not to search anyone attending the meeting that day.

About 2:30 P.M. on Sunday, February 21, Benjamin Karim
opened up the meeting for Malcolm. "Malcolm said, 'How are
you going to open up?' He would always say to follow your mind,
he would never ask me what I was going to say, but this time he
did. And I asked him, 'How do you want me to open up?' I felt so
heavy looking at him; just he and I were there together. So I told
him that I would open up in such a way to prepare the minds of
the audience to accept the fact that he didn't have the charter [for
the OAAU], which he had been promising the members—you can
do that, you can open up in such a way to prepare the minds of
the audience to accept almost anything—and he said okay. The
way I started out was about Columbus as captain of a ship head-
ing towards a destination point when a storm comes up, and
sometimes the captain has to go around the storm and that delays
him. That kind of thing that could delay the captain of the ship
would prepare them for him to tell them that he did not have the
charter."

Karim also remembers how he felt during the opening that
Sunday afternoon. Malcolm had lost his temper, uncharacteristi-
cally. "I never in my eight years as his assistant," says Karim, "I
never did see him lose his temper like he did. It was pressure.
. . . And when I opened up for him that day I felt like a big
gorilla was sitting on top of my shoulders. I believe I felt the same
thing that he did. I felt it because you can work so closely with a
person that you can almost feel what they feel, and you can sense
what they sense. They don't have to tell you, and you can sense
the heaviness of it without that person telling you. I felt it. And I
watched him."

Yuri Kuchiama was watching him too. Malcolm stepped up to the podium at the Audubon Ballroom. He was offering his customary greeting, "Assalaam alaikum," when a disturbance erupted in the auditorium, apparently a heated argument between two men. "I was sitting with my sixteen-year-old son right across from where the disturbance happened"—in the middle of the room, as Kuchiama remembers it—"and then two or three people got up in the first, second, and third rows and pulled out guns and started shooting. The whole place was in chaos. I saw one person pass through the aisle and head toward the stage. I wanted to go up there and be with Malcolm, so I followed this guy who went up to the stage. . . . I'm in one of the pictures that appeared in *Life* magazine, on the floor." Malcolm too had fallen to the floor.

"I watched him," says Benjamin Karim. "I watched him die."

Sonia Sanchez remembers. "I remember exactly where I was. I was in my apartment. It was so weird because it was the morning that I told Larry Neal that I was going to come out to the Audubon Ballroom to see Malcolm; I had seen Neal someplace the night before. It was a gray, cloudy, cold day and I got up late, so I just said, 'Well, I can get up there next week, next Sunday.' I was in my apartment. I had a black and white dinette set in my kitchen and a little black radio in the kitchen on the table, and at that time I still drank coffee. I put some water on the stove, turned the radio on, and I was moving back and forth between the hallway and the kitchen before I settled down to drink my coffee, and a flash came on the radio that Malcolm had been killed. And I stopped. I just stopped what I was doing and I put my head down and I screamed. But I wasn't screaming. No scream came out. And I opened the door to my apartment. I looked up on my floor, but no one was there, and I stood there, and I walked out to the elevator, but no one was there. And I turned around and came back, and I got on the telephone. And all the people I called, their lines were busy, so I knew that they knew, and then I went into the living room and screamed in a way that was not only primal but of such rage, and I said almost, in a sense, like, 'You will regret this; you know you cannot continue to kill these people who love us and need us, and we must not continue to let this happen.' "

For many who mourned him Malcolm's death marked the end of an era. For Claude Lewis, it also marked "the end of the best part of the movement," and it left "an emptiness I have lived with all these years." C. Eric Lincoln felt "not only that the movement had lost a champion but also that the dignity and the hopes of massive numbers of black people had lost a champion." Among those numbers stands Kathryn Gibson; she too counts losses: "It didn't seem like the end of the movement, it seemed like the loss of hope. It seemed like there was no one, like no one would ever fill that void. No one! Not a soul, not a soul. That's how it felt. It was like it was the death of a time, a death of a philosophy, a death of purpose. A death of hope. It was more than a physical death. You had no one to protect you anymore, no one to speak out . . ." Never—"no, never"—did it feel like the end of the movement to Sonia Sanchez; as she says of the assassination and death of Malcolm, "You understand in this business that that happens."

Malcolm certainly understood the business. Benjamin Karim believes that "men like Malcolm and other men like Martin Luther King and other leaders with a mission can sense death, they can sense they are not going to complete [the goals they've set]." They continue nevertheless, despite the threats and skirmishes, the personal losses and costs. "I believe he had less than a hundred and fifty dollars the night he was killed. And one day," Karim recalls, "we were walking in front of the Theresa Hotel, [not many days] before he was assassinated, and he said, 'Brother Benjamin, I just left the insurance company. I wanted to try and get life insurance and they wouldn't give it to me—too high a risk, they said. That tells you how much my life is worth.' And I said, 'Wow,' and he was walking along in these galoshes with every clasp buttoned all the way up, slushing through the snow."

Slushing through the snow, or eating banana splits, or giving a lecture on the swine, or teaching a lesson in charity all the way to Bridgeport, Connecticut, "Malcolm is just as fresh in my mind today as he was twenty-six years ago," Karim avers. "I do not miss him, because I remember. You can't miss someone that you still see in your mind, because the person is still there."

In the minds of those who knew him Malcolm is in many ways still there—quoting Shakespeare or talking softly into the late African night, driving his blue Oldsmobile home to East Elmhurst, letting in the light or creating his own electricity, taking on Harvard, growing a beard. Or keeping a promise and sending twelve postcards from eleven countries to an Asian friend in Harlem. "I have never missed a mission to his gravesite," declares Yuri Kuchiama, "which we do every year on his birthday, May 19," and have been doing every May since his death on February 21, 1965.

That Sunday, "the day he was shot," Dick Schaap remembers, "I went to a party that night at Buddy Hackett's house in New Jersey, and there were a lot of stars there, show-biz types. And for one night I was the star, because all anybody cared about was Malcolm. I was the center of attention. I had just finished writing the obituary, and it was really strange. Obviously, my ego liked everybody hanging on every word I had to say, but it wasn't me. It was Malcolm. And that's what he was like in those days. It's hard to realize now how big he was."

He was big. When the black Muslim leaders, increasingly jealous of Malcolm's exposure in the press, wrested the NOI newspaper, *Muhammad Speaks,* from Malcolm's control and moved it out of the basement of his house in Queens to their national headquarters in Chicago, they also demanded the negatives of all the photographs the paper had printed. "So Malcolm had to come to me and ask me for all my negatives," Robert Haggins recalls. "It hurt him, it really hurt, to do that. He looked at me and said, 'I hate to ask you, because I know photographers don't like to surrender their negatives.' I gave up all of them. He never forgot that, and every chance he got to pay me back for that he did. When he went to Florida and that famous photograph of his family was taken there, he mailed the undeveloped film to me, so I could claim the photographs. I wasn't even there, but I own the negatives. I have a right to sell those pictures only because of what Malcolm did for me.

"And then," Haggins continues, "when he came back from Mecca, he gave me the bag that he had carried all the way into

Mecca. I've got that bag here. And he gave me his camera, I have that camera here. So I have his camera, I have his bag. I'm going to give his camera to his daughter Attallah, I told her I would give it to her, and I want her to have it. But the bag I'm going to keep. That bag went all the way to Mecca. It's up in that closet, and he gave it to me and it's been up in that closet for twenty-five years. It's an old green bag, and it's something that he wanted me to have. So, Malcolm was a good friend of mine, and I tried to serve him with the best means possible. . . .

"He was quite a man, believe me. He taught me how to live. For me Malcolm was the tallest tree in the forest."

II

Getting It On the Record
Conversations With Malcolm X

The Ronald Stokes Incident
*Brother Malcolm on WBAI with Richard Elman**

At 11:15 on Friday night, April 27, 1962, after a meeting of the Muslim mosque in Los Angeles, two of the Muslim brothers were accosted by two white policemen. The brothers were unloading suits from the back of an automobile parked about a block away from the mosque; they worked for a drycleaning establishment. The policemen, however, suspected them of burglary or theft. There was a scuffle. A shot was fired, and an alarm went out. A police squad converged not at the scene of the incident but at the mosque. In the ensuing gunfire seven Muslim brothers were shot. One of the victims, Ronald Stokes, died. The next day Elijah Muhammad dispatched Malcolm to Los Angeles to prevent further violence, and a week later Malcolm himself conducted the funeral services for Stokes.

In this WBAI radio interview with Richard Elman an indignant Malcolm X vividly shares his impressions of these events and considers their consequences. The interview was conducted outside the Manhattan Center on an unusually cold night (for early May), Elman recalls, and was so brief for two reasons: (1) Malcolm, who had just flown in from Los Angeles, was late for a forum at the center (Murray Kempton moderated, and the panel also included Bayard Rustin); and (2) Malcolm was not wearing a coat.

---

* This interview with Malcolm X was conducted for WBAI Radio by Richard Elman in 1962 and given to Columbia Univesity by WBAI Radio in 1977. Richard Elman is a novelist and most recently the author of *Tar Beach*.

ELMAN: Malcolm X, I wonder if you can tell me very briefly what
took place in Los Angeles? You mentioned earlier in the evening
that there was police brutality and there was atrocity committed.
Would you explain what the incident was?

MALCOLM X: There was police brutality and there was atrocity,
and the press was just as atrocious as the police, because they
helped the police to cover it up by propagating a false image
across the country that there was a blazing gun battle which involved Muslims and police shooting at each other. And everyone
who knows Muslims knows that Muslims don't even carry a fin-
gernail file, much less carry guns. So that the blazing gun battle
that the Los Angeles papers were writing about actually consisted
of policemen's guns who were blazing away at unarmed Negroes,
so-called Negroes, whom they murdered and shot down in cold
blood. And how it happened, according to our information—

About 11:15 last Friday night, after the meeting was over, two
brothers who worked for a drycleaner had some clothing in their
car that they were getting to another brother, and two white policemen pulled up to question them, and—in other words, he
probably thought that they were burglars or something or thieves.
And when he stopped to question them, they stopped and began
to give him whatever information he asked. But he got fresh with
them, told them to get up on the curb, which they did, and one
brother in explaining it was talking with his hands, and the officer
told him, don't talk with his hands.

So he took one hand and held it down. So he brought the other
hand, and he was still talking, and the officer grabbed it and
started twisting it, and from the information that we've been able
to gather, the other brother moved in to help him. And when he
moved in to help him, the other policeman moved in and a struggle took place. And while they were struggling with each other, a
dance hall cop, a cop who is the officer on duty in a dance hall,
saw the struggle and he started shooting.

This caused an alarm to go out to all police cars, and instead of
them coming and converging on the place where the incident was
occurring, they went straight to our house of worship, our
mosque, which was a block away. And when they got to the
mosque, they drew up with their guns drawn and shooting. They
were shooting the bullets, not into the air but at the mosque when

they pulled up. And the secretary of the mosque, the one who was shot down by them, being the official, he went up and asked the police what did they want. And it was while he was asking them what did they want that they shot him through the heart. And when he fell to the sidewalk, they beat him in his head and handcuffed him and left him laying there on the sidewalk for forty-five minutes.

And one of the brothers who was in the police car, being taken to the station, overheard one cop say, "What are the ambulances rushing for? There's only niggers been shot."

Then when this same cop got to the station he said to the brother, "I hope you don't feel bad toward me for what I said back there, under the heat of emotion, because some of my best friends are Negroes."

In the shooting that took place, seven men were shot. Seven Muslims were shot. None of them were armed. None of them were struggling. None of them were fighting. None of them were trying to defend themselves at all. And after being taken to the police station, they were held for forty-eight hours and weren't even given hospitalization. We have one now who is completely paralyzed. We just got all of them free last night. One—the one who didn't die was shot an inch above his heart, and the bullet passed through his body. The other, another bullet went through the same person's penis, and went right through his body. A second person was shot through the groin and the hip and the bullet came out the hip. And a third person was shot through the arm. A fourth person had his teeth kicked in, the whole lower region of his jawbone was broken, and his head was battered, and one policeman was bragging about it, he broke his club over a nigger's skull, and the other cop said, "You shoulda had one of the new kind, because then it wouldn't have broken."

Now, these four men whom I just described, when we got them out on bail, the police had them in the police corridor—since they had torn their clothes off of them while they were arresting them, they turned them loose out in the police corridor, with no medical attention whatsoever, and with no one to guide them or help them. This is where we found them. We took them to the hospital, the Avalon Hospital on Avalon and Slauson, and the medical attendants there couldn't believe that these men had received such damages and were held in jail instead of being taken to the hospital immediately.

And later on that night the police discovered that they had let one man go by mistake, and so they sent out an alarm for him. We called the police when we learned that they had mistakenly let one of the brothers go, and told the police that this brother was in the hospital. They went to the hospital. Instead of letting the brother stay there, they took him in custody, and the nurse on duty tried to stop them, and the police attacked her—a nurse who has nothing to do with the case, and you can telephone Mr. Roth, who was the administrator of the hospital, and he will tell you these incidents himself.

So they rearrested this brother, despite the fact that the medical chart said that this man shouldn't be moved and that he should have immediate medical attention if he were to be held in custody, they took him and held him in jail, and we just got him released today. He was held another twenty-four hours with no medication whatsoever.

I should point out too that we have persons in Los Angeles who have police radio and they actually listened to the broadcast that was being sent out to the radio cars. And the radio cars were sent to the mosque, which is our house of worship, instead of being sent to the place where the incident took place.

And one of the officers also was bragging to another officer about, we shot one of their top officials—showing you that when they pulled up there, they did recognize that this brother whom they murdered was the secretary of the temple. And one of them also said, while they had broken down the doors and broken into the place, and they were still shooting inside the mosque, and knocking over chairs and scattering drawers and other debris about the place—they said, "We need to burn the place down, because they're going to declare it subversive pretty soon anyway."

I might add this—that while the men were standing up, after they had submitted to arrest, while they were standing up, the white officers came in and kicked each one of them, to try and get them to react, so that they could execute more violence against them. Because the brothers didn't react to the kicking, then the officers split their coats, their suit coats up the back and their pants, which made their pants drop on the floor. And still the brothers didn't react. Then they came in and started bragging about how they'd just shot four of their brothers and they're laying out there on the ground, what are they going to do about it? And the brothers still didn't react. So the police ordered them and made them walk out of the mosque into the street with their pants dragging on the sidewalk, with their privates hanging down. This was all done to humiliate them, to try and provoke them. And this happened in Los Angeles last Friday night, in the United States of America, not South Africa or France or Portugal or anyplace else or in Russia behind the Iron Curtain, but right here in the United States of America.

ELMAN: I want to find out more about this incident. I wonder if you might answer this. Do you have any particular instructions which you give the brethren regarding, if they are questioned by police under any circumstances?

MALCOLM X: Yes. All Muslims are always told to do just what these brothers did. When the police come up to one of us, no matter what we're doing, we immediately submit to their questioning. If they say, "Come on, let's go to the station house," we go, voluntarily. And you can read in police files across the country that in their own reports, they admit this. The only time there is ever any violence involving Muslims with policemen is when the policemen attack the Muslims. And the only two brothers that night who resisted police were the initial two, and they resisted only to the degree that they could—they had to defend themselves against the violence that the police were executing against them. But the other men who were shot down in front of the mosque, in front of the temple, in front of the house of worship, they were shot down in cold blood, not because they were resisting, but they were shot down while they weren't resisting.

ELMAN: I noticed before when I was going around to do this little program which we're putting together about this whole evening, and the program was in session, when I went up to one of the people who are in the Black Muslim movement and asked them which point of view corresponded to their own, that they were very silent on the question, and that very often, one of the brothers would tap the other and call that to his attention. Would you mind explaining why?

MALCOLM X: Yes. You will find that a Muslim won't answer any of your questions, unless someone, especially about our organization or about our religion, a Muslim is not going to give you any answers, unless there is one person—wherever Muslims are, there is always someone in charge. If there's three, there's someone in charge. If there's four, someone's in charge; if there's two, someone is in charge. And when you come up, if you ask the person who's not in charge, he'll refer you to the one who is in charge. That's our discipline.

ELMAN: It's a somewhat authoritarian group in this respect?

MALCOLM X: We respect authority. Not only do we respect the authority of our own officials, we respect the authority of police officials, and again I say, the police admit this. So when these police say that we were resisting them, the only time a Muslim resists a policeman is when a policeman attacks him. And you have to do something to defend yourself.

ELMAN: One final question, if I may. What course of action do you expect you'll be taking regarding this incident? In Los Angeles?

MALCOLM X: What course of action are we expected to take? In regards to this incident? We believe in God. We believe in justice. We believe in freedom. We believe in equality. And we do believe that God, our God, the Supreme Being, whose proper name is Allah, will execute judgment and justice in whatever way He sees fit, against the people who are guilty of this crime against our people in this country.

And we believe religiously that the tornadoes that tore up the country are all part of God's plan. We believe that God will—every time a Muslim, one Muslim, the least Muslim is in any way molested, we believe that ten of the best persons the molesters have will be taken off the scene by God Himself. By God Himself. In one manner or another.

ELMAN: In the community itself, do you welcome the assistance of groups like the NAACP?

MALCOLM X: The NAACP president in Los Angeles, Ed Warren, was one of the first ones to file, to wire a protest to Attorney General of California Stanley Mosk.

ELMAN: Do you welcome an investigation of the matter?

MALCOLM X: The matter should be investigated. The matter

should be investigated by the Federal Bureau of Investigation. What do they look like, running all over this country investigating things that are of no consequence, and they haven't got sense enough to go into Los Angeles and investigate the Gestapo tactics of the police department out there? What do they look like condemning Eichmann for what he did in Germany or the Nazis for what they did in Germany, and you've got some Gestapo tactics being practiced by the police department in this country against twenty million black people, second class citizens, day in and day out—not only down South but up North. Los Angeles isn't down South. Los Angeles isn't in Mississippi. Los Angeles is in the state of California, which produced Earl Warren, the Chief Justice of the Supreme Court—and Richard Nixon, the man who was Vice President of this country for some eight or nine years and who wants to run for President again.

ELMAN: Thank you very much, Mr. Malcolm X.

The *Playboy* Interview:
Malcolm X speaks with Alex Haley

Playboy *magazine published its interview with Malcolm X in May 1963. At the time Malcolm stood only second in power and authority among the Black Muslims to Elijah Muhammad, the founder of the Nation of Islam who proclaimed himself the One True Messenger of Allah. The interview was conducted by Alex Haley, with whom Malcolm would collaborate the following year in writing* The Autobiography of Malcolm X. *It presents Malcolm at his most articulate, and his candid words may indeed have prompted the shock and outrage that* Playboy *predicts in its prefatory comments on the interview.*

Playboy's *comment's and its "candid conversation with the militant major-domo of the black muslims," as the interview was captioned, follow in their entirety.*

Within the past five years, the militant American Negro has become an increasingly active combatant in the struggle for civil rights. Espousing the goals of unqualified equality and integration, many of these outspoken insurgents have participated in freedom rides and protest marches against their segregationist foes. Today, they face opposition from not one, but two inimical exponents of racism and segregation: the white supremacists and the Black Muslims. A relatively unknown and insignificant radical religious Negro cult until a few years ago, the Muslims have grown into a dedicated, disciplined nationwide movement which runs its own school, publishes its own newspaper, owns stores and restaurants in four major cities, buys broadcast time on fifty radio stations throughout the country, stages mass rallies attended by partisan crowds of ten thousand and more, and maintains its own police force of judo-trained athletes called the Fruit of Islam.

Predicated on the proposition that the black man is morally, spiritually and intellectually superior to the white man, who is called a "devil," Muslim doctrine dooms him to extermination in an imminent Armageddon—along with Christianity itself, which is denounced as an opiate designed to lull Negroes—with the promise of heaven—into passive acceptance of inferior social status. Amalgamating elements of Christianity and Mohammedanism (both of which officially and unequivocally disown it) and spiked with a black-supremacy version of Hitler's Aryan racial theories, Muslimism was founded in 1931 by Elijah Poole, a Georgia-born ex-factory worker who today commands unquestioning obedience from thousands of followers as the Honorable Elijah Muhammad, Messenger of Allah. At the right hand of God's Messenger stands thirty-six-year-old Malcolm Little, a lanky one time dining-car steward, bootlegger, pimp and dope pusher who left prison in 1952 to heed Muhammad's message, abandoned his "slave name," Little, for the symbolic "X" (meaning identity unknown), and took an oath to abstain thereafter from smoking, drinking, gambling, cursing, dancing and sexual promiscuity—as required of every Muslim. The ambitious young man rose swiftly to become the Messenger's most ardent and erudite disciple, and today wields all but absolute authority over the movement and its membership as Muhammad's business manager, troubleshooter, prime minister and heir apparent.

In the belief that knowledge and awareness are necessary and effective antitoxins against the venom of hate, PLAYBOY asked Malcolm X to submit to a cross-examination on the means and ends of his organization. The ensuing interview was conducted at a secluded table in a Harlem restaurant owned by the Muslims. Interrupting his replies occasionally with a sip of black African coffee and whispered asides to deferential aides, the dark-suited minister of Harlem's Muslim Temple Number Seven spoke with candor and—except for moments of impassioned execration of all whites—the impersonal tone of a self-assured corporation executive.

Many will be shocked by what he has to say; others will be outraged. Our own view is that this interview is both an eloquent statement and a damning self-indictment of one noxious facet of rampant racism. As such, we believe it merits publication—and reading.

PLAYBOY: What is the ambition of the Black Muslims?

MALCOLM X: Freedom, justice and equality are our principal ambitions. And to faithfully serve and follow the Honorable Elijah Muhammad is the guiding goal of every Muslim. Mr. Muhammad teaches us the knowledge of our own selves, and of our own people. He cleans us up—morally, mentally and spiritually—and he reforms us of the vices that have blinded us here in the Western society. He stops black men from getting drunk, stops their dope addiction if they had it, stops nicotine, gambling, stealing, lying, cheating, fornication, adultery, prostitution, juvenile delinquency. I think of this whenever somebody talks about someone investigating us. Why investigate the Honorable Elijah Muhammad? They should subsidize him. He's cleaning up the mess that white men have made. He's saving the government millions of dollars, taking black men off of welfare, showing them how to do something for themselves. And Mr. Muhammad teaches us love for our own kind. The white man has taught the black people in this country to hate themselves as inferior, to hate each other, to be divided against each other. Messenger Muhammad restores our love for our own kind, which enables us to work together in unity and harmony. He shows us how to pool our financial resources and our talents, then to work together toward a common objective. Among other things, we have small businesses in most major cities in this country, and we want to create many more. We are taught by Mr. Muhammad that it is very important to improve the black man's economy, and his thrift. But to do this, we must have land of our own. The brainwashed black man can never learn to stand on his own two feet until he is on his own. We must learn to become our own producers, manufacturers and traders: we must have industry of our own, to employ our own. The white man resists this because he wants to keep the black man under his thumb and jurisdiction in white society. He wants to keep the black man always dependent and begging—for jobs, food, clothes, shelter, education. The white man doesn't want to lose somebody to be supreme over. He wants to keep the black man where he can be watched and retarded. Mr. Muhammad teaches that as soon as we separate from the white man, we will learn that we can do without the white man just as he can do without us. The white man knows that once black men get off to themselves and learn they can do for themselves, the black man's full potential will explode and he will *surpass* the white man.

PLAYBOY: Do you feel that the Black Muslims' goal of obtaining "several states" is a practical vision?

MALCOLM X: Well, *you* might consider some things practical that are really impractical. Wasn't it impractical that the Supreme Court could issue a desegregation order nine years ago and there's still only eight percent compliance? Is it practical that a hundred years after the Civil War there's not freedom for black men yet? On the record for integration you've got the President, the Congress, the Supreme Court—but show me your integration, where is it? That's practical? Mr. Muhammad teaches us to be for what's *really* practical—that's separation. It's more natural than integration.

PLAYBOY: In the view of many, that is highly debatable. However: In a recent interview, Negro author-lecturer Louis Lomax said, "Eighty percent, if not more, of America's twenty million Negroes vibrate sympathetically with the Muslims' indictment of the white power structure. But this does not mean we agree with them in their doctrines of estrangement or with their proposed resolutions of the race problem." Does this view represent a consensus of opinion among Negroes? And if so, is it possible that your separationist and anti-Christian doctrine have the effect of alienating many of your race?

MALCOLM X: Sir, you make a mistake listening to people who tell you how much our stand alienates black men in this country. I'd guess actually we have the sympathy of ninety percent of the black people. There are twenty million dormant Muslims in America. A Muslim to us is somebody who is for the black man; I don't care if he goes to the Baptist Church seven days a week. The Honorable Elijah Muhammad says that a black man is born a Muslim by nature. There are millions of Muslims not aware of it now. All of them will be Muslims when they wake up; that's what's meant by the Resurrection.

Sir, I'm going to tell you a secret: the black man is a whole lot smarter than white people think he is. The black man has survived in this country by fooling the white man. He's been dancing and grinning and white men never guessed what he was thinking. Now you'll hear the bourgeois Negroes pretending to be alienated, but they're just making the white man *think* they don't go for what Mr. Muhammad is saying. This Negro that will tell you he's so against us, he's just protecting the crumbs he gets from the white man's table. This kind of Negro is so busy trying to be *like* the white man that he doesn't know what the real masses of his own people are thinking. A fine car and house and clothes and liquor have made a lot think themselves different from their poor black brothers. But Mr. Muhammad says that Allah is going to wake up all black men to see the white man as he really is, and see what Christianity has done to them. The black masses that are waking up don't believe in Christianity anymore. All it's done for black men is to help keep them slaves. Mr. Muhammad is teaching that Christianity, as white people see it, means that whites can have their heaven here on earth, but the black man is supposed to keep believing that when he dies, he'll float up to some city with golden streets and milk and honey on a cloud somewhere. Every black man in North America has heard black Christian preachers shouting about "tomorrow in good old Beulah's Land." But the thinking black masses today are interested in Muhammad's Land. The Promised Land that the Honorable Elijah Muhammad talks about is right here on this earth. Intelligent black men today are interested in a religious doctrine that offers a solution to their problems right now, right here on this earth, while they are alive.

You must understand that the Honorable Elijah Muhammad represents the fulfillment of Biblical prophecy to us. In the Old Testament, Moses lived to see his enemy, Pharaoh, drowned in the Red Sea—which in essence means that Mr. Muhammad will see the completion of his work in his lifetime, that he will live to see victory gained over his enemy.

PLAYBOY: The Old Testament connection seems tenuous. Are you referring to the Muslim judgment day which your organization's newspaper, *Muhammad Speaks,* calls "Armageddon" and prophesies as imminent?

MALCOLM X: Armageddon deals with the final battle between God and the Devil. The Third World War is referred to as Armageddon by many white statesmen. There won't be any more war after then because there won't be any more warmongers. I don't know when Armageddon, whatever form it takes, is supposed to be. But I know the time is near when the white man will be finished. The signs are all around us. Ten years ago you couldn't have *paid* a Southern Negro to defy local customs. The British Lion's tail has been snatched off in black Africa. The Indonesians have booted out such would-be imperialists as the Dutch. The French, who felt for a century that Algeria was theirs, have had to run for their lives back to France. Sir, the point I make is that all over the world, the old day of standing in fear and trembling before the almighty white man is *gone!*

PLAYBOY: You refer to whites as the guilty and the enemy; you predict divine retribution against them; and you preach absolute separation from the white community. Do not these views substantiate that your movement is predicated on race hatred?

MALCOLM X: Sir, it's from Mr. Muhammad that the black masses are learning for the first time in four hundred years the real truth of how the white man brainwashed the black man, kept him ignorant of his true history, robbed him of his self-confidence. The black masses for the first time are understanding that it's not a case of being anti-white or anti-Christian, but it's a case of seeing the true nature of the white man. We're anti-evil, anti-oppression, anti-lynching. You can't be anti- those things unless you're also anti- the oppressor and the lyncher. You can't be anti-slavery and pro-slavemaster; you can't be anti-crime and pro-criminal. In fact, Mr. Muhammad teaches that if the present generation of *whites* would study their own race in the light of their true history, they would be anti-white themselves.

PLAYBOY: Are you?

MALCOLM X: As soon as the white man hears a black man say he's through loving white people, then the white man accuses the black man of hating him. The Honorable Elijah Muhammad doesn't teach hate. The white man isn't *important* enough for the Honorable Elijah Muhammad and his followers to spend any time hating him. The white man has brainwashed himself into believing that all the black people in the world want to be cuddled up next to him. When he meets what we're talking about, he can't believe it, it takes all the wind out of him. When we tell him we don't want to be around him, we don't want to be like he is, he's staggered. It makes him re-evaluate his three-hundred-year myth about the black man. What I want to know is how the white man, with the blood of black people dripping off his fingers, can have the audacity to be asking black people do they hate him. That takes a lot of nerve.

PLAYBOY: How do you reconcile your disavowal of hatred with the announcement you made last year that Allah had brought you "the good news" that 120 white Atlantans had just been killed in an air crash en route to America from Paris?

MALCOLM X: Sir, as I see the law of justice, it says as you sow, so shall you reap. The white man has reveled as the rope snapped black men's necks. He has reveled around the lynching fire. It's only right for the black man's true God, Allah, to defend us—and for us to be joyous because our God manifests his ability to inflict pain on our enemy. We Muslims believe that the white race, which is guilty of having oppressed and exploited and enslaved our people here in America, should and will be the victims of God's divine wrath. All civilized societies in their courts of justice set a sentence of execution against those deemed to be enemies of society, such as murderers and kidnappers. The presence of twenty million black people here in America is proof that Uncle Sam is guilty of kidnapping—because we didn't come here voluntarily on the Mayflower. And four hundred years of lynchings condemn Uncle Sam as a murderer.

PLAYBOY: We question that all-inclusive generalization. To return to your statement about the plane crash, when Dr. Ralph Bunche heard about it, he called you "mentally depraved." What is your reaction?

MALCOLM X: I know all about what Dr. Bunche said. He's always got his international mouth open. He apologized in the UN when black people protested there. You'll notice that whenever the white man lets a black man get prominent, he has a job for him. Dr. Bunche has functioned as a white man's tool, designed to influence international opinion on the Negro. The white man has Negro local tools, national tools, and Dr. Bunche is an international tool.

PLAYBOY: Dr. Bunche was only one of many prominent Negroes who deplored your statement in similar terms. What reply have you to make to these spokesmen for your own people?

MALCOLM X: Go ask their opinions and you'll be able to fill your notebook with what white people want to hear Negroes say. Let's take these so-called spokesmen for the black men by types. Start with the politicians. They never attack Mr. Muhammad personally. They realize he has the sympathy of the black masses. They know they would alienate the masses whose votes they need. But the black civic leaders, they do attack Mr. Muhammad. The reason is usually that they are appointed to their positions by the white man. The white man pays them to attack us. The ones who attack Mr. Muhammad the most are the ones who earn the most. Then take the black religious leaders, they also attack Mr. Muhammad. These preachers do it out of self-defense, because they know he's waking up Negroes. No one believes what the Negro preacher preaches except those who are mentally asleep, or in the darkness of ignorance about the true situation of the black man here today in this wilderness of North America. If you take note, sir, many so-called Negro leaders who once attacked the Honorable Elijah Muhammad don't do so anymore. And he never speaks against them in the personal sense except as a reaction if they speak against him. Islam is a religion that teaches us never to attack, never to be the aggressor—but you can waste somebody if he attacks you. These Negro leaders have become aware that whenever the Honorable Elijah Muhammad is caused by their attack to level his guns against them, they always come out on the losing end. Many have experienced this.

PLAYBOY: Do you admire and respect any other American Negro leaders—Martin Luther King, for example?

MALCOLM X: I am a Muslim, sir. Muslims can see only one leader who has the qualifications necessary to unite all elements of black people in America. This is the Honorable Elijah Muhammad.

PLAYBOY: Many white religious leaders have also gone on record against the Black Muslims. Writing in the official NAACP magazine, a Catholic priest described you as "a fascist-minded hate group," and B'nai B'rith has accused you of being not only anti-Christian but anti-Semitic. Do you consider this true?

MALCOLM X: Insofar as the Christian world is concerned, dictatorships have existed only in areas or countries where you have Roman Catholicism. Catholicism conditions your mind for dictators. Can you think of a single Protestant country that has ever produced a dictator?

PLAYBOY: Germany was predominantly Protestant when Hitler—

MALCOLM X: Another thing to think of—in the twentieth century, the Christian Church has given us two heresies: fascism and communism.

PLAYBOY: On what grounds do you attribute these "isms" to the Christian church?

MALCOLM X: Where did fascism start? Where's the second-largest communist party outside of Russia? The answer to both is Italy. Where is the Vatican? But let's not forget the Jew. Anybody that gives even a just criticism of the Jew is instantly labeled anti-Semite. The Jew cries louder than anybody else if anybody criticizes him. You can tell the truth about any minority in America, but make a true observation about the Jew, and if it doesn't pat him on the back, then he uses his grip on the news media to label you anti-Semite. Let me say just a word about the Jew and the black man. The Jew is always anxious to *advise* the black man. But they never advise him how to solve his problem the way the Jews solved their problem. The Jew never went sitting-in and crawling-in and sliding-in and freedom-riding, like he teaches and helps Negroes to do. The Jews stood up, and stood together, and they used their ultimate power, the economic weapon. That's exactly what the Honorable Elijah Muhammad is trying to teach black men to do. The Jews pooled their money and *bought* the hotels that barred them. They bought Atlantic City and Miami Beach and anything else they wanted. Who owns Hollywood? Who runs the garment industry, the largest industry in New York City? But the Jew that's advising the Negro joins the NAACP, CORE, the Urban League, and others. With money donations, the Jew gains control, then he sends the black man doing all this wading-in, boring-in, even burying-in—everything but buying-in. Never shows him how to set up factories and hotels. Never advises him how to own what he wants. No, when there's something worth owning, the Jew's got it.

PLAYBOY: Isn't it true that many Gentiles have also labored with dedication to advance integration and economic improvement for the Negro, as volunteer workers for the NAACP, CORE and many other interracial agencies?

MALCOLM X: A man who tosses worms in the river isn't necessarily a friend of the fish. All the fish who take him for a friend, who think the worm's got no hook in it, usually end up in the frying pan. All these things dangled before us by the white liberal posing as a friend and benefactor have turned out to be nothing but bait to make us think we're making progress. The Supreme Court decision has never been enforced. Desegregation has never taken place. The promises have never been fulfilled. We have received only tokens, substitutes, trickery and deceit.

PLAYBOY: What motives do you impute to *Playboy* for providing you with this opportunity for the free discussion of your views?

MALCOLM X: I think you want to sell magazines. I've never seen a sincere white man, not when it comes to helping black people. Usually things like this are done by white people to benefit themselves. The white man's primary interest is not to elevate the thinking of black people, or to waken black people, or white people either. The white man is interested in the black man only to the extent that the black man is of use to him. The white man's interest is to make money, to exploit.

PLAYBOY: Is there any white man on earth whom you would concede to have the Negro's welfare genuinely at heart?

MALCOLM X: I say, sir, that you can never make an intelligent judgment without evidence. If any man will study the entire history of the relationship between the white man and the black man, no evidence will be found that justifies any confidence or faith that the black man might have in the white man today.

PLAYBOY: Then you consider it impossible for the white man to be anything but an exploiter and a hypocrite in his relations with the Negro?

MALCOLM X: Is it wrong to attribute a predisposition to wheat before it comes up out of the ground? Wheat's characteristics and nature make it wheat. It differs from barley because of its nature. Wheat perpetuates its own characteristics just as the white race does. White people are born devils by nature. They don't become so by deeds. If you never put popcorn in a skillet, it would still be popcorn. Put the heat to it, it will pop.

PLAYBOY: You say that white men are devils by nature. Was Christ a devil?

MALCOLM X: Christ wasn't white. Christ was a black man.

PLAYBOY: On what Scripture do you base this assertion?

MALCOLM X: Sir, Billy Graham has made the same statement in public. Why not ask *him* what Scripture he found it in? When Pope Pius XII died, *Life* magazine carried a picture of him in his private study kneeling before a black Christ.

PLAYBOY: Those are hardly quotations from Scripture. Was He not reviled as "King of the Jews"—a people the Black Muslims attack?

MALCOLM X: Only the poor, brainwashed American Negro has been made to believe that Christ was white, to maneuver him into worshiping the white man. After becoming a Muslim in prison, I read almost everything I could put my hands on in the prison library. I began to think back on everything I had read and especially with the histories, I realized that nearly all of them read by the general public have been made into white histories. I found out that the history-whitening process either had left out great things that black men had done, or some of the great black men had gotten whitened.

PLAYBOY: Would you list a few of these men?

MALCOLM X: Well, Hannibal, the most successful general that ever lived, was a black man. So was Beethoven; Beethoven's father was one of the blackamoors that hired themselves out in Europe as professional soldiers. Haydn, Beethoven's teacher, was of African descent. Columbus, the discoverer of America, was a half-black man.

PLAYBOY: According to biographies considered definitive, Beethoven's father, Johann, was a court tenor in Cologne; Haydn's parents were Croatian; Columbus's parents were Italian—

MALCOLM X: Whole black empires, like the Moorish, have been whitened to hide the fact that a great black empire had conquered a white empire even before America was discovered. The Moorish civilization—black Africans—conquered and ruled Spain; they kept the light burning in Southern Europe. The word "Moor" means "black," by the way. Egyptian civilization is a classic example of how the white man stole great African cultures and makes them appear today as white European. The black nation of Egypt is the only country that has a science named after its culture: Egyptology. The ancient Sumerians, a black-skinned people, occupied the Middle Eastern areas and were contemporary with the Egyptian civilization. The Incas, the Aztecs, the Mayans, all dark-skinned Indian people, had a highly developed culture here in America, in what is now Mexico and northern South America. These people had mastered agriculture at the time when European white people were still living in mud huts and eating weeds. But white children, or black children, or grownups here today in America don't get to read this in the average books they are exposed to.

PLAYBOY: Can you cite any authoritative historical documents for these observations?

MALCOLM X: I can cite a great many, sir. You could start with Herodotus, the Greek historian. He outright described the Egyptians as "black, with woolly hair." And the American archaeologist and Egyptologist James Henry Breasted did the same thing.

PLAYBOY: You seem to have based your thesis on the premise that all nonwhite races are necessarily black.

MALCOLM X: Mr. Muhammad says that the red, the brown and the yellow are indeed all part of the black nation. Which means that black, brown, red, yellow, all are brothers, all are one family. The white one is a stranger. He's the odd fellow.

PLAYBOY: Since your classification of black peoples apparently includes the light-skinned Oriental, Middle Eastern and possibly even Latin races as well as the darker Indian and Negroid strains, just how do you decide how light-skinned it's permissible to be before being condemned as white? And if Caucasian whites are devils by nature, do you classify people by degrees of devilishness according to the lightness of their skin?

MALCOLM X: I don't worry about these little technicalities. But I know that white society has always considered that one drop of black blood makes you black. To me, if one drop can do this, it only shows the power of one drop of black blood. And I know another thing—that Negroes who used to be light enough to pass for white have seen the handwriting on the wall and are beginning to come back and identify with their own kind. And white people who also are seeing the pendulum of time catching up with them are now trying to join with blacks, or even find traces of black blood in their own veins, hoping that it will save them from the catastrophe they see ahead. But no devil can fool God. Muslims have a little poem about them. It goes, "One drop will make you black, and will also in days to come save your soul."

PLAYBOY: As one of this vast elite, do you hold the familiar majority attitude toward minority groups—regarding the white race, in this case, as inferior in quality as well as quantity to what you call the "black nation"?

MALCOLM X: Thoughtful white people *know* they are inferior to black people. Even Eastland* knows it. Anyone who has studied the genetic phase of biology knows that white is considered recessive and black is considered dominant. When you want strong coffee, you ask for black coffee. If you want it light, you want it weak, integrated with white milk. Just like these Negroes who weaken themselves and their race by this integrating and intermixing with whites. If you want bread with no nutritional value, you ask for white bread. All the good that was in it has been bleached out of it, and it will constipate you. If you want pure flour, you ask for dark flour, whole-wheat flour. If you want pure sugar, you want dark sugar.

PLAYBOY: If all whites are devilish by nature, as you have alleged, and if black and white are essentially opposite, as you have just stated, do you view all black men—with the exception of their non-Muslim leaders—as fundamentally angelic?

MALCOLM X: No, there is plenty wrong with Negroes. They have no society. They're robots, automatons. No minds of their own. I hate to say that about us, but it's the truth. They are a black body with a white brain. Like the monster Frankenstein. The top part is your bourgeois Negro. He's your integrator. He's not interested in his poor black brothers. He's usually so deep in debt from trying to copy the white man's social habits that he doesn't have time to worry about nothing else. They buy the most expensive clothes and cars and eat the cheapest food. They act more like the white man than the white man does himself. These are the ones that hide their sympathy for Mr. Muhammad's teachings. It conflicts with the sources from which they get their white-man's crumbs. This class to us are the fence-sitters. They have one eye on the white man and the other eye on the Muslims. They'll jump whichever way they see the wind blowing. Then there's the middle class of the Negro masses, the ones not in the ghetto, who realize

* James Oliver Eastland, for thirty-five years the Democratic senator from Mississippi, consistently opposed civil rights legislation.

that life is a struggle, who are conscious of all the injustices being done and of the constant state of insecurity in which they live. They're ready to take some stand against everything that's against them. Now, when this group hears Mr. Muhammad's teachings, they are the ones who come forth faster and identify themselves, and take immediate steps toward trying to bring into existence what Mr. Muhammad advocates. At the bottom of the social heap is the black man in the big-city ghetto. He lives night and day with the rats and cockroaches and drowns himself with alcohol and anesthetizes himself with dope, to try and forget where and what he is. That Negro has given up all hope. He's the hardest one for us to reach, because he's the deepest in the mud. But when you get him, you've got the best kind of Muslim. Because he makes the most drastic change. He's the most fearless. He will stand the longest. He has nothing to lose, even his life, because he didn't have that in the first place. I look upon myself, sir, as a prime example of this category—and as graphic an example as you could find of the salvation of the black man.

PLAYBOY: Could you give us a brief review of the early life that led to your own "salvation"?

MALCOLM X: Gladly. I was born in Omaha on May 19, 1925. My light color is the result of my mother's mother having been raped by a white man. I hate every drop of white blood in me. Before I am indicted for hate again, sir—is it wrong to hate the blood of a rapist? But to continue: My father was a militant follower of Marcus Garvey's "Back to Africa" movement. The Lansing, Michigan, equivalent of the Ku Klux Klan warned him to stop preaching Garvey's message, but he kept on and one of my earliest memories is of being snatched awake one night with a lot of screaming going on because our home was afire. But my father got louder about Garvey, and the next time he was found bludgeoned in the head, lying across streetcar tracks. He died soon and our family was in a bad way. We were so hungry we were dizzy and we had nowhere to turn. Finally the authorities came in and we children were scattered about in different places as public wards. I happened to become the ward of a white couple who ran a correctional school for white boys. This family liked me in the way they liked their house pets. They got me enrolled in an all-white school. I was popular, I played sports and everything, and studied hard, and I stayed at the head of my class through the eighth grade. That summer I was fourteen, but I was big enough and looked old enough to get away with telling a lie that I was twenty-one, so I got a job working in the dining car of a train that ran between Boston and New York City.

On my layovers in New York, I'd go to Harlem. That's where I saw in the bars all these men and women with what looked like the easiest life in the world. Plenty of money, big cars, all of it. I could tell they were in the rackets and vice. I hung around those bars whenever I came in town, and I kept my ears and eyes open and my mouth shut. And they kept their eyes on me, too. Finally, one day a numbers man told me that he needed a runner, and I never caught the night train back to Boston. Right there was when I started my life in crime. I was in all of it that the white police and the gangsters left open to the black criminal, sir. I was in numbers, bootleg liquor, "hot" goods, women. I sold the bodies of black women to white men, and white women to black men. I was in dope, I was in everything evil you could name. The only thing I could say good for myself, sir, was that I did not indulge in hitting anybody over the head.

PLAYBOY: By the time you were sixteen, according to the record, you had several men working for you in these various enterprises. Right?

MALCOLM X: Yes, sir. I turned the things I mentioned to you over to them. And I had a good working system of paying off policemen. It was here that I learned that vice and crime can only exist, at least the kind and level that I was in, to the degree that the police cooperate with it. I had several men working and I was a steerer myself. I steered white people with money from downtown to whatever kind of sin they wanted in Harlem. I didn't care what they wanted, I knew where to take them to it. And I tell you what I noticed here—that my best customers always were the officials, the top police people, businessmen, politicians and clergymen. I never forgot that. I met all levels of these white people, supplied them with everything they wanted, and I saw that they were just a filthy race of devils. But despite the fact that my own father was murdered by whites, and I had seen my people all my life brutalized by whites, I was still blind enough to mix with them and socialize with them. I thought they were gods and goddesses

—until Mr. Muhammad's powerful spiritual message opened my eyes and enabled me to see them as a race of devils. Nothing had made me see the white man as he is until one word from the Honorable Elijah Muhammad opened my eyes overnight.

PLAYBOY: When did this happen?

MALCOLM X: In prison. I was finally caught and spent seventy-seven months in three different prisons. But it was the greatest thing that ever happened to me, because it was in prison that I first heard the teachings of the Honorable Elijah Muhammad. His teachings were what turned me around. The first time I heard the Honorable Elijah Muhammad's statement, "The white man is the devil," it just clicked. I am a good example of why Islam is spreading so rapidly across the land. I was nothing but another convict, a semi-illiterate criminal. Mr. Muhammad's teachings were able to reach into prison, which is the level where people are considered to have fallen as low as they can go. His teachings brought me from behind prison walls and placed me on the podiums of some of the leading colleges and universities in the country. I often think, sir, that in 1946, I was sentenced to eight to ten years in Cambridge, Massachusetts, as a common thief who had never passed the eighth grade. And the next time I went back to Cambridge was in March 1961, as a guest speaker at the Harvard Law School Forum. This is the best example of Mr. Muhammad's ability to take nothing and make something, to take nobody and make somebody.

PLAYBOY: Your rise to prominence in the Muslim organization has been so swift that a number of your own membership have hailed you as their articulate exemplar, and many anti-Muslims regard you as the real brains and power of the movement. What is your reaction to this sudden eminence?

MALCOLM X: Sir, it's heresy to imply that I am in any way whatever even equal to Mr. Muhammad. No man on earth today is his equal. Whatever I am that is good, it is through what I have been taught by Mr. Muhammad.

PLAYBOY: Be that as it may, the time is near when your leader, who is sixty-five, will have to retire from leadership of the Muslim movement. Many observers predict that when this day comes, the new Messenger of Allah in America—a role which you have called the most powerful of any black man in the world—will be Malcolm X. How do you feel about this prospect?

MALCOLM X: Sir, I can only say that God chose Mr. Muhammad as his Messenger, and Mr. Muhammad chose me and many others to help him. Only God has the say-so. But I will tell you one thing. I frankly don't believe that I or anyone else am worthy to succeed Mr. Muhammad. No one preceded him. I don't think I could make the sacrifice he has made, or set his good example. He has done more than lay down his life. But his work is already done with the seed he has planted among black people. If Mr. Muhammad and every identifiable follower he has, certainly including myself, were tomorrow removed from the scene by more of the white man's brutality, there is one thing to be sure of: Mr. Muhammad's teachings of the naked truth have fallen upon fertile soil among twenty million black men here in this wilderness of North America.

PLAYBOY: Has the soil, in your opinion, been as fertile for Mr. Muhammad's teachings elsewhere in the world—among the emerging nations of black Africa, for instance?

MALCOLM X: I think not only that his teachings have had considerable impact even in Africa but that the Honorable Elijah Muhammad has had a greater impact on the world than the rise of the African nations. I say this as objectively as I can, being a Muslim. Even the Christian missionaries are conceding that in black Africa, for every Christian conversion, there are two Muslim conversions.

PLAYBOY: Might conversions be even more numerous if it weren't for the somewhat strained relations which are said by several Negro writers to exist between the black people of Africa and America?

MALCOLM X: Perhaps. You see, the American black man sees the African come here and live where the American black man can't. The Negro sees the African come here with a sheet on and go places where the Negro—dressed like a white man, talking like a white man, sometimes as wealthy as the white man—can't go. When I'm traveling around the country, I use my real Muslim name, Malik Shabazz. I make my hotel reservations under that name, and I always see the same thing I've just been telling you. I come to the desk and always see that "here-comes-a-Negro" look.

It's kind of a reserved, coldly tolerant cordiality. But when I say "Malik Shabazz," their whole attitude changes: they snap to respect. They think I'm an African. People say what's in a name? There's a whole lot in a name. The American black man is seeing the African respected as a human being. The African gets respect because he has an identity and cultural roots. But most of all because the African owns some land. For these reasons he has his human rights recognized, and that makes his civil rights automatic.

PLAYBOY: Do you feel this is true of Negro civil and human rights in South Africa, where the doctrine of apartheid is enforced by the government of Prime Minister Verwoerd?

MALCOLM X: They don't stand for anything different in South Africa than America stands for. The only difference is over there they *preach* as well as practice apartheid. America preaches freedom and practices slavery. America preaches integration and practices segregation. Verwoerd is an honest white man. So are the Barnetts, Faubuses, Eastlands and Rockwells.* They want to keep all white people white. And we want to keep all black people black. As between the racists and the integrationists, I highly prefer the racists. I'd rather walk among rattlesnakes, whose constant rattle warns me where they are, than among those Northern snakes who grin and make you forget you're still in a snake pit. Any white man is against blacks. The entire American economy is based on white supremacy. Even the religious philosophy is, in essence, white supremacy. A white Jesus. A white Virgin. White angels. White everything. But a black Devil, of course. The "Uncle Sam" political foundation is based on white supremacy, relegating non-whites to second-class citizenship. It goes without saying that the social philosophy is strictly white supremacist. And the educational system perpetuates white supremacy.

PLAYBOY: Are you contradicting yourself by denouncing white supremacy while praising its practitioners, since you admit that you share their goal of separation?

MALCOLM X: The fact that I prefer the candor of the Southern

---

* Mississippi governor Ross Barnett and Alabama governor Orval Faubus continually defied court ordered desegregation of schools; George Lincoln Rockwell was president of the American Nazi Party.

segregationist to the hypocrisy of the Northern integrationist doesn't alter the basic immorality of white supremacy. A devil is still a devil whether he wears a bed sheet or a Brooks Brothers suit. The Honorable Elijah Muhammad teaches separation simply because any forcible attempt to integrate America completely would result in another Civil War, a catastrophic explosion among whites which would destroy America—and still not solve the problem. But Mr. Muhammad's solution of separate black and white would solve the problem neatly for both the white and black man, and America would be saved. Then the whole world would give Uncle Sam credit for being something other than a hypocrite.

PLAYBOY: Do you feel that the administration's successful stand on the integration of James Meredith into the University of Mississippi has demonstrated that the government—far from being hypocritical—is sympathetic with the Negro's aspirations for equality?

MALCOLM X: What was accomplished? It took fifteen thousand troops to put Meredith in the University of Mississippi. Those troops and three million dollars—that's what was spent—to get one Negro in. That three million dollars could have been used much more wisely by the federal government to elevate the living standards of all the Negroes in Mississippi.

PLAYBOY: Then in your view, the principle involved was not worth the expense. Yet it is a matter of record that President Kennedy, in the face of Southern opposition, championed the appointment of Dr. Robert Weaver as the first Negro Cabinet member. Doesn't this indicate to you, as it does to many Negro leaders, that the administration is determined to combat white supremacy?

MALCOLM X: Kennedy doesn't *have* to fight; he's the president. He didn't have any fight replacing Ribicoff with Celebrezze [as HEW secretary in 1962]. He didn't have any trouble putting Goldberg on the Supreme Court. He hasn't had any trouble getting anybody in but Weaver and Thurgood Marshall. He wasn't worried about Congressional objection when he challenged U.S. Steel. He wasn't worried about either Congressional reaction or Russian reaction or even world reaction when he blockaded Cuba. But when it comes to the rights of the Negro, who helped to put him in office, then he's afraid of little pockets of white resistance.

PLAYBOY: Has *any* American president, in your opinion—Lincoln, FDR, Truman, Eisenhower, Kennedy—accomplished anything for the Negro?

MALCOLM X: None of them have ever done anything for Negroes. All of them have tricked the Negro, and made false promises to him at election times which they never fulfilled. Lincoln's concern wasn't freedom for the blacks but to save the Union.

PLAYBOY: Wasn't the Civil War fought to decide whether this nation could, in the words of Lincoln, "endure permanently half slave and half free"?

MALCOLM X: Sir, many, many people are completely misinformed about Lincoln and the Negro. That war involved two thieves, the North and the South, fighting over the spoils. The further we get away from the actual incident, the more they are trying to make it sound as though the battle was over the black man. Lincoln said that if he could save the Union without freeing the slaves, he would. But after two years of killing and carnage he found out he would *have* to free the slaves. He wasn't interested in the slaves but in the Union. As for the Emancipation Proclamation, sir, it was an empty document. If it freed the slaves, why, a century later, are we still battling for civil rights?

PLAYBOY: Despite the fact that the goal of racial equality is not yet realized, many sociologists—and many Negro commentators—agree that no minority group on earth has made as much social, civil and economic progress as the American Negro in the past hundred years. What is your reaction to this view?

MALCOLM X: Sir, I hear that everywhere almost exactly as you state it. This is one of the biggest myths that the American black man himself believes in. Every immigrant ethnic group that has come to this country is now a genuinely first-class citizen group—every one of them but the black man, who was here when they came. While everybody else is sharing the fruit, the black man is just now starting to be thrown some seeds. It is our hope that through the Honorable Elijah Muhammad, we will at last get the soil to plant the seeds in. You talk about the progress of the Negro—I'll tell you, mister, it's just because the Negro has been in America while *America* has gone forward that the Negro ap-

1963. In Harlem a crowd gathers to hear Malcolm X at an outdoor rally: "He had the ability to hold the minds of thousands of people," says Benjamin Karim, "even in the rain; I have seen thousands of people stand in the rain and listen to Malcolm, and nobody would leave." *UPI/Bettmann*

Brother Minister Malcolm addresses a rally in support of integration efforts in Birmingham, Alabama, at Harlem's Hotel Theresa in May 1963; the gesture is familiar. "It was like you knew you had a big brother," Kathryn Gibson says of the public Malcolm, "who could knock down anybody who messed with you; it was like he was the protector." *UPI/Bettmann Newsphotos*

The protector close up. The balled fist or pointed finger, the raised arm; the indignation and the anger; the rhetoric; the fire, irony, and conviction; the grimace, the snarl: The image. *UPI/Bettmann Newsphotos*

"Malcolm could not have been higher in his life than when he and Cassius Clay were so close," recalls Alex Haley. *Left to right:* World heavyweight champion Cassius Clay (now Muhammad Ali); his brother, Rudolph Valentino Clay; Malcolm X; S. O. Adebo, Nigerian ambassador to the United Nations. The photograph was taken at the United Nations in March 1964, shortly before the rift between Malcolm and Clay. *UPI/Bettmann Newsphotos*

Malcolm with his third daughter, Ilysah, at John F. Kennedy Airport on May 21, 1964. Malcolm has just returned from his spring tour of the Middle East and Africa. *UPI/Bettmann Newsphotos*

Malcolm leaves his house in East Elmhurst, Queens. It was fire
bombed on February 14, 1965. "He called me," Alex Haley
remembers, and "said his home had been bombed . . . and he had
nowhere for his children, his wife and children, to go." *UPI/
Bettmann*

February 21, 1965; outside the Audubon Ballroom in Harlem. Robert Haggins was "late getting to the meeting that Sunday. . . . I was going up those long stairs at the Audubon Ballroom and Malcolm was on a stretcher coming down, and when he got close to me I could see his mouth was opened, his eyes were open, and I knew that he was dead." *UPI/Bettmann*

Betty Shabazz *(right)* stands outside the Audubon Ballroom shortly after her husband's death by hired assassins. *UPI/Bettmann Newsphotos*

At a press conference on February 22 the Honorable Elijah Muhammad, leader of the Nation of Islam, tells reporters that Malcolm X died by the very devices he advocated. Behind Muhammad stand two of his bodyguards. *UPI/Bettmann Newsphotos*

Mourners line the streets outside the Faith Temple Church of God in Harlem during the funeral services for Malcolm on February 27. "It was like it was the death of a time; a death of a philosophy, a death of purpose. A death of hope," says Kathryn Gibson. *UPI/Bettmann Newsphotos*

Malcolm sat for this photograph in 1965, a month or so before his death. *Lawrence Henry Collection*

pears to have gone forward. The Negro is like a man on a luxury commuter train doing ninety miles an hour. He looks out of the window, along with all the white passengers in their Pullman chairs, and he thinks *he's* doing ninety, too. Then he gets to the men's room and looks in the mirror—and he sees he's not really getting anywhere at all. His reflection shows a black man standing there in the white uniform of a dining-car steward. He may get on the 5:10, all right, but he sure won't be getting off at Westport.

PLAYBOY: Is there anything then, in your opinion, that could be done—by either whites or blacks—to expedite the social and economic progress of the Negro in America?

MALCOLM X: First of all, the white man must finally realize that *he's* the one who has committed the crimes that have produced the miserable condition that our people are in. He can't hide this guilt by reviling us today because we answer his criminal acts—past and present—with extreme and uncompromising resentment. He cannot hide his guilt by accusing us, his victims, of being racists, extremists and black supremacists. The white man must realize that the sins of the fathers are about to be visited upon the heads of the children who have continued those sins, only in more sophisticated ways. Mr. Elijah Muhammad is warning this generation of white people that they, too, are also facing a time of harvest in which they will have to pay for the crime committed when their grandfathers made slaves out of us.

But there *is* something the white man can do to avert this fate. He must atone—and this can only be done by allowing black men, those who choose, to leave this land of bondage and go to a land of our own. But if he doesn't want a mass movement of our people away from this house of bondage, then he should separate this country. He should give us several states here on American soil, where those of us who wish to can go and set up our own government, our own economic system, our own civilization. Since we have given over 300 years of our slave labor to the white man's America, helped to build it up for him, it's only right that white America should give us everything *we* need in finance and materials for the next twenty-five years, until our own nation is able to stand on its feet. Then, if the western hemisphere is attacked by outside enemies, we would have both the capability and the motivation to join in defending the hemisphere, in which we would then have a sovereign stake.

The Honorable Elijah Muhammad says that the black man has served under the rule of all the other peoples of the earth at one time or another in the past. He teaches that it is now God's intention to put the black man back at the top of civilization, where he was in the beginning—before Adam, the white man, was created. The world since Adam has been white—and corrupt. The world of tomorrow will be black—and righteous. In the white world there has been nothing but slavery, suffering, death and colonialism. In the black world of tomorrow, there will be *true* freedom, justice and equality for all. And that day is coming— sooner than you think.

PLAYBOY: If Muslims ultimately gain control as you predict, do you plan to bestow *"true* freedom" on white people?

MALCOLM X: It's not a case of what would we do, it's a case of what would God do with whites. What does a judge do with the guilty? Either the guilty atone, or God executes judgment.

Minister Malcolm
A conversation with Kenneth B. Clark

In June 1963 Kenneth B. Clark interviewed Malcolm X on American television. Dynamic, outspoken, charismatic, compelling, Malcolm had become the most visible—and powerful—representative of the Honorable Elijah Muhammad and the Black Muslim movement. In this interview he discusses with conviction and authority the phenomenon of the Muslims in America in the early sixties—their goals, their stands, their philosophy, his ministry.

In his book The Negro Protest *(1963) Clark introduces the interview as follows:*

"Malcolm X is a punctual man. He arrived at the television studio, with two of his closest advisers, at the precise time of our appointment. He and his friends were immaculately dressed, with no outward sign of their belonging to either a separate sect or the ministry. Minister Malcolm X (and he insists on being called 'Minister Malcolm') is a tall, handsome man in his late thirties. He is clearly a dominant personality whose disciplined power seems all the more evident in contrast to the studied deference paid him by his associates. He is conscious of the impression of power which he seeks to convey, and one suspects that he does not permit himself to become too casual in his relations with others.

"Although Minister Malcolm X seems proud of the fact that he did not go beyond the eighth grade, he speaks generally with the vocabulary and the tone of a college-educated person. Happy when this is pointed out to him, he explains that he has read extensively since joining the Black Muslim movement. His role as the chief spokesman for this movement in the New York-Washington region is, he insists, to raise the level of pride and accomplishment in his followers.

"Malcolm X has been interviewed on radio, television, and by newspapermen probably more than any other Negro leader during

the past two years. He shows the effects of these interminable interviews by a professional calm, and what appears to be an ability to turn on the proper amount of emotion, resentment, and indignation, as needed. One certainly does not get the impression of spontaneity. On the contrary, one has the feeling that Minister Malcolm has anticipated every question and is prepared with the appropriate answer, an answer which is consistent with the general position of the Black Muslim movement, as defined by the Honorable Elijah Muhammad.

"We began the interview by talking about Malcolm X's childhood."

MALCOLM X: I was born in Omaha, Nebraska, back in 1925—that period when the Ku Klux Klan was quite strong in that area at that time—and grew up in Michigan, partially. Went to school there.

CLARK: What part of Michigan?

MALCOLM X: Lansing. I went to school there—as far as the eighth grade. And left there and then grew up in Boston and in New York.

CLARK: Did you travel with your family from Omaha to Michigan to Boston?

MALCOLM X: Yes. When I was born—shortly after I was born—the Ku Klux Klan gave my father an ultimatum—or my parents an ultimatum—about remaining there, so they left and went to——

CLARK: What was the basis of this ultimatum?

MALCOLM X: My father was a Garveyite, and in those days, you know, it wasn't the thing for a black man to be outspoken or to deviate from the accepted stereotype that was usually considered the right image for Negroes to fulfill or reflect.

CLARK: Of all the words that I have read about you, this is the first time that I've heard that your father was a Garveyite. And, in fact, he *was* an outspoken black nationalist in the nineteen twenties?

MALCOLM X: He was both a Garveyite and a minister, a Baptist minister. In those days you know how it was and how it still is; it has only changed in the method, but the same things still exist: whenever a black man was outspoken, he was considered crazy or dangerous. And the police department and various branches of the law usually were interwoven with that Klan element, so the Klan had the backing of the police, and usually the police had the backing of the Klan, same as today.

CLARK: So in effect your father was required, or he was forced—

MALCOLM X: Yes, they burned the house that we lived in in Omaha, and I think this was in 1925, and we moved to Lansing, Michigan, and we ran into the same experience there. We lived in an integrated neighborhood, by the way, then. And it only proves that whites were as much against integration as they are now, only then they were more openly against it. And today they are shrewd in saying they are for it, but they still make it impossible for you to integrate. So we moved to Michigan and the same thing happened: they burned our home there. And he was—like I say—he was a clergyman, a Christian; and it was Christians who burned the home in both places—people who teach, you know, religious tolerance and brotherhood and all of that.

CLARK: Did you start school in Michigan?

MALCOLM X: Yes.

CLARK: How long did you stay in Michigan?

MALCOLM X: I think I completed the eighth grade while I was still in Michigan.

CLARK: And then where did you go?

MALCOLM X: To Boston.

CLARK: Did you go to high school in Boston?

MALCOLM X: No, I have never gone to high school.

CLARK: You've never gone to high school?

MALCOLM X: The eighth grade was as far as I went.

CLARK: That's phenomenal.

MALCOLM X: Everything I know above the eighth grade, I've learned from Mr. Muhammad. He's been my teacher, and I think he's a better teacher than I would have had had I continued to go to the public schools.

CLARK: How did you meet Mr. Muhammad?

MALCOLM X: I was—when I was in prison, in 1947, I first heard about his teaching, about his religious message. And at that time I was an atheist, myself. I had graduated from Christianity to agnosticism on into atheism.

CLARK: Were the early experiences in Nebraska and Michigan where, as you say, Christians burned the home of your father, who was a Christian minister—were these experiences the determinants of your moving away from Christianity?

MALCOLM X: No, no, they weren't, because despite those experiences, I, as I said, lived a thoroughly integrated life. Despite all the experiences I had in coming up—and my father was killed by whites at a later date—I still thought that there were some good white people; at least the ones *I* was associating with, you know, were supposed to be different. There wasn't any experience, to my knowledge, that opened up my eyes, because right up until the time that I went to prison, I was still integrated into the white society and thought that there were some good ones.

CLARK: Was it an integrated prison?

MALCOLM X: It was an integrated prison at the prison level, but the administrators were all white. You usually find that in any situation that is supposed to be based on integration. At the low level they integrate, but at the administrative or executive level you find whites running it.

CLARK: How long did you stay in prison?

MALCOLM X: About seven years.

CLARK: And you were in prison in Boston. And this is where you got in touch with—

MALCOLM X: My family became Muslims, accepted the religion of Islam, and one of them who had spent pretty much—had spent quite a bit of time with me on the streets of New York out here in Harlem had been exposed to the religion of Islam. He accepted it, and it made such a profound change in him. He wrote to me and was telling me about it. Well, I had completely eliminated Christianity. After getting into prison and having time to think, I could see the hypocrisy of Christianity. Even before I went to prison, I had already become an atheist and I could see the hypocrisy of Christianity. Most of my associates were white; they were either Jews or Christians, and I saw hypocrisy on both sides. None of them really practiced what they preached.

CLARK: Minister Malcolm—

MALCOLM X: Excuse me, but despite the fact that I had detected this, my own intellectual strength was so weak, or so lacking, till I was not in a position to really see or come to a conclusion concerning this hypocrisy until I had gotten to where I could think a little bit and had learned more about the religion of Islam. Then I could go back and remember all of these experiences and things that I had actually heard—discussions that I had participated in myself with whites. It had made everything that Mr. Muhammad was saying add up.

CLARK: I see.

MALCOLM X: He was the one who drew the line and enabled me to add up everything and say that this is this, and I haven't met anyone since then who was capable of showing me an answer more strong or with more weight than the answer that the Honorable Elijah Muhammad has given.

CLARK: I'd like to go back just a little to your life in prison. What was the basis—how did you—

MALCOLM X: Crime. I wasn't framed. I went to prison for what I did, and the reason that I don't have any hesitation or reluctance whatsoever to point out the fact that I went to prison: I firmly believe that it was the Christian society, as you call it, the Judaic-Christian society, that created all of the factors that send so many so-called Negroes to prison. And when these fellows go to prison there is nothing in the system designed to rehabilitate them. There's nothing in the system designed to reform them. All it does is—it's a breeding ground for a more professional type of criminal, especially among Negroes. Since I saw, detected, the reluctance on the part of penologists, prison authorities, to reform men and even detected that—noticed that after a so-called Negro in prison tries to reform and become a better man, the prison authorities are more against *that* man than they were against him when he was completely criminally inclined, so this is again hypocrisy. Not only is the Christian society itself religious hypocrisy, but the court system is hypocrisy, the entire penal system is hypocrisy. Everything is hypocrisy. Mr. Muhammad came along with his religious gospel and introduced the religion of Islam and showed the honesty of Islam, showed the justice in Islam, the freedom in Islam. Why naturally, just comparing the two, Christianity had already eliminated itself, so all I had to do was accept the religion of Islam. I know today what it has done for me as a person.

CLARK: I notice that the Black Muslim movement has put a great deal of time, effort, and energy in seeking recruits within the prisons.

MALCOLM X: This is incorrect.

CLARK: It is incorrect?

MALCOLM X: It is *definitely* incorrect.

CLARK: Eric Lincoln's book—

MALCOLM X: Well, Lincoln is incorrect himself. Lincoln is just a Christian preacher from Atlanta, Georgia, who wanted to make some money, so he wrote a book and called it *The Black Muslims in America*. We're not even Black Muslims. We are black people in a sense that "black" is an adjective. We are black people who are Muslims because we have accepted the religion of Islam, but what Eric Lincoln shrewdly did was capitalize the letter "b," and made "black" an adjectival noun and then attached it to "Muslim," and now it is used by the press to make it appear that this is the name of an organization. It has no religious connotation or religious motivation or religious objectives.

CLARK: You do not have a systematic campaign for recruiting or rehabilitating?

MALCOLM X: No, no.

CLARK: What about rehabilitation?

MALCOLM X: The reason that the religion of Islam has spread so rapidly in prison is because the average so-called Negro in prison has had experiences enough to make him realize the hypocrisy of everything in this society, and he also has experienced the fact that the system itself is not designed to rehabilitate him or make him turn away from crime. Then when he hears the religious teaching of the Honorable Elijah Muhammad that restores to him his racial pride, his racial identity, and restores to him also the desire to be a man, to be a human being, he reforms himself. And this spreads so rapidly among the so-called Negroes in prison that, since the sociologist and the psychologists and the penologist and the criminologist have all realized their own inability to rehabilitate the criminal, when Mr. Muhammad comes along and starts rehabilitating the criminal with just the religious

gospel, it's a miracle. They look upon it as a sociological phenomenon or psychological phenomenon, and it gets great publicity.

CLARK: You do not, therefore, have to actively recruit.

MALCOLM X: The Honorable Elijah Muhammad has no active
effort to convert or recruit men in prison any more so than he
does Negroes, period. I think that what you should realize is that
in America there are twenty million black people, all of whom are
in prison. You don't have to go to Sing Sing to be in prison. If
you're born in America with a black skin, you're born in prison,
and the masses of black people in America today are beginning to
regard our plight or predicament in this society as one of a prison
inmate. And when they refer to the president, he's just another
warden to whom they turn to open the cell door, but it's no different. It's the same thing, and just as the warden in the prison
couldn't rehabilitate those men, the president in this country
couldn't rehabilitate or change the thinking of the masses of black
people. And as the Honorable Elijah Muhammad has been able
to go behind the prison walls—the physical prison walls—and
release those men from that which kept them criminals, he likewise on a mass scale throughout this country—he is able to send
his religious message into the so-called Negro community and
rehabilitate the thinking of our people and make them conquer
the habits and the vices and the evils that had held us in the
clutches of this white man's society.

CLARK: I think, Minister Malcolm, what you have just said brings
me to trying to hear from you directly your ideas concerning the
philosophy of the Black Muslim movement. Among the things
that have been written about this movement, the things which
stand out are the fact that this movement preaches hatred for
whites; that it preaches black supremacy; that it, in fact, preaches,
or if it does not directly preach, it accepts the inevitability of
violence as a factor in the relationship between the races. Now—

MALCOLM X: That's a strange thing. You know, the Jews here in
this city rioted last week against some Nazi, and I was listening to
a program last night where the other Jew—where a Jewish commentator was congratulating what the Jews did to this Nazi, com-
plimenting them for it. Now no one mentioned violence in connection with what the Jews did against these Nazis. But these
same Jews, who will condone violence on their part or hate some-

one whom they consider to be an enemy, will join Negro organizations and tell Negroes to be nonviolent; that it is wrong or immoral, unethical, unintelligent for Negroes to reflect some kind of desire to defend themselves from the attacks of whites who are trying to brutalize us. The Muslims who follow the Honorable Elijah Muhammad don't advocate violence, but Mr. Muhammad does teach us that any human being who is intelligent has the right to defend himself. You can't take a black man who is being bitten by dogs and accuse him of advocating violence because he tries to defend himself from the bite of the dog. If you notice, the people who are siccing the dogs on the black people are never accused of violence; they are never accused of hate. Nothing like that is ever used in the context of a discussion when it's about them. It is only when the black man begins to explode and erupt after he has had too much that they say that the black man is violent, and as long as these whites are putting out a doctrine that paves the way to justify their mistreatment of blacks, this is never called hate. It is only when the black man himself begins to spell out the historic deeds of what whites have been doing to him in this country that the shrewd white man with his control over the news media and propaganda makes it appear that the black people today are advocating some kind of hate. Mr. Muhammad teaches us to love each other, and when I say love each other— love our own kind. This is all black people need to be taught in this country because the only ones whom we don't love are our own kind. Most of the Negroes you see running around here talking about "love everybody"—they don't have any love whatsoever for their own kind. When they say, "Love everybody," what they are doing is setting up a situation for us to love white people. This is what their philosophy is. Or when they say, "Suffer peacefully," they mean suffer peacefully at the hands of the white man, because the same nonviolent Negroes are the advocators of nonviolence. If a Negro attacks one of them, they'll fight that Negro all over Harlem. It's only when the white man attacks them that they believe in nonviolence, all of them.

CLARK: Mr. X, is this a criticism of the Reverend Martin Luther King, Jr.?

MALCOLM X: You don't have to criticize Reverend Martin Luther King, Jr. His actions criticize him.

CLARK: What do you mean by this?

MALCOLM X: Any Negro who teaches other Negroes to turn the other cheek is disarming that Negro. Any Negro who teaches Negroes to turn the other cheek in the face of attack is disarming that Negro of his God-given right, of his moral right, of his natural right, of his intelligent right to defend himself. Everything in nature can defend itself, and is right in defending itself, except the American Negro. And men like King—their job is to go among Negroes and teach Negroes "Don't fight back." He doesn't tell them, "Don't fight each other." "Don't fight the white man" is what he's saying in essence, because the followers of Martin Luther King, Jr., will cut each other from head to foot, but they will not do anything to defend themselves against the attacks of the white man. But King's philosophy falls upon the ears of only a small minority. The majority or masses of black people in this country are more inclined in the direction of the Honorable Elijah Muhammad than Martin Luther King, Jr.

CLARK: Is it not a fact though—

MALCOLM X: *White* people follow King. *White* people pay King. *White* people subsidize King. *White* people support King. But the masses of black people don't support Martin Luther King, Jr. King is the best weapon that the white man, who wants to brutalize Negroes, has ever gotten in this country, because he is setting up a situation where, when the white man wants to attack Negroes, they can't defend themselves, because King has put this foolish philosophy out—you're not supposed to fight or you're not supposed to defend yourself.

CLARK: But, Mr. X, is it not a fact that Reverend King's movement was successful in Montgomery—

MALCOLM X: You can't tell me that you have had success—excuse me, sir.

CLARK: Was it not a success in Birmingham?

MALCOLM X: No, no. What kind of success did they get in Birmingham? A chance to sit at a lunch counter and drink some coffee with a cracker—that's success? A chance to—thousands of little children went to jail; they didn't get out, they were bonded out by King. They had to *pay* their way out of jail. That's not any kind of advancement or success.

CLARK: What is advancement from the point of view of the Muslims?

MALCOLM X: Any time dogs have bitten black women, bitten black children—when I say dogs, that is four-legged dogs and two-legged dogs have brutalized thousands of black people—and the one who advocates himself as their leader is satisfied in making a compromise or a deal with the same ones who did this to these people only if they will offer him a job, one job, downtown for one Negro or things of that sort, I don't see where there's any kind of success, sir; it's a sellout. Negroes in Birmingham are in worse condition now than they were then because the line is more tightly drawn. And to say that some moderate—to say that things are better now because a different man, a different white man, a different Southern white man is in office now, who's supposed to be a moderate, is to tell me that you are better off dealing with a fox than you were when you were dealing with a wolf. The ones that they were dealing with previously were wolves, and they didn't hide the fact that they were wolves. The man that they got to deal with now is a fox, but he's no better than the wolf. Only he's better in his ability to lull the Negroes to sleep, and he'll do that as long as they listen to Dr. Martin Luther King, Jr.

CLARK: What would be the goals, or what are the goals of the Black Muslim movement? What would the Black Muslim movement insist upon in Birmingham, in Montgomery, and in Jackson, Mississippi, etc.?

MALCOLM X: Well, number one, the Honorable Elijah Muhammad teaches us that the solution will never be brought about by politicians, it will be brought about by God, and that the only way the black man in this country today can receive respect and recognition of other people is to stand on his own feet, get something for himself and do something for himself; and the solution that God has given the Honorable Elijah Muhammad is the same as the solution that God gave to Moses when the Hebrews in the Bible were in a predicament similar to the predicament of the so-called Negroes here in America today, which is nothing other than a modern house of bondage, or a modern Egypt, or a modern Babylon. And Moses' answer was to separate these slaves from their slave master and show the slaves how to go to a land of their own where they would serve a God of their own and a religion of their own and have a country of their own in which they could feed themselves, clothe themselves, and shelter themselves.

CLARK: In fact then, you're saying that the Black Muslim movement—

MALCOLM X: It's not a Black Muslim movement.

CLARK: All right, then—

MALCOLM X: We are black people who are Muslims because we believe in the religion of Islam.

CLARK: —this movement which you so ably represent actually desires separation.

MALCOLM X: Complete separation; not only physical separation but moral separation. This is why the Honorable Elijah Muhammad teaches the black people in this country that we must stop drinking, we must stop smoking, we must stop committing fornication and adultery, we must stop gambling and cheating and using profanity, we must stop showing disrespect for our women, we must reform ourselves as parents so we can set the proper example for our children. Once we reform ourselves of these immoral habits, that makes us more godly, more godlike, more righteous. That means we are qualified then, to be on God's side, and it puts God on our side. God becomes our champion then, and it makes it possible for us to accomplish our own aims.

CLARK: This movement then, is not particularly sympathetic with the integrationist goals of the NAACP, CORE, Martin Luther King, Jr., and the student nonviolent movement.

MALCOLM X: Mister Muhammad teaches us that integration is only a trick on the part of the white man today to lull Negroes to sleep, to lull them into thinking that the white man is changing and actually trying to keep us here; but America itself, because of the seeds that it has sown in the past against the black man, is getting ready to reap the whirlwind today, reap the harvest. Just as Egypt had to pay for its crime that it committed for enslaving the Hebrews, the Honorable Elijah Muhammad teaches us that America has to pay today for the crime that is committed in enslaving the so-called Negroes.

CLARK: There is one question that has bothered me a great deal about your movement, and it involves just a little incident. Rock-

well, who is a self-proclaimed white supremacist and American Nazi, was given an honored front row position at one of your—
MALCOLM X: This is incorrect.
CLARK: Am I wrong?
MALCOLM X: This is a false statement that has been put out by the press. And Jews have used it to spread anti-Muslim propaganda throughout this country. Mister Muhammad had an open convention to which he invited anyone, black and white. (And this is another reason why we keep white people out of our meetings.) He invited everyone, both black and white, and Rockwell came. Rockwell came the same as any other white person came, and when we took up a collection, we called out the names of everyone who made a donation. Rockwell's name was called out the same as anybody else's, and this was projected to make it look like Rockwell was financing the Muslims. And secondly, Rockwell came to another similar meeting. At this meeting Mister Muhammad gave anyone who wanted to oppose him or congratulate him an opportunity to speak. Rockwell spoke; he was not ever allowed up on the rostrum; he spoke from a microphone from which other whites spoke at the same meeting. And again, the Jewish press, or the Jewish who are a part of the press—Jewish *people* who are part of the press—used this as propaganda to make it look like Rockwell was in cahoots with the Muslims. Rockwell, to us, is no different from any other white man. One of the things that I *will* give Rockwell credit for: he preaches and practices the same thing. And these other whites running around here posing as liberals, patting Negroes on the back—they think the same thing that Rockwell thinks, only they speak a different talk, a different language.
CLARK: Minister Malcolm, you have mentioned the Jews and the Jewish press and Jewish propaganda frequently in this discussion. It has been said frequently that an important part of your movement is anti-Semitism. I have seen you deny this.
MALCOLM X: No. We're a—
CLARK: Would you want to comment on this?
MALCOLM X: No, the followers of Mr. Muhammad aren't anti-anything but anti-wrong, anti-exploitation, and anti-oppression. A lot of the Jews have a guilty conscience when you mention exploitation because they realize that they control ninety per cent of the

businesses in every Negro community from the Atlantic to the Pacific and that they get more benefit from the Negro's purchasing power than the Negro himself does or than any other white or any other segment of the white community does, so they have a guilt complex on this. And whenever you mention exploitation of Negroes, most Jews think that you're talking about them, and in order to hide what they are guilty of, they accuse you of being anti-Semitic.

CLARK: Do you believe the Jews are more guilty of this exploitation that are—

MALCOLM X: Jews belong to practically every Negro organization Negroes have. Arthur B. Spingarn, the head of the NAACP, is Jewish. Every organization that Negroes—When I say the head of the NAACP, the *president* of the NAACP is Jewish. The same Jews wouldn't let you become the president of the B'nai B'rith or their different organizations.

CLARK: Thank you very much. You have certainly presented important parts of your movement, your point of view. I think we understand more clearly now some of your goals, and I'd like to know if we could talk some other time, if you would tell me a little about what you think is the future of the Negro in America other than separation.

MALCOLM X: Yes. As long as they have interviews with the Attorney General and take Negroes to pose as leaders, all of whom are married either to white men or white women, you'll always have a race problem. When Baldwin took that crew with him to see Kennedy, he took the wrong crew. And as long as they take the wrong crew to talk to that man, you're not going to get anywhere near any solution to this problem in this country.

Chickens, Snakes and Duck Eggs
Making history and parables with Robert Penn Warren

Early in December 1963 Malcolm X referred to the Kennedy assassi-nation as a case of the chickens coming home to roost. For this remark he was suspended from his Muslim ministry for ninety days by Elijah Muhammad. Shortly after the suspension a reflective, self-possessed but fiery and intellectually nimble Malcolm X spoke with Robert Penn Warren about blood damnation, separatism, the logic of history, snakes and nonselective reprisals. The excerpt that follows originally appeared in Warren's book Who Speaks for the Negro? *(1965).*

This morning, in Suite 128 of the Theresa Hotel, he is no longer the heir apparent to Elijah Muhammad, he is merely himself. But that fact—as he stands there across the expanse of bare, ill-swept floor, conferring with the ominous attendant—is not to be ig-nored. I am watching him, and he knows I am watching him, but he gives no sign. He has the air of a man who can be himself with many eyes on him.

Finally he beckons to me. The attendant takes my raincoat and hat and hangs them in a little closet, and acknowledges my thanks with a reserved inclination of the head. Minister Malcolm X leads me into a long, very narrow room made by partitioning off the end of the big room where the blackboard is. The only furniture is a small table and two chairs, set face-to-face, under a series of windows that give over the street. Malcolm X tells me that he has only a few minutes, that he has found that you waste a lot of time with reporters and then you don't get much space. It is the same remark that Whitney Young made to me at our first interview; only he had said, "enough space for the Urban League to justify it."

I begin by asking if the Negro's sense of a lack of identity is the key for the appeal of the Black Muslim religion.

MALCOLM X: Yes. Besides teaching him (the American Negro) that Islam is the best religion, since the main problem that Afro-Americans* have is a lack of cultural identity, it is necessary to teach him that he had some type of identity, culture, civilization before he was brought here. But now, teaching him about his historic and cultural past is not his religion. The two have to be separated.

WARREN: What about the matter of personal identity as distinguished from cultural and blood identity?

MALCOLM X: The religion of Islam actually restores one's human feelings—human rights, human incentives—his talent. It brings out of the individual all of his dormant potential. It gives him the incentive to develop, to be identified collectively in the brotherhood of Islam with the brothers in Islam; at the same time this also gives him the—it has the psychological effect of giving him incentive as an individual.

WARREN: One often encounters among Negroes a deep suspicion of any approach which involves anything like the old phrase "self-improvement" and a Negro's individual responsibility. You take a different line.

MALCOLM X: Definitely. Many of the Negro leaders actually suffer themselves from an inferiority complex, even though they say they don't, and because of this they have subconscious defensive

---

* For the Black Muslims, the word *Negro* is a white invention, a badge of slavery. Ordinarily the Muslim will, if he uses the word at all, preface it with "so-called." Afro-Americans or Black Men is preferred. As Malcolm X puts it: "If you call yourself 'white,' why should I not call myself 'black'? Because you have taught me that I am a 'Negro'! Now then, if you ask a man his nationality and he says he is German, that means he comes from a nation called Germany. . . . The term he uses to identify himself connects him with a nation, a language, a culture and a flag. Now if he says his nationality is 'Negro' he has told you nothing—except possibly that he is not good enough to be 'American.' . . . No matter how light or how dark we are, we call ourselves 'black' . . . and we don't feel we have to make apologies about it." (C. Eric. Lincoln, *The Black Muslims in America.*)

But in the course of the conversation Malcolm X begins to use "Negro."

mechanisms, so that when you mention self-improvement, the implication is that the Negro is something distinct and different and therefore needs to improve himself. Negro leaders resent this being said, not because they don't know that it's true but they're thinking—they're looking at it personally, they think the implication is directed at them, and they duck this responsibility, whereas the only real solution to the race problem is a solution that involves individual self-improvement and collective self-improvement.

"Self-improvement," for the Black Muslims, then, carries no stigma of Booker T. Washington or Uncle Tom. And the reason I take to be clear: the purpose of the self-improvement is not to become "worthy" to integrate with the white man, to be "accepted" by him—to integrate with "a burning house"—but to become worthy of the newly discovered self, as well as of a glorious past and a more glorious future. The question asked by Lorraine Hansberry and James Baldwin—"Who wants to integrate with a burning house?"—with its repudiation of white values, has some of the emotional appeal of the Black Muslim prophecy of destruction for the "white devils" and the glory of the Black Kingdom to come. In a more subtle form we find the same appeal in the role that some Negro workers in the Movement assume: the role of being the regenerator of society, not working merely for integration into white society but for the redemption of society— a repudiation, and a transcendence, of white values that gives something of the satisfaction that may be found in the Black Muslim promise of Armageddon, and a perfect world thereafter. It assumes, not equality, but superiority—superiority to, at least, the present-day white man.

I am thinking of the freedom the Black Muslim enjoys in accepting the doctrine of self-improvement, and then of the complex—and sometimes unfree—reaction the white man has to the Negro's assumption of the role of regenerator, even as I ask Malcolm X about his own conversion.

MALCOLM X: That was in prison. I was in prison and I was an atheist. In fact, one of the persons who started me to thinking seriously was an atheist—a Negro inmate whom I had heard in discussion with white inmates and who was able to hold his own at all levels; and it was he who switched my reading habits in the direction away from fiction to nonfiction, so that by the time one of my brothers [who had become a Muslim in Detroit] told me about Islam, I was open-minded and I began to read in that direction. One of the things that appealed to me was in Islam a man is honored as a human being and not measured by the color of his skin.

I think of Lolis Elie, back in his office in New Orleans, his voice full of controlled violence as he says: "At what point—when will it be possible for white people to look at black people as human beings?"

Elie had said that he was reading Black Muslim literature. And the thing that drives him is what had driven Malcolm X to his conversion.

WARREN: Was your conversion fast or slow—a flash of intuition?

MALCOLM X: It was fast. I took an about-turn overnight.

WARREN: Really overnight?

MALCOLM X: Yes. And while I was in prison. I was indulging in all types of vice right within the prison, and I never was ostracized as much by the penal authorities while I was participating in all the evils of the prison as they tried to ostracize me after I became a Muslim.

WARREN: If Islam teaches the worth of all men without reference to color, how does this relate to the message of black superiority and the doom of the white race?

MALCOLM X: The white race is doomed not *because* it's white but because of its misdeeds. If people listen to what Muslims declare they will find that, even as Moses told Pharoah, you are doomed if you don't do so-and-so. Always the *if* is there. Well, it's the same way in America. When the Muslims deliver the indictment of the American system, it is not the white man per se that is being doomed.

I discovered that that pale, dull yellowish face that had seemed so veiled, so stony, as though beyond all feeling, had flashed into its merciless, leering life—the sudden wolfish grin, the pale pink lips drawn hard back to show the strong teeth, the unveiled glitter of the eyes beyond the lenses, giving the sense that the lenses were only part of a clever disguise, that the eyes need no help, that they suddenly see everything.

He has made his point.

I study his grin, then say: "There's no blood damnation, then?"

MALCOLM X: No, but it's almost impossible to separate the actions—to separate the criminal exploitation and criminal oppression of the American Negro from the color of the skin of the oppressor. So he thinks he's being condemned because of the color of his skin.

WARREN: Can any person of white blood—even one—be guiltless?

MALCOLM X: Guiltless?

WARREN: Yes.

MALCOLM X: You can answer it this way, by turning it around. Can any Negro who is the victim of the system escape the collective stigma that is placed upon all Negroes in this country? And the answer is "No." Well, the white race in America is the same way. As individuals it is impossible to escape the collective crime.

WARREN: Let's take an extreme case—your reaction to it. A white child of three or four—an age below decisions or responsibility—is facing death before an oncoming truck.

MALCOLM X: The white child, although he has not committed any of the deeds that have produced the plight the Negro finds himself in, is he guiltless? The only way you can determine that is to take a Negro child who is only four years old—can he escape, though he's only four years old, can he escape the stigma of segregation? He's only four years old.

WARREN: Let's put the Negro child in front of the truck, and put a white man there who leaps—risks his own life—to save the child. What is your attitude toward him?

MALCOLM X: It wouldn't alter the fact that after the white man saved the little black child he couldn't take that little black child into many restaurants right along with him. That same white man would have to toss that child back into discrimination, segregation.

WARREN: Let's say that white man is willing to go to jail to break segregation. Some white men have. What about him then?
MALCOLM X: My personal attitude is that he has done nothing to solve the problem.
WARREN: But what is your attitude toward his moral nature?
MALCOLM X: I'm not even interested in his moral nature. Until the problem is solved, we're not interested in anybody's moral nature.

How close is this, I wonder, looking back, to what James Forman had said? "It's what the social effect is of what a person is doing that's important," he had said. Does he mean to imply that moral value equates, simply, with consequence? Many people have believed that. Machiavelli, for one; Bishop Paley, who wrote *Evidences of Christianity,* for another; Stalin, for another. I wonder if—and how deeply and in what sense—Forman believes this. I do not need to wonder about Malcolm X.

For behind all his expert illogic there is a frightful, and frightfully compelling, clarity of feeling—one is tempted to say logic. Certainly a logic of history. Of history conceived of as doom.

So, even as I ask Malcolm X if he could call that white man who goes to jail a friend, I know that his answer will be "No."

MALCOLM X: If his own race were being trampled upon as the race of Negroes are being trampled upon, he would use a different course of action to protect his rights [different from going to jail].
WARREN: What course of action?
MALCOLM X: I have never seen white people who would sit—would approach a solution to their own problems nonviolently. It's only when they are so-called fighting for the rights of the Negroes that they nonviolently, passively and lovingly, you know, approach the situation. Those types of whites who are always going to jail with Negroes are the ones who tell Negroes to be loving and kind and patient and be nonviolent and turn the other cheek.

He would not call him a friend. And I think of an article in the *Village Voice*—"View from the Back of the Bus" by Marlene

Nadle—reporting the dialogue on a bus to Washington for the March, in August 1963:

> Frank Harman (a young man, white, member of the Peace Corps) was asked why, since he was white, he wanted to go to Nigeria. He replied, "I want to help those people because they are human beings."
>
> Suddenly Wayne (a Negro) shouted, "If this thing comes to violence, yours will be the first throat we slit. We don't need your kind. Get out of our organization."
>
> Completely baffled by the outburst, Frank kept repeating the questions, "What's he talking about? What did I say?"
>
> Wayne, straining forward tensely, screamed, "We don't need any white liberals to patronize us!"
>
> Other Negroes joined in. "We don't trust you." "We don't believe you're sincere." "You'll have to prove yourself."
>
> Frank shouted back, "I don't have to prove myself to anyone but myself."
>
> "We've been stabbed in the back too many times."
>
> "The reason white girls come down to civil rights meetings is because they've heard of the black man's reputation of sex."
>
> "The reason white guys come down is because they want to rebel against their parents."

Poor Frank Harman, he doesn't know what kind of test he has to pass. But Malcolm X could tell him.

MALCOLM X: If I see a white man who was willing to go to jail or throw himself in front of a car in behalf of the so-called Negro cause, the test that I would put to him, I'd ask him, "Do you think Negroes—when Negroes are being attacked—they should defend themselves even at the risk of having to kill the one who's attacking them?" If that white man told me, yes, I'd shake his hand.

But what would this mean, this hand-shaking? If the demand Malcolm X makes is merely that the white man recognize his right of self-defense (which the law already defines for him and which the NAACP supports), then he might go around shaking hands all day and not exhaust the available supply. If by "defend themselves" he means the business of Armageddon, then he will find few hands to shake. But in any case, what does the hand-shaking mean if he maintains that the white man, and the white man's system, can't change from the iniquity which he attributes to him?

MALCOLM X: It is the system itself that is incapable of producing freedom for the twenty-two million Afro-Americans. It is like a chicken can't lay a duck egg. A chicken can't lay a duck egg because the system of the chicken isn't constructed in a way to produce a duck egg; and the political and economic system of this country is absolutely incapable of producing freedom and justice and equality and human dignity for the twenty-two million Afro-Americans.

WARREN: You don't see in the American system the possibility of self-regeneration?

MALCOLM X: No.

We come to the separatism, the independent nation, to Africa —the dream or the reality.

MALCOLM X: The solution for the Afro-American is twofold—long-range and short-range. I believe that a psychological, cultural, and philosophical migration back to Africa will solve our problems. Not a physical migration, but a cultural, psychological, philosophical migration back to Africa—which means restoring our common bond—will give us the spiritual strength and the incentive to strengthen our political and social and economic position right here in America, and to fight for the things that are ours by right on this continent. And at the same time this will give incentive to many of our people to also visit and even migrate physically back to Africa, and those who stay here can help those who go back and those who go back can help those who stay here, in the same way as the Jews who go to Israel.

WARREN: What about the short-range?

MALCOLM X: Immediate steps have to be taken to re-educate our people—a more real view of political, economic, and social conditions, and self-improvement to gain political control over every community in which we predominate, and also over the economy of that same community.

WARREN: That is, you are now thinking of localities—communities in the United States—being operated by Negroes, not of a separate state or nation?

MALCOLM X: No. Separating a section of America for Afro-Americans is similar to expecting a heaven in the sky after you die.

WARREN: You now say it is not practical?

MALCOLM X: To say it is not practical one has to also admit that integration is not practical.

WARREN: I don't follow that.

MALCOLM X: In stating that a separate state is not practical I am also stating that integration—forced integration as they have been making an effort to do for the last ten years—is also just as impractical.

WARREN: To go back—you are thinking simply of Negro-dominated communities?

MALCOLM X: Yes, and once the black man becomes the political master of his own community, it means that the politicians will also be black, which means that he will be sending black representatives even at the federal level.

WARREN: What do you think of the Negroes now holding posts at the federal level?

MALCOLM X: Window dressing.

WARREN: Ralph Bunche too?

MALCOLM X: Any Negro who occupies a position that was given him by the white man—if you analyze his function, it never enables him to really take a firm, militant stand. He opens his mouth only to the degree that the political atmosphere will allow him to do so.

In my opinion, mature political action is the type of action that enables the black people to see the fruits that they should be receiving from the politicians, and thereby determine whether or not the politician is really fulfilling his function, and if he is not they can then set up the machinery to remove him from the position by whatever means necessary. He either produces or not, and he's out one way or another.

WARREN: There's only one way to put a politician out, ordinarily —to vote him out.

MALCOLM X: I think the black people have reached the point

where they should reserve the right to do whatever is necessary to exercise complete control over the politicians of their community by whatever means necessary.

I ask him if he believes in political assassination, and he turns the hard, impassive face and veiled eyes upon me, and says: "I wouldn't know anything about that."

He has only said: ". . . reserve the right to do whatever is necessary to exercise complete control . . . by whatever means necessary." What is "reserve the right"? What is "complete control"? What is "whatever means necessary"? Who knows?

Malcolm X has always been a master of the shadowy phrase, the faintly shaken veil, the charged blankness into which the white man can project the images of guilt or fear. He is also a master of parable.

WARREN: What about the matter of nonselective reprisal?
MALCOLM X: Well, I'll tell you, if I go home and my child has blood running down her leg and someone tells me a snake bit her, I'm going out and kill snakes, and when I find a snake I'm not going to look and see if he has blood on his jaws.
WARREN: You mean you'd kill any snake you could find?
MALCOLM X: I grew up in the country, on a farm. And whenever a snake was bothering the chickens, we'd kill snakes. We never knew which was the snake did it.
WARREN: To read your parable, then, you would advocate nonselective reprisals?
MALCOLM X: I'm just telling you about snakes.

His Best Credentials
On the air with Joe Rainey

"Malcolm X Splits With Muhammad" announced The New York Times *on March 8, 1964. On March 20 Malcolm discussed the implications of his break with the Nation of Islam on Joe Rainey's phone-in radio show,* Listening Post, *which was broadcast at 11:15* P.M. *out of Philadelphia on station WDAS.*

The program opened with a prepared statement by Malcolm X. It expresses Malcolm's desire first of all not to fight other black organizations or their leaders but to "find a common approach, a common solution to a common problem." Malcolm then announces his plan to organize the Muslim Mosque, Incorporated, in order to forward a political and social philosophy of black nationalism. Blacks, says Malcolm, must gain control of the politics as well as the politicians in their own communities. To that end, Malcolm calls for young blood, new ideas, more militancy and racial solidarity. Whereas Malcolm would encourage his people to be "peaceful and law-abiding," he asserts too that "the time has come for the American Negro to fight back in self-defense whenever and wherever he is being unjustly and unlawfully attacked. And if the government thinks that I'm wrong for saying this, then let the government start doing its job."

Malcolm's opening statement, then, is his dedication to the battle of African-Americans for their civil rights. He makes it clear, however, that he speaks with no pretensions to divinity (as did Muhammad). He confesses to a lack of formal education and of particular professional expertise. But, Malcolm emphatically assures his audience, he is sincere, and "my sincerity is my best credential."

That sincerity is everywhere apparent both in Malcolm's responses to Joe Rainey and in his replies to the radio listeners' questions. Their broadcast was recorded by an agent of the FBI, and what follows is the transcript from the FBI file on the Muslim Mosque, Incorporated.

JOE RAINEY: Well, number one, the emphasis that you're placing on self-defense is contrary to the belief that many people advance in relation to taking an aggressive side. In other words what you're advocating is self-defense. You're not advocating that people buy guns and start shooting up places, are you?

MALCOLM X: No, all I said was, if you notice, in areas where the government is either unable or unwilling, then it's time for the so-called Negro to be a man as others are men and defend himself. If you read the Constitution, Article II, from the original amendments, the Bill of Rights, it says this: "a well-regulated militia being necessary to the security of a free state, the right of the people to keep and bear arms shall not be infringed." We're not telling anybody to break the law, but we're telling the so-called Negroes to read the Constitution, and in the context of his constitutional rights he should do whatever is necessary to defend himself, especially since the government itself has proven its inability or else its unwillingness to come to the rescue and defend our people when they are being unjustly attacked.

JOE RAINEY: What is the difference in the philosophy of the Muslims under Muhammad and the philosophy that you're preaching now?

MALCOLM X: None, because the Honorable Elijah Muhammad in his speech in 1959 said that the Negro should take the Justice Department, the Constitution, the Church, and Christianity and put them in the garbage can and then use the garbage can to fight back. Well, if I can fight with a garbage can I can fight with a rifle, and I'd rather shoot bullets at my enemy than shoot garbage at my enemy. I don't think that anything I'm saying conflicts with anything that the Honorable Elijah Muhammad teaches. In fact, I believe that I'm his number one follower: and as I mentioned in my opening statement, it was true that I ran into some opposition within the movement. And since I love the Honorable Elijah Muhammad and what he is teaching, I felt that I could better expedite his program and carry it into practice by keeping free and clear of those forces which I knew existed. So the purpose of the Muslim Mosque, Incorporated, will be to launch an action program in the community to show our people how to solve our own problems right now. It's true we are going somewhere: we're all going back home. But before we go back home we still have to eat, we still have to sleep, we still have to have clothes and jobs and education. So we are evolving an action program that will enable us to take the techniques of the Honorable Elijah Muhammad and carry it into practice right now in the so-called Negro community and eliminate some of the ills, the social ills and political ills and the economic ills, that keep our people imprisoned and trapped there in the ghetto.

JOE RAINEY: Well, are there differences existing between you and Elijah Muhammad at this point?

MALCOLM X: I have no differences whatsoever with the Honorable Elijah Muhammad. I still, as I told you, think I am one of his most faithful followers.

JOE RAINEY: Does he have any differences with you?

MALCOLM X: Well, I haven't been in touch with the Honorable Elijah Muhammad now in about two weeks, and if there are differences then I submit to these differences. I am in no way in opposition to him.

JOE RAINEY: I read and saw a picture today relative to the severing of some type of relationship that existed between you and Cassius Clay. I had been reading, of course, up to that time and had been hearing about a very close relationship that existed. And then all of a sudden out of a clear blue sky, I see this picture; it was in one of the New York papers, of Elijah Muhammad with Clay and Clay making a statement to some effect that he was more or less severing relations with you, even though you still were his friend.

MALCOLM X: I don't think that Cassius has ever made any statement, negative statement, concerning me, nor have I made any concerning him. We are brothers, and in the initial statement that I made to the press I pointed out that my hope and prayer is that all Muslims who follow the Honorable Elijah Muhammad will continue to follow him. But my intent and purpose is to take what I have learned from the Honorable Elijah Muhammad and teach it among the twenty-two million non-Muslims, so-called Negroes in this country. And Cassius, being a follower of the Honorable Elijah Muhammad, still is, but he and I are closer than brothers. In fact, I spent probably the most important hours of his life, preceding the fight . . .

JOE RAINEY: But the question I am actually asking is if there is a difference now in the association from what was prior to the fight.

MALCOLM X: No, no difference, we are still brothers. I doubt that you will get any words out of him that will in any way depict any difference. We are still brothers, very close brothers. In fact, at this same time last night we were breaking bread together.

JOE RAINEY: That should substantiate what you are saying. I wish I was breaking bread with somebody right now, as hungry as I am.

MALCOLM X: I would like to say this about Cassius. Cassius is a remarkable person. I knew that Cassius was going to win the championship.

JOE RAINEY: How did you know?

MALCOLM X: Well, when you get to know him you can see the man is one hundred percent man. He is very shrewd, for one thing, and his public image and his private image are as different as night and day. Cassius knew that he never could get a shot at the title by remaining quiet, and he put on an act that the public went for a thousand percent. He is an extremely intelligent young man, and he has more depth than a person would ever realize. He has a very pure heart, free heart toward people. He loves children, and he loves people, actually. He gets his strength from people. When he would be walking through the streets of Miami if no one was around he seemed distant and far away and deep, but as soon as he gets around a crowd of people you can see the strength coming right out in him. And he is a strong race man, not a racist. He has strong love for his people, and one of the things that made the public not realize he would win—as soon as it was mentioned that Cassius was a Muslim or implied rather that he was a Muslim the white reporters were so prejudiced that they lost their ability to be objective. And I noticed that whenever they would come around the gym while he was in training, instead of asking Cassius something about the fight or his athletic ability they would be asking him questions about politics and race and things of that sort. When they would go to Sonny's camp they would ask Sonny questions about his muscles or how he feels physically, but reporters from all over the world would be questioning Cassius concerning his views on the relationship the Chinese, perhaps, on the mainland and those on Formosa, or the problems that exist in Africa or the European Common Market.

They were able to recognize that Cassius had a mind of his own; not only was he champ caliber physically, but intellectually he was the same thing.

JOE RAINEY: How do you account, if you can, for his failure to pass his Draft Board examination for the United States Army?

MALCOLM X: Well, I'll tell you. I'm very reluctant to pass any comment on it. I know someone was really in a very paradoxical position when they were faced with the possibility of the heavyweight champion of the world and a black man too taking a stand on the basis of his conscience. It was a very precarious position for a lot of people to be in, so I'm inclined to be very thankful for him that it came out as it did.

JOE RAINEY: You mean that you fear that if he had enlisted something might happen to him?

MALCOLM X: No, I think any black man today who is twenty-two years old who faces the possibility of being drafted into an army to fight for a philosophy that has fallen short where he's concerned, that man is really faced with a grave question. And almost every young, so-called Negro today when it comes time for him to be drafted asks himself what is he being drafted for. What does he have to fight for? The young generation is asking that question. Now preceding generations were supposed to be militant and all that, but they allowed themselves to be drafted to fight for something that they never received. And I think that most youth today—that is among our people—are asking themselves just what are they fighting for, what did their father fight for, what did their uncle fight for. And if they didn't get what they fought for how does this present generation know that it will get what it's being called upon to fight for. And not only that, if these young Negroes aren't allowed to fight in Mississippi, it says here in the news that just came out where the Klan is burning Negroes, shooting Negroes, terrorizing Negroes, and then these Negro leaders are telling these young Negroes to turn the other cheek, be nonviolent, and love their enemy. Well, you got the young generation now thinking, and they are asking themselves why should they be nonviolent in Mississippi and allow this government to draft them and send them to be violent in South Vietnam or in Germany somewhere. If it's right to be violent abroad, it's right to be violent at home. And if it's right to be nonviolent at home, then the government should expect these young Negroes to be nonviolent when it comes time to be drafted.

JOE RAINEY: You made some mention a little earlier relative to your desire to work with a number of other organizations in their program. Am I quoting it correctly now when I say that? Just exactly what do you mean in view of the fact that you have in the past differed with some of the philosophies as advanced by such organizations as the NAACP, the organization of Dr. King, the Student Nonviolent Coordinating Committee? You have disagreed in the past with their philosophy; are you now approving of what they do?

MALCOLM X: No. Krushchev and John F. Kennedy disagreed with each other on philosophy, but they were able to exchange wheat with each other. And if white people with differences can get together I think it's time for us so-called Negroes to submit. Some of our differences can be submitted, and we can get together in areas that we have in common. And the Honorable Elijah Muhammad has always said that in areas where we can work with the so-called civil rights groups without compromising our religious philosophy we should get our heads together. So I was involved just this week in the school boycott in New York, *not* because I believe in integration, but I am against segregation. I realize that the segregated school system produces crippled children that are crippled when it comes to education. So my involvement in the boycott is that I agree with the civil rights leaders that it is an inferior education. And, therefore, I will work with them in this particular field against a segregated school system. But at the same time they believe in integration and I believe in separation. Where we don't agree we won't bring that up. We only bring up where we do agree, and once we eliminate that we'll get to our disagreements later on.

Both of us believe that quality education is needed in the so-called Negro community. Now we disagree on integration, but we agree on quality education. We believe that the so-called Negro schools should have better facilities, that we should have better teachers, that we should have better books. Where we agree let us work toward trying to bring that about, but where we disagree, again on integration, let's not bring that up.

So all I have said to these civil rights groups is start at the things where we can agree and let's get together on that, and leave the things where we don't agree in the closet until a later date.

JOE RAINEY: What has been the reaction of the leaders of the groups that you have mentioned recently: the NAACP, the Urban League, King's group and so forth. How have they reacted?

MALCOLM X: Well, I was in Chester, Pennsylvania a week ago tomorrow, Saturday; I was involved in a conference in which a cross section of civil rights leaders were represented. Gloria Richardson was there, Landry who headed the school boycott in Chicago was there, several others. Stanley Branche hosted the meeting, of Chester. The young chap from down in Maryland where they had so much trouble a few weeks ago, there was a cross section represented, and they agreed to form a group called ACT. The initials mean nothing; the word is what they are using, ACT. And this organization is going to be free to act whenever, wherever, whatever men are necessary to get a job done, and Landry of Chicago was chosen as the chairman. It was quite a milestone. I believe in the whole struggle. And I was invited to address the group, and my address was designed to show them that as long as they call themselves a civil rights group and fight the battle at a civil rights level they are alienating much of the assistance that they could get. But if they would expand the entire civil rights struggle to a human rights level where different members of the United Nations can step in and lend their support, in fact, they put it on a level by which the groups can take it to the United Nations Committee on Human Rights. They actually make it a much broader battle, and they get help from many different quarters.

At this point Joe Rainey gave the telephone number of the station and asked for questions and comments from the listening audience.

JOE RAINEY: Is this a nationwide outfit now? This is a nationwide organization.

MALCOLM X: The strangest thing is I have gotten a flood of mail from student groups from coast to coast, expressing a desire to become active with us, and although we have Islam as our religion, black nationalism is our political philosophy. Our social philosophy is black nationalism, our economic philosophy is black nationalism, which means that the political philosophy of black nationalism means that the so-called Negro controls the politics and the politicians of his own community. The economic philosophy of black nationalism means that our people should be re-educated into the importance of economics and the importance of controlling the economy in the community in which we live. And the social so that we can create jobs for our own kind instead of having to boycott and picket and beg the white man to give us jobs. And the social philosophy of black nationalism involves the emphasis upon the culture of the black man, which will be designed to connect us with our cultural roots, to restore the racial dignity necessary for us to love our own kind and be in unity and harmony with our own kind and strike at the evils and vices that strike at the moral fiber of our own community and our own society. The social philosophy of black nationalism encourages the black man to elevate his own society instead of trying to force himself into the unwanted presence of the white society.

JOE RAINEY: Now you made mention earlier of the Negro chasing false leaders. You didn't use the term "false leaders," but you said that there are politicians that are not leading them up the right street, that they should dispose of them. Now I was under the impression that the Muslims do not vote. Do they vote?

MALCOLM X: Well, if you check again, every edition of Elijah Muhammad's newspaper has on the back of it his programs, and if a person reads it carefully they will find there is leeway there or latitude there that will enable anyone who really understands his program the latitude to take action in whatever area necessary to uplift the level of the so-called Negro community, whether it is in the field of politics, whether it is in the field of economics, or whether it is in the social and civic affairs of their community. And it is the failure to properly understand what the Honorable Elijah Muhammad is teaching that has caused the Nation of Islam to reach a sort of impasse as far as its growth is concerned. So I feel it is my understanding of what the Honorable Elijah

Muhammad is teaching that it is within what he teaches to take an active part in the politics of the community, especially right here in Philadelphia. I was here with him, I think in October, when he pointed out that it was time for the Negroes to come together and unite and sweep out of office all of the—as he called them—"Uncle Tom" politicians. You can't sweep anybody out of office without voting. You can't vote without registering, but there are too many Muslims who are sitting around . . .

JOE RAINEY: Well, does the average Muslim vote? I'm still under the impression that they do not.

MALCOLM X: They do what they understand, and too many Muslims don't understand what the Honorable Elijah Muhammad is teaching. And there are interorganizational blocs that make it almost impossible for the Muslim who is in there to have freedom of thought to the extent where he can really understand what Mr. Muhammad is teaching so that he can become involved in the action programs of the community.

JOE RAINEY: I have a certificate of registration from one of my friends here.

MALCOLM X: He's a Muslim. Usually in the past Muslims have kept their politics to themselves. But you'll find there's a lot of young Muslims who want action and who are aggressive, who are progressive, who have an education and who want to take part in these things to uplift the standard of the so-called Negro community.

JOE RAINEY: What sort of action do they want?

MALCOLM X: Action that will get results, any kind of action that will get results. If a man wants freedom he shouldn't be confined to certain tactics. Freedom is something that's so dear that someone that doesn't have it should reserve the right to use whatever technique or tactic that is necessary to bring about this freedom.

If George Washington and Jefferson and Hamilton and Patrick Henry and the founding fathers of this country had been confined to certain tactics, why these people wouldn't even have a country. This would still be England or New England.

A FEMALE LISTENER: Would you ask Malcolm X for me if he intends to hold any public speaking rallies here in Philadelphia anytime soon, and if he intends to set up any headquarters here. Thank you.

MALCOLM X: The Muslim Mosque, Incorporated, which is presently headquartered in New York, will definitely be here in Philadelphia also. There are a large number of our people who have already expressed the desire to organize into groups to work in conjunction with those of us who are organizing in New York. We are interested in all people. We don't care whether you are a Christian or a Jew or a gentile or whatever the case may be; if you are fed up with the conditions that the black people are suffering in this country, and you want to take an active part, then we are interested in helping you organize so that we can get together, work together, and get the problem solved.

A MALE LISTENER: All of us are people who support in all respects Malcolm's traditions on the freedom movement. I would like to ask him two questions. First, what are his feelings concerning the issue in which Robert Williams of Monroe raised the issues that he did raise. And secondly, I feel that there are differences among the various groups, different meanings to the freedom movement, of radical organizations which are predominantly white, which he feels give—that is does he feel that some radical groups are more amenable to his position than others?

MALCOLM X: Concerning Robert Williams, who is a very good friend of mine who was exiled to Cuba, primarily because he was teaching the so-called Negroes in I think it's South Carolina, Monroe, or North Carolina, to defend themselves, he was exiled down to Cuba. He made some mistakes. For one thing, all of the civil rights groups united against him. All of the integrationist groups united against him. They allowed themselves to be used by the government against Robert Williams. Well, this was two or three years ago, and most of our people today are becoming more mature. Many of our people who were, say, fourteen four years ago are eighteen today, and a whole new world of thought has opened up unto them as they mature towards this higher age level. You know, just a new thinking period and I have gotten response, as I say, from high school students as well as college students, all of whom are changing in their outlook in this whole struggle. So that we feel that we are well on the popular side or that we have the masses on our side when we come to the conclusion that it is time to take a stand on these injustices. Robert Williams was just a couple years ahead of his time; but he laid a good groundwork, and he will be given credit in history for the stand that he took prematurely.

Now we don't think that our stand is premature. We think that now things have gotten to the point, especially behind the March on Washington last year, which was probably the century's greatest fizzle and probably the most unproductive move that was ever made by so many people.

JOE RAINEY: Why do you call it a fizzle?

MALCOLM X: Fizzle—what did it produce? They went down, they sang some songs, they marched around. They went and marched between the feet of the two dead presidents, Lincoln and, what's his name, Washington. They carried signs, they shouted. When they left Washington the civil rights bill hadn't passed yet. In fact . . .

JOE RAINEY: Well, it hasn't passed yet, but a lot of people are going to claim the civil rights bill, when it passes, if it does, that it would not have passed if it had not been for the March on Washington.

MALCOLM X: Well, Mr. Rainey, I was in Washington at the time of the march, and I heard the leaders talking about, this was in August, I heard the leaders talking, saying to others we will be back. And they said we'll be back in September. And at that time they thought the bill would come up in September. September passed, October passed, November passed, the President passed, December passed, the year passed, and the bill itself hasn't passed yet. So everything has passed except that which is supposed to help Negroes. So the march was a fizzle. In fact, I heard Bayard Rustin on a radio program in New York a couple weeks ago pointing out that someone had challenged him concerning what the march had produced. His explanation was this: that since last year in June and July and August there was so much talk about the potential violence and explosion, he said that once everybody began to look toward the march in August this would channel their frustrations. And the march in itself was an escape valve permitting the Negro to give vent to his feelings, which automatically nullified or neutralized that explosive potential. So what Byard was saying was the March on Washington was successful due to that it stopped the explosion, but it didn't give the

Negro anything that the march was supposed to produce. And so this is why I say that.

And now concerning the gentleman's other question about all these white groups, the white groups that want to help can help, but they can't join. The white man who wants to join in with Negroes does nothing but castrate the effort of those Negroes; when whites join Negro groups they aren't joining the Negroes and they end up by controlling the group that the Negro is supposed to be controlling. The day of whites at the helm of Negro movements is long gone. It's over. So we the Muslim Mosque, Incorporated, are interested in establishing a movement that will be under the complete control and the direction of black people themselves. And eventually the young ones, the new generation, that doesn't have a stake in this present structure and therefore they don't mind doing whatever is necessary to change the structure. Most of the older generation of Negroes have a stake. They have crumbs that they get from the structure, and therefore they are not trying to change it. They are trying to be accepted into the same old crumby structure or corrupt structure. But the youth, the young generation, wants to fix it where it cannot any longer exploit and suppress us.

Final Views

Getting it on the record
with Claude Lewis

These final views offered by Malcolm X to Claude Lewis appeared in a Special Report of The National Leader *on June 2, 1983. In his introduction to the piece Claude Lewis, then the editor and publisher of the* Leader *(he is now a syndicated columnist for* The Philadelphia Inquirer*), wrote that this interview "places Malcolm in perspective and reveals how much he changed toward the end of his life, though that change was rarely reflected in the daily press."*

Claude Lewis had interviewed Malcolm X eighteen years earlier, in December 1964, just six weeks before the assassination. At that time Lewis was a reporter at the New York Post, *and Malcolm, as Lewis writes in his introduction, "was worried. He knew he hadn't long to live. The word had been given. But he had much to get done in whatever time was left. . . . He wanted to get something 'on the record.' . . ."*

Malcolm telephoned Lewis at the Post *offices late one night and requested the interview. They met at the 22 West Coffee Shop on 135th Street in New York City, which, as Lewis writes, "was crowded with people he knew and who respected him. He wanted to be among friends throughout his final days. . . . [They] sat in a booth along with Malcolm's personal bodyguard. The outspoken leader reflected [on] many concerns, including his image, his organization, his public stance and his impending death."*

CLAUDE LEWIS: I notice you're growing a beard. What does that mean? Is it a symbol of anything?

MALCOLM X: It has no particular meaning, other than it probably reflects a change that I've undergone and am still undergoing.

CLAUDE LEWIS: Then will you shave it off one day?

MALCOLM X: Certainly. I might leave it on forever, or I might shave it off in the morning. I'm not dogmatic about anything. I don't intend to get into any more straitjackets.

CLAUDE LEWIS: What do you mean, any *more* straitjackets?

MALCOLM X: I don't intend to let anybody make my mind become so set on anything that I can't change it according to the circumstances and conditions that I happen to find myself in.

CLAUDE LEWIS: I see. You've been traveling a good deal recently. Can you tell me a little bit about the experiences relative to your movement? Where you've been and . . .

MALCOLM X: Well I was in Cairo, in Mecca, Arabia; in Kuwait, in Beirut, Lebanon; Khartoum, Sudan; Addis Ababa in Ethiopia, Nairobi in Kenya, Zanzibar, Dar es Salaam in what is now Tanzania and Lagos, Nigeria; Accra in Ghana, Monrovia in Liberia and Conakry in Guinea, and Algiers in Algeria. And during my tour of those various cities, or countries, I spent an hour and a half with President Nasser in Egypt; I spent three hours with President Nyerere president of Tanganuika or Tanzania; I spent several days with Jomo Kenyatta and in fact I flew with Jomo Kenyatta and Prime Minister Milton Obote of Uganda from Tanganyika, from Dar es Salaam to Kenya. I saw Azikwe and I had an audience with Azikwe; also with President Nkrumah and I lived three days in Sekou Toure's house in Conakry. And I cite this to show that everywhere I went I found people at all levels of government and out of government with open minds, open hearts, and open doors.

CLAUDE LEWIS: I see. How long was the trip?

MALCOLM X: I was away almost five months.

CLAUDE LEWIS: And do you think you've learned very much?

MALCOLM X: Oh yes, I've learned a great deal. Because in each country that I visited, I spoke with people at all levels. I had an open mind. I spoke with heads of state, I spoke with their ministers, I spoke with cabinet members, I spoke with kings; I was the guest of State again when I re-visited Saudi Arabia, I spoke with members of King Faisal's family—I don't know how many foreign ministers I spoke with in the Middle East and in Africa and all of them discussed our problems quite freely.

CLAUDE LEWIS: The Negro problem in America?

MALCOLM X: Oh yes, yes!

CLAUDE LEWIS: Did they seem to know much about it?

MALCOLM X: Oh yes. Not only did they seem to know much about it, but they were very sympathetic with it. In fact, it's not an accident that in the United Nations during the debate on the Congo problem in the Security Council, that almost every one of the African foreign ministers tied in what was happening in the Congo with what's happening in Mississippi.

CLAUDE LEWIS: Do you think this changes the minds of any of the Mississippians here in this country?

MALCOLM X: Well, the Mississippian—it's not a case of changing the mind of the Mississippian as much as it's a case of changing the mind of the Americans. The problem is not a Mississippi problem, it's an American problem.

CLAUDE LEWIS: Do you think that it's getting any better, the situation here?

MALCOLM X: No! It'll never get any better until our people in this country learn how to speak the same language that the racists speak. If a man speaks French, you can't talk to him in German. In order to communicate, you have to use the same language he's familiar with. And the language of the racist in the South is the language of violence. It's the language of brutality, and power and retaliation.

CLAUDE LEWIS: You think this is what the Negro should subscribe to?

MALCOLM X: The Negro should—if he's going to communicate —subscribe to whatever language the people use that he's trying to communicate with. And when you're dealing with racists, they only know one language. And if you're not capable of adopting that language or speaking that language, you don't need to try and communicate with those racists.

CLAUDE LEWIS: Dr. Martin Luther King, the other night, was honored in Harlem after receiving the Nobel Peace Prize. And he said, if I can quote him, "If blood must flow on the streets, brothers, let it be ours."

MALCOLM X: I was sitting in the audience. I heard him say that.

CLAUDE LEWIS: What do you think of that statement?

MALCOLM X: I think that if there's going to be a flowing of blood, that it should be reciprocal. The flow of blood should be two ways. Black people shouldn't be willing to bleed, unless white people are willing to bleed. And black people shouldn't be willing to be nonviolent, unless white people are going to be non-violent.

CLAUDE LEWIS: Well, do you think the majority of Americans are nonviolent?

MALCOLM X: No. If the majority of Americans were nonviolent, America couldn't continue to exist as a country. Is America nonviolent in the Congo, or is she nonviolent in South Vietnam? You can't point to a place where America's nonviolent. The only people that they want to be nonviolent are American Negroes. We're supposed to be nonviolent. When the world becomes nonviolent, I'll become nonviolent. When the white man becomes nonviolent, I'll become nonviolent.

CLAUDE LEWIS: I've heard talk recently about Negroes getting money together and hiring a mafia to take care of some of the murderers . . .

MALCOLM X: You don't need to hire a mafia but units should be trained among our people who know how to speak the language of the Klan and the Citizens Council. And at any time any Ku Klux Klan inflicts any kind of brutality against any Negro, we should be in a position to strike back. We should not go out and initiate violence against whites indiscriminately, but we should *absolutely* be in a position to retaliate against the Ku Klux Klan and the White Citizens Council. Especially, since the government seems to be incapable or unwilling to curtail the activities of the Klan.

CLAUDE LEWIS: Can you tell me a little bit about your new program, if you have a new program?

MALCOLM X: We're not unveiling our new program until January. But I will say this, that the Organization of Afro-American Unity, which I'm the chairman of, intends to work with any group that's trying to bring about maximum registration of Negroes in this country. We will not encourage Negroes to become registered Democrats or Republicans. We feel that the Negro should be an independent, so that he can throw his weight either way. He should be nonaligned. His political philosophy should be the same as that of the African, absolute neutrality or nonalignment. When the African makes a move, his move is designed to benefit Africa. And when the Negro makes a move, our move should be designed to benefit us; not the Democratic party or the Republican party or some of these machines.

So, our program is to make our people become involved in the mainsteam of the political structure of this country but not politically naïve. We think that we should be educated in the science of politics so that we understand the very workings of it, what it should produce, and who is responsible when that which we are looking for doesn't materialize.

CLAUDE LEWIS: Do you tell people what they want to hear, essentially?

MALCOLM X: I tell them what I've got on my mind to tell them, whether they like it or not. And I think that most people would have to agree. I don't think anybody could ever accuse me of telling people just what they want to hear. Because most of them don't want to hear what I'm . . . (chuckle), especially white people.

CLAUDE LEWIS: Do you think the Negro can succeed in America through the vote?

MALCOLM X: Well, independence comes only by two ways; by ballots or by bullets. What you read historically—historically you'll find that everyone who gets freedom, they get it through ballots or bullets. Now naturally everyone prefers ballots, and even I prefer ballots but I don't discount bullets. I'm not interested in either ballots or bullets, I'm interested in freedom.

I'm not interested in the means, I'm interested in the objective. So I believe that black people should get free by ballots or bullets. If we can't use ballots to get free, we should use bullets. Yes, yes, I believe that black people should be just as quick to use bullets as ballots.

The white man has not given us anything. It's not something that is his to give. He is not doing us a favor when he permits us a few liberties. So I don't think we should approach it like that; I don't think we should approach our battle like we're battling a friend. We're battling an *enemy*. Anybody who stands in the way of the black man being free is an enemy of the black man, and should be dealt with as an enemy.

CLAUDE LEWIS: Would you say there are some blacks in that group?

MALCOLM X: Oh, yes. A lot of black people in that group. But they are not independent, they're puppets. You don't worry about the puppet, you worry about the puppeteer.

CLAUDE LEWIS: You've been threatened; do you take those threats lightly?

MALCOLM X: I don't take anything lightly. I don't take *life* lightly. But I never worry about dying. I don't see how a Negro can start worrying about dying at this late date. But I think that Negro organizations that talk about killing other Negroes should first go and talk to somebody about practicing some of their killing skill on the Ku Klux Klan and the White Citizens Council.

CLAUDE LEWIS: What do you think of Dr. King?

MALCOLM X: He's a man. He's a human being that is trying to keep Negroes from exploding, so white folk won't have too much to worry about.

CLAUDE LEWIS: Would you say that he's getting in the way of Negro progress?

MALCOLM X: Of Negro what?

CLAUDE LEWIS: Progress?

MALCOLM X: Well the Negro will never progress nonviolently.

CLAUDE LEWIS: What were your thoughts when King was receiving the (Peace) award last week?

MALCOLM X: Well, to me it represented the fact that the struggle of the Negro in this country was being endorsed at the international level and that it was looked upon as a problem that affects the peace of the world. And it was looked upon as a human problem or a problem for humanity, rather than just a Mississippi problem or an American problem.

To me, King getting that Nobel Peace Prize—it wasn't King getting it—it represented the awareness on the part of the world that the race problem in America could upset the peace of the world. And this is true.

If King can get—see I don't think that King got the prize because *he* had solved our people's problem, cause *we* still got the problem. He got the Peace Prize, and *we* got the problem. And so I don't think he should have gotten the medal for that. On the other hand, if Negroes can get it nonviolently, good.

CLAUDE LEWIS: Are you in favor of that?

MALCOLM X: I'm not in favor of anything that doesn't get the solution. But if Negroes can get freedom nonviolently, good. But that's a dream. Even King calls it a dream. But I don't go for no dream. And the only way that you can think Negroes can get it nonviolently, is dream. But when you get out here and start facing the reality of it, Negroes are the victims of violence every day. So I'd rather get violent, right along with the white man.

CLAUDE LEWIS: Have you ever received an award of any kind for your work?

MALCOLM X: No . . . Yes, I've received an award. Whenever I walk the street and I see people ready to get with it. That's my reward (chuckle). Whenever people come out, they know in advance what I'm going to talk about. And if they show any sign of interest in it or agreement with it, that's my reward. And when they show that they're fed up with this slow pace, you know, that's my reward.

CLAUDE LEWIS: When King received his medal, did you sort of wish that it was yours?

MALCOLM X: I don't want the white man giving me medals. If I'm following a general, and he's leading me into battle, and the enemy begins to give him awards, I get suspicious of him. Especially if he gets the peace award before the war is over.

CLAUDE LEWIS: You don't propose that Negroes leave the U.S.?

MALCOLM X: I propose that we have the right to do whatever is necessary to bring about an answer to our problem. And whatever is necessary, if it's necessary to leave to get a solution then we should leave. If we can get a solution staying here, then we should stay. The main thing we want is a *solution.*

CLAUDE LEWIS: Well, do you think things have changed very much since you grew up?

MALCOLM X: They've changed in this sense. If you're a butler for a poor white man, you're a butler and you live but so well and you eat but so well. But if your master becomes rich, you begin to eat better and you begin to live better, but you're still a butler. And the only change that has been made in this society—we occupied a menial position twenty years ago. Our position hasn't changed. Our condition has changed somewhat, but our position hasn't changed. And the change that has been brought about, has been only to the extent that this country has changed. The white man got richer, we're living a little better. He got more power, we got a little more power, but we're still at the same level in his system. You understand what I'm saying?

CLAUDE LEWIS: Oh yes. Oh yes.

MALCOLM X: Our position has never changed. If you sit at the back of the plane and it's going a hundred miles an hour, and you're on the back of the plane, well it can start going a thousand miles an hour; you're going faster, but you're still at the back of the plane. And that's the same way with the Negro in this society, we started out at the rear and we're still in the rear. Society is going faster, but we're still in the rear. And we think we've made progress because *they've* made progress.

CLAUDE LEWIS: Why do you stay in America? Wouldn't it be easier for you to . . .

MALCOLM X: I was offered some good positions in several countries that I went to. Good positions, that would solve my problems personally. But I feel pretty much responsible for much of the action and energy that has been stirred up among our people for rights and for freedom. And I think I'd be wrong to stir it up and then run away from it myself.

CLAUDE LEWIS: Do you expect further riots next year?

MALCOLM X: Yes. I expect that the miracle of 1964 was the degree of restraint that Negroes displayed in Harlem. The miracle of 1964 was the ability of the Negroes to restrain themselves and contain themselves. Because there is no place where Negroes are more equipped and capable of retaliation than right here in Harlem.

CLAUDE LEWIS: Can you give me a capsule opinion of some of the following people? Adam Clayton Powell.

MALCOLM X: Powell is actually the most independent black politician in America. He's in a better position to do more for black people than any other politician.

CLAUDE LEWIS: Is he doing it?

MALCOLM X: And the reason that he's in that position is because he's in an area where people support him. They support him, whereas many other Negro politicians don't get that type of support. People in Harlem are just independent-minded. They just vote for a black man, whether the machine likes it or not. So Powell is in a tremendous position. And with his position also goes responsibility. I think that he should see his responsibilities with the same clarity that he sees his powerful position.

CLAUDE LEWIS: What about Roy Wilkins?

MALCOLM X: Well, I heard Roy say at the rally the other night that he was three-fourths or one-fourth Scandinavian. And he seemed to be lost in that Scandinavian dream somewhat, that night.

CLAUDE LEWIS: Martin Luther King, well—we've talked about him.

MALCOLM X: Well, everytime I hear Martin he's got a dream. And I think the Negro leaders have to come out of the clouds, and wake up, and stop dreaming and start facing reality.

CLAUDE LEWIS: Do you ever think of Whitney Young?

MALCOLM X: Whitney seems to be more down to earth, but he doesn't spend enough time around Negroes. He seems to be down to earth; he's a young man for one thing. But not enough Negroes know him. When I say he needs to be around Negroes, not enough Negroes know Whitney Young. Whitney Young could walk around Harlem all day long and probably no more than five people would know who he was. And he's supposed to be one of our leaders. So he should make himself more known to those who are following him.

CLAUDE LEWIS: Where are you headed from here? Where do you think your future lies?

MALCOLM X: I think one of the most sincere of those big six is James Farmer. You missed asking me about him. I think James Farmer seems to . . . He seems sincere. And I get the impression when I watch Farmer that he could be another Mandela. Mandela, you know, was a man who advocated nonviolence in South Africa, until he saw that it wasn't getting anywhere and then Mandela stepped up and had to resort to tactical violence. Which showed that Mandela was for the freedom of his people. He was more interested in the end than he was the means. Whereas many of the Negro leaders are more strait-jacketed by the means rather than by the end.

CLAUDE LEWIS: Where are you headed? What do you suppose your future is from here?

MALCOLM X: I have no idea.

CLAUDE LEWIS: You have no idea?

MALCOLM X: I have no idea. I'm for freedom. I can capsulize how I feel. I'm for the freedom of the twenty-two million Afro-Americans *by any means necessary. By any means necessary!* I'm for freedom. I'm for a society in which our people are recognized and respected as human beings and I believe that we have the right to resort to *any means necessary* to bring that about. So when you ask me where I'm headed, how can I say? I'm headed in any direction that will bring us some immediate results. Nothing wrong with that!

CLAUDE LEWIS: I think it's going to take a tremendous public relations job to change your image. And you may not be interested in changing your image, but everybody else is. I agree with a lot that you say, but I don't see how people can sign up with you.

MALCOLM X: They don't need to sign up. The most effective part of the trees are the roots. And they're signed up with the tree but you don't ever see them. They're always beneath the ground. And the reason that you never see me worry about my image is because that image puts me in a better position than anybody else. Because I'm able to walk through the street or anywhere else and really find out where people are at. In a silent sort of way, I know where they are, in a silent sort of way. I think that the sympathies are deeply rooted, many of them. Plus also it puts me in a position wherever I go, people know where I stand in advance. And doors that would normally be closed for American Negroes, I don't find them closed for me anywhere. It doesn't make any difference. Anywhere.

CLAUDE LEWIS: So you're saying because of your outspokenness, your honesty . . .

MALCOLM X: People know where I stand. They know where I stand. And you see I'm not standing in an unjust position. This is the thing. Whatever I say I'm *justified.* If I say the Negroes should get out of here right tomorrow and go to war, I'm justified. Really! It may sound *extreme,* but you can't say it's not *justified.* If I say right now that we should go down and shoot fifteen Ku Klux Klansmen in the morning, you may say well that's insane, but you can't say that I'm not justified. This is what I mean. I think that the stand that I'm taking is justified. Many others might not take it.

CLAUDE LEWIS: What I'm trying to do is find out if there is a new Malcolm X?

MALCOLM X: Well, there is a new one in the sense that, perhaps in approach. My travels have broadened my scope, but it hasn't changed me from speaking my mind. I can get along with white people who can get along with me. But you don't see me trying to get along with *any* white man who doesn't want to get along with me. I don't believe in that. Now you got to get another religion.

CLAUDE LEWIS: When you get old and retire . . .

MALCOLM X: I'll never get old.

CLAUDE LEWIS: What does that mean?

MALCOLM X: Well, I'll tell you what it means. You'll find very few people who feel like I feel that live long enough to get old. I'll tell you what I mean and why I say that. When I say by any means necessary, I mean it with all my heart, and my mind and my soul. But a black man should give his life to be free, but he should also be willing to take the life of those who want to take his. It's reciprocal. And when you really think like that, you don't live long. And if freedom doesn't come to your lifetime, it'll come to your children. Another thing about being an old man, that never has come across my mind. I can't even see myself old.

CLAUDE LEWIS: Well, how would you like to be remembered by your black brothers and sisters around the world—twenty years from now?

MALCOLM X: Sincere. In whatever I did or do, even if I make mistakes, they were made in sincerity. If I'm wrong, I'm wrong in sincerity. I think that the best a person can be—he can be *wrong*, but if he's sincere you can put up with him. But you can't put up with a person who's *right*, if he's insincere. I'd rather deal with a person's sincerity, and respect a person for their sincerity than anything else. Especially when you're living in a world that's so hypocritical.

This is an era of hypocrisy. The times that we live in can rightfully be labeled, the Era of Hypocrisy. When white folks pretend that they want Negroes to be free, and Negroes pretend to white folks that they really believe that white folks want them to be free (laughter). An Era of Hypocrisy, brother. You fool me and I fool you. This is the game that the white man and the Negro play with each other. You pretend that you're my brother and I pretend that I really believe you believe you're my brother (laughter).

CLAUDE LEWIS: Do you think there are going to be more killings and more bombings in Mississippi and Alabama?

MALCOLM X: In the North as well as the South. There might be even more in the North because I'll tell you one of the dangers of Martin Luther King. King himself is probably a good man, means well and all that. But the danger is that white people use King. They use King to satisfy their own fears. They blow him up. They give him power beyond his actual influence. Because they want to believe within themselves that Negroes are nonviolent and patient, and long suffering and forgiving. White people want to believe that so bad, 'cause they're so guilty. But the danger is, when they blow up King and fool themselves into thinking that Negroes are really nonviolent, and patient, and long suffering, they've got a powder keg in their house. And instead of them trying to do something to defuse the powder keg, they're putting a blanket over it, trying to make believe that this is no powder keg; that this is a couch that we can lay on and enjoy.

So that's it. Whatever I do, whatever I did, whatever I've said, was all done in sincerity. That's the way I want to be remembered because that's the way it is. . . .

Whatever Is Necessary
The last television interview, with Pierre Berton

On January 19, 1965, just a month before his death, Malcolm X made a television appearance—his last, as it turned out—in Toronto, where he was interviewed by Pierre Berton.

Recalling that interview, Berton speculates "on the kind of man Malcolm X might have become, had an assassin's bullet not struck him down, for what he had to say to me clearly foreshadows the philosophy of 'black power' which became the rallying cry of Negro activists in the summer of 1966. When I talked to him, Malcolm X seemed to be going through a period of reassessment. The break with his leader had obviously shaken him; his journey to Islam had affected him profoundly.

"He seemed to me to be two men," Berton continues, "as so many demagogues are. On the platform, he was a fiery orator, given to explosive statements under the intoxicating influence of the crowd. In the quiet of the TV studio, he was a different man—soft-spoken, comparatively moderate, almost reasonable—even prepared to hedge. Was this just one side of a complex and inscrutable character, or had the break with the Muslims changed him? I began by asking him about his former mentor and the reasons for the rift between them."

MALCOLM X: Well, he represented himself to us as a prophet who had been visited by God, who had been taught by God, who had been given an analysis of the problems concerning black people in America by God, and also a solution by the same God, and as long as I believed in him as a man, I actually thought that he had been taught and commissioned by God to solve the problems of our people in America. Then I came into the knowledge of something in his own personal life that he admitted to me when I confronted him with it. But when it came to him taking the steps that a man would take to correct this mistake, I found that his own ability to be a man was lacking. When I ceased to respect him as a man, I could see that he also was not divine. There was no God with him at all.

BERTON: I take it you don't want to discuss this specific thing in his personal life?

MALCOLM X: Well, discussing it might keep your show from going on the air.

BERTON: All right, we won't discuss it; but there seemed to me at the time that there were other reasons given for your break with Elijah Muhammad. At the time of President Kennedy's assassination, you made a speech that seemed to indicate that you were pleased that he had been assassinated. Certainly at that time, Elijah Muhammad indicated that you had been fired or suspended from the Black Muslim movement. How about that?

MALCOLM X: I had taken a subject as my topic that day, an approach that was designed to show that the seeds that America had sown—in enslavement, in many of the things that followed since then—all of these seeds were coming up today; it was harvest time. At the end of this particular lecture, during the question-and-answer period, somebody asked me what I thought of the assassination of President Kennedy. In line with the topic that I had just been discussing, I pointed out that it was a case of the chickens coming home to roost, by which I meant that this was the result of seeds that had been sown, that this was the harvest. This was taken out of context, and reported in one of the papers, and Elijah Muhammad, who had been waiting for me to make a move that would enable him to suspend me and get the support of the public in doing so, took advantage of that opportunity. He gave the impression that I was saying something against the president himself, because he felt that the public wouldn't go along with that.

BERTON: How did you feel, personally, about the president's assassination in that connection? Were you bothered about it? Were you angered by it? Or were you jubilant?

MALCOLM X: No. I was realistic, in that being at the forefront of this struggle of the black man in America—in his quest for respect as a human being—I had seen the many-faceted repercussions of this hate taking a grip on the American public. I think that many of the politicians took advantage of it and exploited it for their own personal benefit. So to me the whole thing was a case of politics, hate, and a combination of other things.

BERTON: There seems to me to have been a fair amount of hate in the Black Muslim movement itself.

MALCOLM X: Well, I won't deny that. But, at the same time, I don't think that the Black Muslim movement and its hate can be classified as the same degree or type of hate you find in the American society itself, because the hate, so-called, that you see among black people is a reaction to the hate of the society which has rejected us. In that sense it is not hate.

BERTON: I'm not saying that the hate, or whatever it is, isn't understandable. I'm asking if it's effective to fight hate with hate?

MALCOLM X: In my opinion, I think that it is not fair to classify the reaction of people who are oppressed as hate. They are reacting to the hate of the society they have had put upon them or practiced against them.

BERTON: Well, let me ask you about your reaction on another occasion; I'd like to see if you still feel the same way. That's when the planeload of people from Atlanta, Georgia, crashed and 121 were killed. If the papers reported you correctly, you were fairly jubilant about that—because these were white Southerners who had gone to their deaths. Am I right in saying that you had expressed such a sentiment at that time?

MALCOLM X: This was another reaction to the hate that the American society collectively has practiced against the black people in that particular country.

BERTON: Well, how do you feel about it now? Are you sorry you made that kind of statement, or do you still feel the same way?

MALCOLM X: Well, I would probably not now make the same statement. But I cannot see where I was not justified in making the statement at that time. It was made just after the police in Los Angeles had shot up the Negro community and had killed a Muslim and shot seven others who were unarmed and who had no weapons at all. And the court system, the entire city power structure, seemed to be lined up against the Negro community in general and the Muslim Mosque in particular. I think I was justified. I had mentioned in the courtroom, during the coroner's inquest, that if the court system was not capable of producing justice for black people in this country, then I was thankful, as a religious man, that there is a God in Heaven who could bring out justice in cases like this. A couple of days later, when that airplane dropped out of the sky in France, I didn't think it was a coincidence that it was from Georgia and that practically everybody aboard it was from Georgia. Georgia is a state that has a record for having enslaved and lynched and maimed more black human beings than any other state in America other than Mississippi.

BERTON: You felt that this was the hand of God?

MALCOLM X: I felt it was the hand of God. I felt that it was a sign. A couple of days later, Billy Graham was holding one of his crusades in Chicago, and he pointed out at the same time that it was an act of God, that it was God's hand doing this. Now, when Graham said this, they didn't call it hate. When *I* say it, then I'm supposed to be a fanatic and an extremist.

BERTON: Well, of course, he didn't express any jubilation over the death of 121 people. But let me ask you this about your God, Mr. X. Has he got any color? Is he black?

MALCOLM X: No.

BERTON: Is he white?

MALCOLM X: As a Black Muslim, who believed what Elijah Muhammad taught, I regarded God just as he taught, as a black man. Having since gone into the Muslim world and got a better understanding of the religion of Islam, I believe that God is the supreme being, and that color plays no part in his particular being.

BERTON: In fact, isn't the God of the Muslims and of the Jews and the Christians really the same God?

MALCOLM X: If they believe in the God who created the universe, then we all believe in the same God. I believe in the God who created the universe. Muslims call him Allah. Christians, perhaps, call him Christ, or by some other name. Jews call him Jehovah, and in referring to him they mean "the creative." We are all referring to the same God.

BERTON: Now, let me switch the subject briefly, and ask you

what you mean when you say that the Black Muslims are not militant enough. Your new organization, I take it, will be more militant than the Black Muslims. In what way?

MALCOLM X: Well, the Black Muslim movement, number one, professes to be a religious movement. They profess the religion of Islam. But the Muslim world rejected the Black Muslim movement as a bona fide Islamic group, so it found itself maneuvered into a religious vacuum—or a sort of religious hybrid. At the same time, the government of the United States tried to maneuver the Black Muslim movement, with the press, into an image that was political instead of religious. So the Black Muslim movement came to be known as a political group. Yet, at the same time, it didn't vote; it didn't take part in any politics; it didn't involve itself actively in the civil rights struggle; so it became a political hybrid as well as a religious hybrid. Now, on the other hand, the Black Muslim movement attracted the most militant black American, the young, dissatisfied, uncompromising element that exists in this country—drawing them in yet, at the same time, giving them no part to play in the struggle other than moral reform. It created a lot of disillusion, dissatisfaction, dissension, and eventually division. Those who divided are the ones that I'm a part of. We set up the Muslim Mosque, which is based upon orthodox Islam, as a religious group so that we could get a better understanding of our religion; but being black Americans, though we are Muslims, who believe in brotherhood, we also realized that our people have a problem in America that goes beyond religion. We realized that many of our people aren't going to become Muslim; many of them aren't even interested in anything religious; so we set up the Organization of Afro-American Unity as a nonreligious organization which all black Americans could become a part of and play an active part in striking out at the political, economic, and social evils that all of us are confronted by.

BERTON: That "striking out," what form is it going to take? You talk of giving the Ku Klux Klan a taste of its own medicine. This is in direct opposition to the theory of nonviolence of Dr. Martin Luther King, who doesn't believe in striking back. What do you mean by "a taste of its own medicine"? Are you going to burn fiery crosses on their lawns? Are you going to blow up churches with the Ku Klux Klan kids in them? What are you going to do?

MALCOLM X: Well, I think that the only way that two different races can get along with each other is, first, they have to understand each other. That cannot be brought about other than through communication—dialogue—and you can't communicate with a person unless you speak his language. If the person speaks French, you can't speak English or German.

BERTON: We have that problem in our country, too.

MALCOLM X: In America, our people have so far not been able to speak the type of language that the racists understand. By not speaking that language, they fail to communicate, so that the racist element doesn't really believe that the black American is a human being—part of the human family. There is no communication. So I believe that the only way to communicate with that element is to be in a position to speak their language.

BERTON: And this language is violence?

MALCOLM X: I wouldn't call it violence. I think that they should be made to know that, any time they come into a black community and inflict violence upon members of that black community, they should realize in advance that the black community can speak the same language. Then they would be less likely to come in.

BERTON: Let's be specific here: suppose that a church is bombed. Will you bomb back?

MALCOLM X: I believe that any area of the United States, where the federal government has shown either its unwillingness or inability to protect the lives and the property of the black American, then it is time for the black Americans to band together and do whatever is necessary to see that we get the type of protection we need.

BERTON: "Whatever is necessary?"

MALCOLM X: I mean just that. *Whatever is necessary.* This does not mean that we should go out and initiate acts of aggression indiscriminately in the white community. But it does mean that, if we are going to be respected as human beings, we should reserve the right to defend ourselves by whatever means necessary. This is recognized and accepted in any civilized society.

BERTON: Let me ask you a specific question again and see if I can get a specific answer from you. There are some people going to go on trial in Mississippi for the murder of three civil rights workers. There are some witnesses who identify them as murderers, but the general feeling is they'll get off. Will you do anything about this if they get off?

MALCOLM X: I wouldn't say.

BERTON: You don't want to say?

MALCOLM X: Because, then, if something happened to them, they would blame me. But I will say that in a society where the law itself is incapable of bringing known murderers to justice, it's historically demonstrable that the well-meaning people of that society have always banded together in one form or another to see that their society was protected against repetitious acts by these same murderers.

BERTON: What you're talking about here is a vigilante movement.

MALCOLM X: There have been vigilante movements forming all over America in white communities, but the black community has yet to form a vigilante committee. This is why we aren't respected as human beings.

BERTON: Are you training men to use aggressive methods? Are you training men as the Black Muslim movement trained the elite core known as the Fruit of Islam? Have you got trainees operating now who know how to fight back?

MALCOLM X: Yes.

BERTON: Who know how to use knuckle-dusters and guns?

MALCOLM X: Yes, oh yes. The black man in America doesn't need that much training. Most of them have been in the army—have already been trained by the government itself. They haven't been trained to think for themselves and, therefore, they've never used this training to protect themselves.

BERTON: Have you got a specific cadre of such young, tough guys working for you or operating under your aegis?

MALCOLM X: We're not a cadre, nor do we want it to be felt that we want to be tough. We're trying to be human beings, and we want to be recognized and accepted as human beings. But we don't think humanity will recognize us or accept us as such until humanity knows that we will do everything to protect our human ranks, as others will do for theirs.

BERTON: Are you prepared to send flying squads into areas where the Negroes have been oppressed without any legal help?

MALCOLM X: We are prepared to do whatever is necessary to see that our people, wherever they are, get the type of protection that the federal government has refused to give them.

BERTON: Okay. Do you still believe that all whites are devils and all blacks saints, as I'm sure you did under the Black Muslim movement?

MALCOLM X: This is what Elijah Muhammad teaches. No, I don't believe that. I believe as the Koran teaches, that a man should not be judged by the color of his skin but rather by his conscious behavior, by his actions, by his attitude towards others and his actions towards others.

BERTON: Now, before you left Elijah Muhammad and went to Mecca and saw the original world of Islam, you believed in complete segregation of the whites and the Negroes. You were opposed both to integration and to intermarriage. Have you changed your views there?

MALCOLM X: I believe in recognizing every human being as a human being, neither white, black, brown nor red. When you are dealing with humanity as one family, there's no question of integration or intermarriage. It's just one human being marrying another human being, or one human being living around and with another human being. I may say, though, that I don't think the burden to defend any such position should ever be put upon the black man. Because it is the white man collectively who has shown that he is hostile towards integration and towards intermarriage and towards these other strides towards oneness. So, as a black man, and especially as a black American, I don't think that I would have to defend any stand that I formerly took. Because it's still a reaction of the society and it's a reaction that was produced by the white society. And I think that it is the society that produced this that should be attacked, not the reaction that develops among the people who are the victims of that negative society.

BERTON: But you no longer believe in a Black State?

MALCOLM X: No.

BERTON: In North America?

MALCOLM X: No. I believe in a society in which people can live like human beings on the basis of equality.

BERTON: So you have been changed considerably by your visit to the Muslim world and specifically to Mecca. Did this produce violent emotions within yourself? When people lose their faith or change their faith or renew their faith, they usually suffer terrible internal conflicts.

MALCOLM X: Oh, yes. I will confess readily that it's impossible to believe as strongly in a man as I believed in Elijah Muhammad and have him disappoint me—or disappoint anyone else for that matter—and not create a great deal of internal conflict. One of the things that I am thankful for about the religion of Islam is that it is sufficiently strong in itself so that when one broadens one's understanding of it, it gives one the inner strength to face up to some of these crises or tests that one encounters.

BERTON: There has been talk, I think by you and by Elijah Muhammad, about an Armageddon in the United States by 1984. I'm wondering if you still believe that, and why that particular date?

MALCOLM X: I don't frankly. Much of what Elijah Muhammad has taught I don't think he believes in himself. I say that and can easily defend it sitting opposite him. But, where an ultimate clash between East and West is concerned, well, I think that an objective analysis of events taking place on this earth today points towards some type of ultimate showdown. You can call it a political showdown or even a showdown between the economic systems that exist on this earth, which almost boil down along racial lines. I do believe that there will be a clash between East and West. I believe that there will ultimately be a clash between the oppressed and those that do the oppressing. I believe that there will be a clash between those who want freedom, justice, and equality for everyone, and those who want to continue the systems of exploitation. I believe that there will be that kind of clash, but I don't think that it will be based upon the color of the skin, as Elijah Muhammad has taught it. However, I do think you'll find that the European powers, which are the former colonial powers, if they're not able to readjust their feeling of superiority towards the darker skinned people, whom they have been made to think are inferior, then the lines can easily be drawn. They can easily be lumped into racial groups, and it will be a racial war.

III

The Man, the Myth
and the Mission
Reflections on Malcolm X

Initial Reactions on the Assassination of Malcolm X

by *Eldridge Cleaver*

This excerpt from black radical Eldridge Cleaver's Soul on Ice *(1968) is dated June 19, 1965; it was written in Folsom Prison. Cleaver here pays tribute to an "irresistible" Malcolm X not only for the man he was but more so for the truth he uttered. With that truth, Cleaver avers, Malcolm awakened twenty million African Americans into self-consciousness, into their blackness, and in their blackness they found their pride; or, as Cleaver elsewhere wrote, "Black history began with Malcolm X."*

Sunday is Movie Day at Folsom Prison and I was sitting in the darkened hulk of Mess Hall No. 1—which convicts call "The Folsom Theatre"—watching Victor Buono in a movie called *The Strangler,* when a convict known as Silly Willie came over to where I was sitting and whispered into my ear:

"Brother J sent me in to tell you it just came over the TV that Malcolm X was shot as he addressed a rally in New York."

For a moment the earth seemed to reel in orbit. The skin all over my body tightened up. "How bad?" I asked.

"The TV didn't say," answered Silly Willie. The distress was obvious in his voice. "We was around back in Pipe Alley checking TV when a special bulletin came on. All they said was Malcolm X was shot and they were rushing him to the hospital."

"Thanks," I said to Silly Willie. I felt his reassuring hand on my shoulder as he faded away in the darkness. For a moment I pondered whether to go outside and get more information, but something made me hang back. I remember distinctly thinking that I would know soon enough. On the screen before me, Victor Buono had a woman by the throat and was frantically choking the last gasping twitches of life out of her slumping body. I was thinking that if Malcolm's wounds were not too serious, that if he recovered, the shooting might prove to be a blessing in disguise: it would focus more intensified attention on him and create a windfall of sympathy and support for him throughout America's black ghettos, and so put more power into his hands. The possibility that the wounds may have been fatal, that as I sat there Malcolm was lying already dead, was excluded from my mind.

After the movie ended, as I filed outside in the long line of convicts and saw the shocked, wild expression on Brother J's face, I still could not believe that Malcolm X was dead. We mingled in the crowd of convicts milling around in the yard and were immediately surrounded by a group of Muslims, all of whom, like myself, were firm supporters of Malcolm X. He's dead, their faces said, although not one of them spoke a word. As we stood there in silence, two Negro inmates walked by and one of them said to us, "That's a goddam shame how they killed that man! Of all people, why'd they kill Malcolm? Why'n't they kill some of them Uncle-Tomming m.f.'s? I wish I could get my hands on whoever did it." And he walked away, talking and cursing to his buddy.

What does one say to his comrades at the moment when The Leader falls? All comment seems irrelevant. If the source of death is so-called natural causes, or an accident, the reaction is predictable, a feeling of impotence, humbleness, helplessness before the forces of the universe. But when the cause of death is an assassin's bullet, the overpowering desire is for vengeance. One wants to strike out, to kill, crush, destroy, to deliver a telling counterblow, to inflict upon the enemy a reciprocal, equivalent loss. But whom does one strike down at such a time if one happens to be in an anonymous, amorphous crowd of convicts in Folsom Prison and The Leader lies dead thousands of miles away across the continent?

"I'm going to my cell," I told the tight little knot of Muslims. "Allah is the Best Knower. Everything will be made manifest in time. Give it a little time. *Assalaam alaikum.*"

"*Wa-Alaikum salaam,*" the Brothers returned the salutation

and we shook hands all around, the double handshake which is very popular among Muslims in California prisons. (It is so popular that one sometimes grows weary of shaking hands. If a Muslim leaves a group for a minute to go get a drink of water, he is not unlikely to shake hands all around before he leaves and again when he returns. But no one complains and the convention is respected as a gesture of unity, brotherly love, and solidarity—so meaningful in a situation where Muslims are persecuted and denied recognition and the right to function as a legitimate religion.) I headed for my cell. I lived in No. 5 Building, which is Folsom's Honor Unit, reserved for those who have maintained a clean record for at least six months. Advantages: a larger cell, TV every Wednesday, Saturday, and Sunday night, less custodial supervision, easier ingress and egress. If while living in the Honor Unit you get into a "beef" which results in action against you by the disciplinary committee, one of the certain penalties is that you are immediately kicked out of No. 5 Building.

As I walked along the first tier toward my cell, I ran into Red, who lived near me on the tier.

"I guess you heard about Malcolm?"

"Yeah," I said. "They say he got wasted."

Red, who is white, knew from our many discussions that I was extremely partial to Malcolm, and he himself, being thoroughly alienated from the *status quo,* recognized the assassination for what it was: a negative blow against a positive force. Red's questions were the obvious ones: Who? Why? The questions were advanced tentatively, cautiously, because of the treacherous ground he was on: a red-headed, blue-eyed white man concerned by an event which so many others greeted with smiles and sighs. I went into my cell.

Although I heard it blared over the radio constantly and read about it in all the newspapers, days passed during which my mind continued to reject the fact of Malcolm's death. I existed in a dazed state, wandering in a trance around Folsom, drifting through the working hours in the prison bakery; and yet I was keen to observe the effect of the assassination on my fellow inmates. From most of the whites there was a leer and a hint of a smile in the eyes. They seemed anxious to see a war break out between the followers of Elijah and the followers of Malcolm.

There are only a few whites in Folsom with whom I would ever discuss the death of Malcolm or anything else besides baseball or the weather. Many of the Mexican-Americans were sympathetic, although some of them made a point, when being observed by whites, of letting drop sly remarks indicating they were glad Malcolm was gone. Among the Negroes there was mass mourning for Malcolm X. Nobody talked much for a few days. The only Negroes who were not indignant were a few of the Muslims who remained loyal to Elijah Muhammad. They interpreted Malcolm's assassination as the will of Allah descending upon his head for having gone astray. To them, it was Divine chastisement and a warning to those whom Malcolm had tempted. It was not so much Malcolm's death that made them glad; but in their eyes it now seemed possible to heal the schism in the movement and restore the monolithic unity of the Nation of Islam, a unity they looked back on with some nostalgia.

Many Negro convicts saw Malcolm's assassination as a historic turning point in black America. Whereas Negroes often talk heatedly about wiping out all the so-called Negro leaders whom they do not happen to like or agree with, this was the first significant case of Negro leader-killing that anyone could remember. What struck me is that the Negro convicts welcomed the new era. If a man as valuable to us as Malcolm could go down, then as far as I was concerned so could any other man—myself included. Coming a week after the alleged exposé of the alleged plot to dynamite the Statue of Liberty, Washington Monument, and the Liberty Bell, a plot supposedly hatched by discontented blacks, the assassination of Malcolm X had put new ideas in the wind with implications for the future of black struggle in America.

I suppose that like many of the brothers and sisters in the Nation of Islam movement, I also had clung to the hope that, somehow, the rift between Malcolm X and Elijah Muhammad would be mended. As long as Brother Malcolm was alive, many Muslims could maintain this hope, neatly overlooking the increasing bitterness of their rivalry. But death made the split final and sealed it for history. These events caused a profound personal crisis in my life and beliefs, as it did for other Muslims. During the bitter time of his suspension and prior to his break with Elijah Muhammad, we had watched Malcolm X as he sought frantically to reorient himself and establish a new platform. It was like watching a master do a dance with death on a highstrung tightrope. He pirouetted, twirled, turned somersaults in the air—but he landed firmly on his feet and was off and running. We watched it all, seeking a cause to condemn Malcolm X and cast him out of our hearts. We read all the charges and countercharges. I found Malcolm X blameless.

It had been my experience that the quickest way to become hated by the Muslims was to criticize Elijah Muhammad or disagree with something he wrote or said. If Elijah wrote, as he has done, that the swine is a poison creature composed of one-third rat, one-third cat, and one-third dog and you attempted to cite scientific facts to challenge this, you had sinned against the light, that was all there was to it. How much more unlikely was it, therefore, that Muslims would stand up and denounce Elijah himself, repudiate his authority and his theology, deny his revelation, and take sides against him, the Messenger of Almighty God Allah? I never dreamed that someday I would be cast in that hapless role.

After Malcolm made his pilgrimage to Mecca, completing a triumphal tour of Africa and the Near East, during which he received the high honors of a visiting dignitary, he returned to the U.S.A. and set about building his newly founded Organization of Afro-American Unity. He also established the Muslim Mosque, Inc., to receive the Muslims he thought would pull away from Elijah. The Muslim Mosque would teach Orthodox Islam, under the direction of Sheikh Ahmed Hassoun from the Holy City of Mecca. Grand Sheik Muhammad Sarur Al-Sabban, secretary-general of the Muslim World League, had offered the services of Sheikh Ahmed, according to the Los Angeles *Herald-Dispatch,* to "help Malcolm X in his efforts to correct the distorted image that the religion of Islam has been given by hate groups in this country."

I began defending Malcolm X. At a secret meeting of the Muslims in Folsom, I announced that I was no longer a follower of Elijah Muhammad, that I was throwing my support behind Brother Malcolm. I urged everyone there to think the matter over and make a choice, because it was no longer possible to ride two horses at the same time. On the wall of my cell I had a large, framed picture of Elijah Muhammad which I had had for years. I took it down, destroyed it, and in its place put up, in the same frame, a beautiful picture of Malcolm X kneeling down in the Mohammed Ali Mosque in Cairo, which I clipped from the *Saturday Evening Post*. At first the other Muslims in Folsom denounced me; some I'd known intimately for years stopped speaking to me or even looking at me. When we met, they averted their eyes. To them the choice was simple: Elijah Muhammad is the hand-picked Messenger of Allah, the instrument of Allah's Will. All who oppose him are aiding Allah's enemies, the White Devils. Whom do you choose, God or the Devil? Malcolm X, in the eyes of Elijah's followers, had committed the unforgivable heresy when, changing his views and abandoning the racist position, he admitted the possibility of brotherhood between blacks and whites. In a letter sent back to the U.S. from the Holy Land, Malcolm X had stated:

> You may be shocked by these words coming from me, but I have always been a man who tries to face facts and to accept the reality of life as new experiences and knowledge unfold it. The experiences of this pilgrimage have taught me much and each hour in the Holy Land opens my eyes even more. . . . I have eaten from the same plate with people whose eyes were the bluest of blue, whose hair was the blondest of blond and whose skin was the whitest of white . . . and I felt the sincerity in the words and deeds of these "white" Muslims that I felt among the African Muslims of Nigeria, Sudan and Ghana.

Many of us were shocked and outraged by these words from Malcolm X, who had been a major influence upon us all and the main factor in many of our conversions to the Black Muslims. But there were those of us who were glad to be liberated from a doctrine of hate and racial supremacy. The onus of teaching racial supremacy and hate, which is the white man's burden, is pretty hard to bear. Asked if he would accept whites as members of his Organization of Afro-American Unity, Malcolm said he would accept John Brown if he were around today—which certainly is setting the standard high.

At the moment I declared myself for Malcolm X, I had some

prestige among the Muslims in the prisons of California, because of my active role in proselytizing new converts and campaigning for religious freedom for Muslim convicts. We sent a barrage of letters and petitions to the courts, governmental officials, even the United Nations.

After the death of Brother Booker T.X, who was shot dead by a San Quentin prison guard, and who at the time had been my cell partner and the inmate Minister of the Muslims of San Quentin, my leadership of the Muslims of San Quentin had been publicly endorsed by Elijah Muhammad's west coast representative, Minister John Shabazz of Muhammad's Los Angeles Mosque. This was done because of the explosive conditions in San Quentin at the time. Muslim officials wanted to avert any Muslim-initiated violence, which had become a distinct possibility in the aftermath of Brother Booker's death. I was instructed to impose an iron discipline upon the San Quentin Mosque, which had continued to exist despite the unending efforts of prison authorities to stamp it out. Most of the Muslims who were in prison during those days have since been released. I was one of the few remaining, and I was therefore looked upon by the other Muslims as one who had sacrificed and invested much in the struggle to advance the teachings of Elijah Muhammad. For that reason, my defection to Malcolm X caused a great deal of consternation among the Muslims of Folsom. But slowly, Malcolm was getting his machine together and it was obvious to me that his influence was growing. Negro inmates who had had reservations about Malcolm while he was under Elijah's authority now embraced him, and it was clear that they accepted Malcolm's leadership. Negroes whom we had tried in vain for years to convert to Elijah's fold now lined up with enthusiasm behind Malcolm.

I ran a regular public relations campaign for Malcolm in Folsom. I saw to it that copies of his speeches were made and circulated among Negro inmates. I never missed a chance to speak favorably about Malcolm, to quote him, to explain and justify what he was trying to do. Soon I had the ear of the Muslims, and it was not long before Malcolm had other ardent defenders in Folsom. In a very short time Malcolm became the hero of the vast majority of Negro inmates. Elijah Muhammad was quickly becoming irrelevant, passé.

Malcolm X had a special meaning for black convicts. A former prisoner himself, he had risen from the lowest depths to great heights. For this reason he was a symbol of hope, a model for thousands of black convicts who found themselves trapped in the vicious PPP cycle: prison-parole-prison. One thing that the judges, policemen, and administrators of prisons seem never to have understood, and for which they certainly do not make any allowances, is that Negro convicts, basically, rather than see themselves as criminals and perpetrators of misdeeds, look upon themselves as prisoners of war, the victims of a vicious, dog-eat-dog social system that is so heinous as to cancel out their own malefactions: in the jungle there is no right or wrong.

Rather than owing and paying a debt to society, Negro prisoners feel that they are being abused, that their imprisonment is simply another form of the oppression which they have known all their lives. Negro inmates feel that they are being robbed, that it is "society" that owes them, that should be paying them, a debt.

America's penology does not take this into account. Malcolm X did, and black convicts know that the ascension to power of Malcolm X or a man like him would eventually have revolutionized penology in America. Malcolm delivered a merciless and damning indictment of prevailing penology. It is only a matter of time until the question of the prisoner's debt to society versus society's debt to the prisoner is injected forcefully into national and state politics, into the civil and human rights struggle, and into the consciousness of the body politic. It is an explosive issue which goes to the very root of America's system of justice, the structure of criminal law, the prevailing beliefs and attitudes toward the convicted felon. While it is easier to make out a case for black convicts, the same principles apply to white and Mexican-American convicts as well. They too are victimized, albeit a little more subtly, by "society." When black convicts start demanding a new dispensation and definition of justice, naturally the white and Mexican-American convicts will demand equality of treatment. Malcolm X was a focus for these aspirations.

The Black Muslim movement was destroyed the moment Elijah cracked the whip over Malcolm's head, because it was not the Black Muslim movement itself that was so irresistibly appealing to the true believers. It was the awakening into self-consciousness of twenty million Negroes which was so compelling. Malcolm X articulated their aspirations better than any other man of our time. When he spoke under the banner of Elijah Muhammad he was irresistible. When he spoke under his own banner he was still irresistible. If he had become a Quaker, a Catholic, or a Seventh-Day Adventist, or a Sammy Davis-style Jew, and if he had continued to give voice to the mute ambitions in the black man's soul, his message would still have been triumphant: because what was great was not Malcolm X but the truth he uttered.

The truth which Malcolm uttered had vanquished the whole passle of so-called Negro leaders and spokesmen who trifle and compromise with the truth in order to curry favor with the white power structure. He was stopped in the only way such a man can be stopped, in the same way that the enemies of the Congolese people had to stop Lumumba, by the same method that exploiters, tyrants, and parasitical oppressors have always crushed the legitimate strivings of people for freedom, justice, and equality— by murder, assassination, and mad-dog butchery.

What provoked the assassins to murder? Did it bother them that Malcolm was elevating our struggle into the international arena through his campaign to carry it before the United Nations? Well, by murdering him they only hastened the process, because we certainly are going to take our cause before a sympathetic world. Did it bother the assassins that Malcolm denounced the racist straitjacket demonology of Elijah Muhammad? Well, we certainly do denounce it and will continue to do so. Did it bother the assassins that Malcolm taught us to defend ourselves? We shall not remain a defenseless prey to the murderer, to the sniper and the bomber. Insofar as Malcolm spoke the truth, the truth will triumph and prevail and his name shall live; and insofar as those who opposed him lied, to that extent will their names become curses. Because "truth crushed to earth shall rise again."

So now Malcolm is no more. The bootlickers, Uncle Toms, lackeys, and stooges of the white power structure have done their best to denigrate Malcolm, to root him out of his people's heart, to tarnish his memory. But their million-worded lies fall on deaf ears. As Ossie Davis so eloquently expressed it in his immortal eulogy of Malcolm:

If you knew him you would know why we must honor him: Malcolm was our manhood, our living, black manhood! This was his meaning to his people. And, in honoring him, we honor the best in ourselves. . . . However much we may have differed with him—or with each other about him and his value as a man, let his going from us serve only to bring us together, now. Consigning these mortal remains to earth, the common mother of all, secure in the knowledge that what we place in the ground is no more now a man —but a seed—which, after the winter of our discontent will come forth again to meet us. And we will know him then for what he was and is—a Prince—our own black shining Prince!—who didn't hesitate to die, because he loved us so.

We shall have our manhood. We shall have it or the earth will be leveled by our attempts to gain it.

Malcolm X
Mission and Meaning
by Robert Penn Warren

By his own wits, ingenuity and devices a young man of humble origin triumphs over the considerable odds against him to rise out of ignominy into unforeseen success and fame. It's an old story; it's an American story. As the American poet, critic and essayist Robert Penn Warren sees it, it is also Malcolm Little's story. Martyrdom, Warren argues, thrust Malcolm X into the American popular consciousness so that his final significance lies less in the history he made than in the myth he became. Warren's essay was originally published in The Yale Review *of December 1966.*

James Farmer, lately the National Director of the Congress of Racial Equality, has called Malcolm X a "very simple man." Elijah Poole, better known to the Black Muslims as Muhammad and, indeed, as Allah, called him a "star gone astray." An editorial writer of the *Saturday Evening Post* put it: "If Malcolm X were not a Negro, his autobiography would be little more than a journal of abnormal psychology, the story of a burglar, dope pusher, addict and jailbird—with a family history of insanity—who acquires messianic delusions and sets forth to preach an upside-down religion of 'brotherly' hatred." Carl Rowan, a Negro, lately the director of the United States Information Service, substantially agreed with that editorial writer when he said, in an interview after Malcolm's assassination, that he was "an ex-convict, ex-dope peddler who became a racial fanatic." Another editorial writer, that of the *Daily Times* of Lagos, Nigeria, called him a martyr.

Malcolm X may have been, in varying perspectives, all these

things. But he was also something else. He was a latter-day example of an old-fashioned type of American celebrated in grammar school readers, commencement addresses, and speeches at Rotary Club lunches—the man who "makes it," the man who, from humble origins and with meager education, converts, by will, intelligence, and sterling character, his liabilities into assets. Malcolm X was of that breed of Americans, autodidacts and homemade successes, that has included Benjamin Franklin, Abraham Lincoln, P. T. Barnum, Thomas A. Edison, Booker T. Washington, Mark Twain, Henry Ford, and the Wright brothers. Malcolm X would look back on his beginnings and, in innocent joy, marvel at the distance he had come.

But in Malcolm X the old Horatio Alger story is crossed, as has often been the case, with another typical American story. America has been prodigally fruitful of hot-gospellers and prophets—from Dr. Graham and his bread, Amelia Bloomer and her bloomers, Emerson and the Oversoul, and Brigham Young, on to F.D.R. and the current Graham, Billy. Furthermore, to round out his American story and insure his fame, Malcolm X, like John Brown, Abraham Lincoln, Joseph Smith (the founder of Mormonism), and John Fitzgerald Kennedy, along with a host of lesser prophets, crowned his mission with martyrdom. Malcolm X fulfills, it would seem, all the requirements—success against odds, the role of prophet, and martyrdom—for inclusion in the American pantheon.

Malcolm Little, who was to become Malcolm X and El-Hajj Malik El-Shabazz, was born in Omaha, Nebraska, on May 19, 1925. All omens were right, and all his background. He was the seventh child of his father. One night during the pregnancy of his mother, hooded Ku Klux Klansmen, mounted and brandishing rifles and shotguns, surrounded the house, calling for the father to come out; the mother faced them down and persuaded them of the fact that her husband was not at home. The mother, a West Indian who looked white, was ashamed, not proud, of the white blood. The father, a Baptist preacher, was a militant follower of Marcus Garvey, and this was to lead to another attack on the Little home, in 1929, in Lansing, Michigan, this time by the Black Legion, which except for black robes was indistinguishable from the Klan; the house burned to the ground, while white police and firemen looked on. The memory of that night stayed with Malcolm from childhood—that and the pictures his father showed him of Marcus Garvey "riding in a fine car, a big black man dressed in a dazzling uniform with gold braid on it, and he was wearing a thrilling hat with tall plumes," and the Garveyite meetings at which his father presided and which always ended with the exhortation, "Up, you mighty race, you can accomplish what you will!" The people would chant these words after Malcolm's father.

To complete the picture of the preparation of the hero for his mission, his father, who had seen two brothers killed by white men and a third lynched, was found, one night, on a streetcar track, with skull crushed and body cut almost across. Negroes in Lansing—and the son all his life—believed that he had been attacked by white men, and then laid on the track. Malcolm always believed that he, too, would meet a violent death. When he first became aware of the long stalk, which was to end in gunfire in the Audubon Ballroom, Malcolm might accept it, then, as a fulfillment of old omens and intuitions.

In spite of the powerful image of the father, the pictures of Garvey in uniform, and the tales of black kings, Malcolm's early notion of Africa was still one "of naked savages, cannibals, monkeys and tigers and steaming jungles." He says that that he never understood why. But that statement must be an example, in a form more bland than usual, of his irony, for a large part of his autobiography (*The Autobiography of Malcolm X,* with the assistance of Alex Haley, New York City: The Grove Press, 1966) is devoted to explaining *why*—that is, by the white man's "brainwashing"; and then explaining *how,* step by step, he came to the vision of another Africa, and of another self, different from the hustler, pimp, dope-addict, dope-pusher, burglar, and, by his own account, generally degraded and vice-ridden creature known as "Satan," who, in 1948, in Concord Prison, in Massachusetts, heard, in a letter from his brother Philbert, of the "natural religion for the black man." The religion was called the "Nation of Islam."

This autobiography is "told" to Alex Haley, a Negro, a retired twenty-year man of the Coast Guard turned journalist. From 1963 up to the assassination, Haley saw Malcolm for almost daily sessions when Malcolm was in New York, and sometimes accompanied him on his trips. Haley's account of this period, of how he slowly gained Malcolm's confidence and how Malcolm himself discovered the need to tell his story, is extremely interesting and, though presented as an Epilogue, is an integral part of the book; but the main narrative has the advantage of Malcolm's tone, his characteristic movement of mind, and his wit, for Haley has succeeded admirably in capturing these qualities, as can be checked by the recollection of Malcolm's TV appearances and conversation and by his taped speeches (*Malcolm X Speaks: Selected Speeches and Statements,* edited by George Breitman, New York: Merit Publishers, 1966).

The *Autobiography* and the speeches are an extraordinary record of an extraordinary man. They are, among other things, a record that may show a white man (or some Negroes, for Malcolm would say that many Negroes do not know the nature of their own experience) what it means to be a Negro in America, in this century, or at least what it so dramatically meant to one man of unusual intelligence and powerful personality. Being a Negro meant being "black"—even if black was no more than a metaphor for Malcolm, who was himself "marigny," a dull yellowish skin, pale enough to freckle, pale eyes, hair reddish-coppery. He had been "Detroit Red" in his hustling days.

To be black, metaphorically or literally, meant, according to Malcolm, to wear a badge of shame which was so mystically and deeply accepted that all the practical injustices the white world might visit upon the black would seem only a kind of inverted justice, necessary in the very nature of things, the working out of a curse. The black man had no history, no country, no identity; he was alienated in time and place; he lived in "self-hate," and being unable to accept "self," he therefore was willing to accept, supine or with random violence, his fate. This was the diagnosis of his own plight, as Malcolm learned it from the "Nation of Islam."

As for the cure, what he found was the doctrine of the Black Muslims. This involved a history of creation and a metaphysic which made the black man central and dominant, and a secular history of kingly achievement in Africa. The divine and secular histories provided a justification for the acceptance of the black "self." In addition, the doctrine provided an understanding of the iniquity of the white man which would account for the black man's present lot and would, at the same time, mobilize an unquenchable hate against him. Total withdrawal from the white man and all his works was the path to virtue, until the day of Armageddon when he would be destroyed. Meanwhile, until the Chosen People had been relieved of the white man's presence, the black man was presented with a practical program of life: thrift, education, cleanliness, diet (no pork, for example, pork being a "nigger" food), abstemiousness (no alcohol or tobacco), manners and courtesy, puritanical morality and reverence for the home and Muslim womanhood—a general program of "wake up, clean up, and stand up." In fact, on the practical side, in spite of the hatred of the white man and contempt for his culture, the Black Muslim doctrine smuggled into the life of the Negro slum the very virtues which had made white middle-class America what it was—i.e., successful.

After Malcolm's death Dr. Kenneth B. Clark, the Negro psychologist and the author of an important book called *Dark Ghetto,* said that he had been "cut down at the point when he seemed on the verge of achieving the position of respectability he sought." In the midst of the gospel of violence and the repudiation of the white world, even in the Black Muslim phase, there appears now and then the note of yearning. In the *Autobiography* we find, for instance, this passage: "I was the invited speaker at the Harvard Law School Forum. I happened to glance through a window. Abruptly, I realized that I was looking in the direction of the apartment house that was my old burglary group's hideout. . . . And there I stood, the invited speaker, at Harvard."

Malcolm, still in prison, gave up pork and tobacco, and undertook a program of reading in the good library there available. He read in Plato, Aristotle, Schopenhauer, Kant, Nietzsche, and the "Oriental philosophers." He read and reread the Bible, and could match quotations with a Harvard Seminary student who conducted a class for prisoners. He studied *The Loom of Language,* by Frederick Bodmer, and memorized Grimm's Law. He read Durant's *Story of Civilization,* H. G. Wells' *Outline of History,* Herodotus, Fannie Kimball, *Uncle Tom's Cabin,* Gandhi, Gregor Mendel, pamphlets of the "Abolitionist Anti-Slavery Society of New England," and J. A. Rogers' *Sex and Race.* He was trying to find the black man's place—and his own—in history, trying, in other words, to document the doctrine of the Black Muslims. He wrote regularly to Muhammad to tell what he had found. While he was still in prison Malcolm also had a vision. He had written an appeal to Muhammad to reinstate his brother Reginald, suspended as a Muslim for "improper relations" with the secretary of the New York temple. That night he spent in desperate prayer. The next night he woke up and saw a man sitting, there in the cell, in a chair by him. "He had on a dark suit, I remember. I could see him as plainly as I see anyone I look at. He wasn't black, and he wasn't white. He was light-brown-skinned, an Asiatic cast of countenance, and he had oily black hair. . . . I had no idea whatsoever who he was. He just sat there. Then suddenly as he had come, he was gone." The color of the man in the vision is an interesting fact. So is his immobility and silence.

When Malcolm Little came out of prison, he was Malcolm X, the "X," according to the practice of the Black Muslims, standing for the true name lost long ago in Africa to take the place of the false white name that had been forced on him. He had been reborn, and he now entered upon his mission. Soon he was an accredited minister of Muhammad, the official defender of the faith and the intellectual spokesman of the movement. His success, and especially the fact that he was invited to colleges, where Muhammad would never be invited, led to jealousy and, as Malcolm reports, contributed to his "silencing" as soon as a good justification appeared.

Malcolm X was not the only man drawn from the lower depths to be reborn in the Nation of Islam. It is generally admitted that the record of rehabilitation by the Black Muslims of dope addicts, alcoholics, prostitutes, and criminals makes any other method seem a waste of time. They have, it would seem, found the nerve center that, once touched, can radically change both the values and the way of life for a number of Negroes in America; and it is important here to use the phrase "Negroes in America" with special emphasis, and no other locution, for those redeemed by the Black Muslims are those who have been only *in,* but not *of,* America, those without country, history, or identity. The Black Muslims have found, then, a principle that, if not of universal validity (or, in one perspective, isn't it? for white as well as for black?), at least involves a truth of considerable psychological importance. That truth is, indeed, shrouded in metaphysical mumbo-jumbo, political and economic absurdity, and some murderous delusions, but even these elements have a noteworthy symbolic relation to the central truth. It is reported that Martin Luther King, after seeing Malcolm X on TV, remarked: "When he starts talking about all that's been done to us, I get a twinge of hate, of identification with him. But hate is not the only effect." A man as intelligent, as cultivated, and as experienced as James Farmer has testified in his recent book *Freedom When?* that the Black Muslims and Malcolm X have had a very important impact on his own thinking and in helping to change his basic views of the Negro Revolution, especially on the question of "blackness" and on the nature of integration and the Negro's role in an open society.

If this is the case, then the story of Malcolm X assumes an added dimension. It shows the reader the world in which that truth can operate; that is, it shows the kind of alienation to which this truth is applicable. It shows, also, the human quality of the operation, a man in the process of trying to understand his plight, and to find salvation, by that truth. But there is another aspect to the *Autobiography.* Malcolm X was a man in motion, he was a seeker, and that motion led, in the end, away from orthodox Black Muslim doctrine. The doctrine had been, he said, a straitjacket. He was now in the process of stripping away, perhaps unconsciously, the mumbo-jumbo, the absurdities, and the murderous delusions. He was trying, as it were, to locate the truth that had saved him, and divest it of the irrelevancies. In the end, he might have come to regard the religion that, after his break with the Black Muslims, he had found in Mecca as an irrelevancy, too. Certainly, just before his death he could say that his "philosophy" was still changing. Perhaps what Mecca gave him, for the time being at least, was the respectability, the authority, of the established thing. But he might have finally found that authority in himself, for he could speak as a man whose very existence was witness to what he said. Something of that purely personal authority comes through in these books.

Malcolm X had, in his last phase, lost the mystique of blackness so important to the Black Muslims; he had seen the blue-eyed and fair-haired pilgrims in Mecca. He was no longer a separatist in the absolute sense of the Black Muslims. He had become enough of an integrationist to say: "I believe in recognizing every human being as a human being . . . and when you are dealing with humanity as a family, there's no question of integration or intermarriage. It's just one human being marrying another human being or one human being living around with another human being." And just before his death he had made a down payment on a house, in Long Island, in a largely Jewish neighborhood. He no longer saw the white man as the "white devil"—metaphysically evil; and he was ready, grudgingly, not optimistically, and with a note of threat, to grant that there was in America a chance, a last chance, for a "bloodless revolution." He was ready to work with other Negro organizations, even those which he had most derided, to try to find common ground and solutions at a practical level.

Certain ideas were, however, carried over from the Black Muslim days. The question of "identity" remained, and the question of race pride and personal self-respect divested of chauvinism, and with this the notion of "wake up, clean up, and stand up," the notion of self-reliance, self-improvement, self-discipline. If he could say such things, which smacked of the discredited philosophy of Booker T. Washington, and which few other civil rights leaders would dare to utter, it was because he did so in the context of his intransigence vis-à-vis the white world and his radical indictment of white society. Even in the last phase, even if he believed in "recognizing every human being as a human being," and no longer took the white man to be metaphysically evil, his indictment of white society was still radical; unless that society could really be regenerated, the chance for the "bloodless revolution" was gone.

This radical indictment leads to what may be the greatest significance of Malcolm X, his symbolic role. He was the black man who looked the white man in the eye and forgave nothing. If the white man had turned away, in shame or indifference, from the awful "forgiveness" of a Martin Luther King, he still had to face the unforgivingness, with its shattering effect on his accustomed view of himself and with the terrifying discovery, as Malcolm's rage brought his own rage forth, of the ultimate of which he himself would, under pressure, be capable. To put it another way,

Malcolm X let the white man see what, from a certain perspective, he, his history, and his culture looked like. It was possible to say that that perspective was not the only one, that it did not give the whole truth about the white man, his history, and his culture, but it was not possible to say that the perspective did not carry *a* truth, a truth that was not less, but more, true for being seen from the angle of Small's Paradise in Harlem or of the bedroom to which "Detroit Red," the "steerer," brought the "Ivy League fathers" to be ministered to by the big black girl, whose body had been greased to make it look "shinier and blacker" and whose Amazonian hand held a small plaited whip.

On the afternoon of Sunday, February 21, 1965, at a meeting of his struggling new Organization of Afro-American Unity, in the Audubon Ballroom, on West 166th Street, in Harlem, Malcolm X rose to speak and uttered the ritual greeting, *"Assalaam alaikum,* brothers and sisters!" He was immediately cut down by shotgun and revolver fire from assassins waiting in the front of the audience. At 3:30 at the Columbia-Presbyterian Hospital, he was pronounced dead. Three men—Talmadge Hayer, Norman 3X Butler, and Thomas 15X Johnson—were arrested in the case and tried for first-degree murder. Thayer denied Black Muslim connections, but Thomas 15X was identified as a member and Norman 3X as a lieutenant in the "Fruit of Islam"—the bodyguards of Elijah Muhammad. After deliberating for twenty hours a jury found them guilty, and all three were given life sentences.

What would have been Malcolm's role had he lived? Perhaps, as some Negro leaders said shortly before his death, he had no real organization, and did not have the talent to create one. Perhaps his being in motion was only, as some held, a result of confusion of mind, a groping that could not be trusted to bring results. Perhaps, as James Farmer had put it, Malcolm, for all his talk, was not an activist; he had managed all along to be out of harm's way whenever harm was brewing, and he was afraid of the time when he "would have to chirp or get off the perch."

But perhaps the new phase of the Negro Revolution, with the violence of the great city slums, might have given him his great chance. He might have, at last, found himself in action. He might have found himself committed to blind violence, but on the other hand he might have had the power to control and canalize action and do something to reduce the danger of the Revolution's degenerating into random revolt. For, in spite of all the gospel of intransigence, Malcolm had always had a governing idea of a constructive role for the Negro, some notion of a society. After all, he had personal force, as no one who ever spent as little as ten minutes with him would have doubted: charisma, to use the fashionable word, and that to a degree possessed by no other leader except Martin Luther King. And he had one great asset which Martin Luther King does not have: he was from the lower depths and possessed the authority of one who had both suffered and conquered the depths.

Whatever the future might have held for him had he lived, his actual role was an important one, and in one sense the importance lay in his *being* rather than his *doing*. He was a man of passion, depth, and scale—and his personal story is a moving one. There is the long struggle. There is the sense of desperation and tightening entrapment as, in the last days, Malcolm recognized the dilemma developing in his situation. The "so-called moderate" civil rights leaders, he said, dodged him as "too militant," and the "so-called militants" dodged him as "too moderate." Haley reports that he once exclaimed "They won't let me turn the corner! I'm caught in a trap!" For there is a trap in the story, a real and lethal one. There is the gang of Black Muslims covering his every move in the Statler Hilton at Los Angeles, the mysterious Negro men who tried to get his room number at the Hilton in New York City, and the sinister telephone call to his room in the hotel the morning of his death. There is the bombing of his house, and his despairing anger when the event was widely taken as a publicity stunt. There is his remark to Haley, as he asked to read the manuscript of his book for a last, unnecessary time: "I just want to read it one more time, because I don't expect to read it in finished form"—wanting, as it were, to get a last sense of the shape of his own life as he felt the trap closing. There is, as with a final accent of pathos, the letter by his six-year-old daughter Attallah (named for the Scourge of God), written just after his death: "Dear Daddy, I love you so. O dear, O dear, I wish you wasn't dead." But entrapment and pathos was not all. He had been bred to danger. When he stepped on the platform that Sunday afternoon, in the face of odds which he had more shrewdly estimated than anybody else, he had nerve, confidence, style. He made his last gesture.

As one reads the *Autobiography*, one feels that, whatever the historical importance of Malcolm Little, his story has permanence, that it has something of tragic intensity and meaning. One feels that it is an American story bound to be remembered, to lurk in the background of popular consciousness, to reappear some day in a novel, on the stage, or on the screen. No—the right medium might be the ballad. Malcolm was a figure out of the anonymous depth of the folk, and even now, in a slum bedroom or in the shadowy corner of some bar, fingers may be tentatively picking the box, and lips fumbling to frame the words that will mean, long after our present problems are resolved and forgotten, the final fame, and the final significance.

Malcolm X
Witness for the Prosecution
by Peter Goldman

In the preface to The Death and Life of Malcolm X *Peter Goldman comments on his attempt as a biographer "to resist the temptation to crowd [Malcolm] into some neat little box and label him nationalist, or socialist, or militant, or hate-monger, or any of the other names in which we have tried in the past to contain his protean life and intelligence." Instead, Goldman would define Malcolm X "minimally"— as "neither saint nor sinner but a good and gifted man struggling imperfectly toward daylight," a man whose "past killed him just as he was triumphing over it." The essay that follows was adapted by Goldman from his biography on Malcolm X and was first published in the book* Black Leaders of the Twentieth Century *(1982).*

For the thirteen impassioned years of his ministry, Malcolm X was a witness for the prosecution against white America—a "field nigger," he called himself, giving incendiary voice to the discontents of our urban black underclass. Everything about Malcolm was an accusation: his Muslim faith, his militant politics, his self-made manhood, even the name he took in token of his renunciation of white society and his embrace of black Islam. He was a dissonant and mostly misunderstood figure in his own public lifetime, a bitter and cynical counterpoint to the orthodox civil rights movement in its romantic high of the 1950s and 1960s; he stood apart, dimly perceived as a racist and demagogue inflaming the black lumpenproletariat to revenge its grievances in blood. Only with his death and the movement's discouraged exhaustion could Malcolm be seen more nearly as he was: a revolutionary of the soul who, by word and charismatic example, helped awaken a proud and assertive new black consciousness among the grand-sons and granddaughters of slaves.

Even then, Malcolm has had to survive his admirers—to pass, that is, through a kind of posthumous canonization that carica-tured him almost as unrecognizably as his prior media image as a hate-monger. He was neither thinker nor planner nor tactician but rather, by his own definition, a "black Billy Graham"—a revi-valist calling souls to Allah and blackness as Graham summoned them to Christ. He made his fiery witness for a dozen years in the ministry of the late Messenger Elijah Muhammad and his Lost-Found Nation of Islam in the Wilderness of North America, the then anti-white doomsday sect better known to us as the Black Muslims; only slowly and with intense pain did he cast off its trammeling dogmas and strike out for a single year on his own, searching America, Africa, and the Middle East for the uncreated conscience of a race. The search was still unfinished at his death, at age thirty-nine, as El Hajj Malik El-Shabazz, an accredited minister of orthodox Sunni Islam and a happily unconstrained agitator against the way things were. He passed in that quest from the belief on faith that all white people are devils to the convic-tion on the available evidence that American white society is irre-mediably racist. But the shadings of gray that stole into his black-and-white world view in his last year of life never softened the bleak landscape of his politics. Malcolm was, before anything else, a public moralist—a scold whose private manner was gentle-manly, even priestly, but whose aspect to the world was one of implacable and uncompromising fury.

As moralist, he was a voice of quite another sort than his con-temporary, Martin Luther King, Jr.—a voice of that estranged backstreet black community where the churchly southern style has not traveled well. He spoke a fluent, downtown English when he needed to, but his first language was a slurred and cynical ghetto black, and his first source of authority was that the ghetto recognized so much of itself in him. His life was, as he wrote in his *Autobiography,* a "chronology of changes"—a series of provi-sional identities that he did not live to complete. He began it, in 1925, as Malcolm Little, the fourth of eight children of a fragile West Indian woman and a fiery black preacher devoted with equal

heat to the Baptist gospels and the secular teachings of the nationalist Marcus Garvey. Malcolm was born the year Garvey went
to prison for mail fraud, and his boyhood was a casualty of the
Garvey movement's subsequent rout; white vigilantes harried the
Littles out of Omaha, Nebraska, burned their home in Lansing,
Michigan, and finally mobbed Malcolm's father, beating him
nearly lifeless and leaving him to die under the wheels of a streetcar. The family disintegrated thereafter, and Malcolm, stormy
and rebellious, wound up in the foster care of a white couple—a
beneficence that was the beginning of his education in white folk-
ways and, later, the object of his unsparing rage. He described the
interlude in a televised debate with black journalist Louis Lomax
in 1964:

LOMAX: Are all white men immoral, Minister Malcolm? Is there
not one good one?
MALCOLM: I haven't met all of them. Those whom I have met
are the type I would say are insincere. Now if there are some
sincere whites somewhere, it's those that I haven't met yet.
LOMAX: How about the woman . . . that took you in when you
were a little boy and put you on the road to learning something?
MALCOLM: . . . My presence in that home was like a cat or a
parrot or any type of pet that they had. You know how you'll be
around whites and they'll discuss things just like you're not there.
I think [Ralph] Ellison calls it the *Invisible Man* and [James] Bald-
win calls it *Nobody Knows My Name*. My presence in that home
was not the presence of a human being.
LOMAX: But she did feed you.
MALCOLM: You feed your cat.
LOMAX: She clothed you.
MALCOLM: You clothe any kind of pet that you might have.
LOMAX: And you impute to her no humanitarian motivation?
MALCOLM: No. Not today.

That pitiless wrath had been Malcolm's personal salvation,
once Elijah Muhammad and his little nation in the wilderness
taught him what it was and how to use it. His life till then had
been a descent into hell. He dropped out of school as soon as he
finished the eighth grade, ran away east to Boston and later Har-

lem, and drifted through a series of menial jobs into the zoot-suited, bop-gaited life of a street hustler. Malcolm Little became Detroit Red, then Big Red, dealing (and using) drugs, running numbers slips and bootleg whiskey, steering white customers to black brothels, burglarizing homes, and sticking up stores. "I loved the devil," he said later. "I was trying as hard as I could to be white." There is some evidence that he tended to inflate his size in the hustler underground for pedagogical effect; he is only dimly remembered by old-timers on the street, and then principally as having been a "john-walker"—a curbside shill for a Harlem whorehouse. But his degradation was complete and was ultimately certified by the Commonwealth of Massachusetts with an eight-to-ten-year sentence for burglary—a severe penalty then thought commensurate with the fact that one of his accomplices was his white mistress.

His redemption began in prison with his exposure to Muhammad's ghetto theology and its Damascene central revelation: that white people were a race of devils created for the torment of the black sons and daughters of Allah. Muhammad said he had this on the word of God Himself, who had appeared in the black slums of Detroit in 1930 in the person of a silk peddler named Wallace D. Fard and announced himself as "the one the world has been expecting for the past two thousand years." His teachings took root in a little communion of country southern blacks flung north, like Muhammad himself, in the great black diaspora of the 1920s. He found Muhammad, then Elijah Poole, a particularly apt and willing pupil—a fragile man whose sleepy eyes and faltering speech masked a keen native wit and a certain genius for the main chance. When Fard disappeared in 1934—or, as believers prefer, when he returned to Mecca to prepare for the end of the world—Muhammad stood first in the line of succession; the fountainhead of the extraordinary authority he held for forty years thereafter was that he had known Allah and been personally ordained his last Messenger, "missioned" by him to lead his people out of bondage to their white slavemasters and back to their lost Zion "in the East."

Outsiders commonly found Muhammad's cultish scriptures rather quaint; even believers in the parting of the Red Sea or the miracle of the loaves and fishes smiled at the revelation that whites were a bleached-out, blue-eyed mutant race created by a dissident black scientist named Yacub and set loose to subjugate black people to its satanic pleasure. But, as James Baldwin once wrote, Muhammad's theology was "no more indigestible than the more familiar brand asserting that there is a curse on the sons of Ham," and for some fraction of black America, as for Malcolm himself, it had the force of empirical truth. Stripped of its exotica and its hyperbole, Muhammad's message was that white slavers had destroyed the black civilizations of Africa and reduced black men and women to chattel; had stripped them of their culture, their religion, even their names; had taught them to speak a foreign tongue, worship a "spook" Christian God, and call themselves Smith, Jones, Powell, Bunche, and King; had reduced them from African blacks to "so-called American Negroes," wallowing in the white man's vices and obedient to the white man's unthreatening Negro leaders; had, in sum, murdered them spiritually, emotionally, and morally. What Muhammad asked, and what Malcolm demanded in his name, was that blacks understand what they had in common—the color of their skins and the enmity it provoked against them. "You don't catch hell because you're a Methodist or a Baptist," Malcolm told a black audience in 1963. "You don't catch hell because you're a Democrat or a Republican; you don't catch hell because you're a Mason or an Elk, and you sure don't catch hell because you're an American, because if you were an American you wouldn't catch no hell. You catch hell because you are a black man."

What the Muslims thus offered black people was an alternative to the religious positions then available to them: to accept the fallen state of one's people as the judgment of God or to extrapolate from it that God does not exist. The message was much misunderstood by white people, who heard only the Nation's imprecations against the devil and saw only the scowling, paramilitary face it turned outward to the world; the Muslims were accordingly deemed a threat to the peace and good order of our society and were already under surveillance by the Federal Bureau of Investigation, among other police agencies, when Malcolm left prison and joined the ministry in 1952. It was a case of mistaken identity. The Muslims belonged more nearly to the tradition of Booker T. Washington than of Nat Turner; they practiced a kind of quietist

withdrawal from the black struggle, leading peaceful and abstemi-
ous lives, tithing to the Nation and the Messenger, building a
business empire once valued at seventy million dollars on a base
of small retail stores and streetcorner newspaper sales.

But Malcolm saw and exploited the uses of rage as an organizing principle akin in force, for example, to the divinity of Christ or
the labor theory of value; he promoted it brilliantly and, once the
mass media discovered his extraordinary star quality, made the
Nation a force in our national life far beyond its enrolled membership of around ten thousand. At his dazzling peak, it was easy
to forget that he was a prison-educated man schooled in the language by copying words out of a dictionary and introduced to
wisdom by the revelations of Fard; he became a regular on the
talk shows, a lecturer on the university tour—only Barry Goldwater had more bookings in Malcolm's day—and a figure in the
diplomatic lounge of the United Nations. He praised Elijah
Muhammad second only to Allah for his success, and for years he
meant it; in private, he spoke of himself as "a little Charlie Mc-
Carthy sitting on the Messenger's knee"; in public, he dropped
the old man's name so often—once a minute, by his own accurate
count—that it sometimes came out "the Honorbubble Elijah
Muhammad." But he was in the process creating a style of leadership and a pitch of demand all his own—a politics in which dema-
goguery was a legitimate means of struggle and "responsibility" a
form of treason. The responsible leaders, he said, were responsible to whites, not blacks. "They controlled you, but they have
never incited you or excited you," he said at a rally in 1963. "They
controlled you. They contained you. They have kept you on the
plantation."

The Malcolm style was finally too successful; his militance agi-
tated the calm of Muhammad's courtiers, who saw it as bad for
business, and his gifts for and easy access to the media excited
their jealousies. With their encouragement, what had been a fa-
ther-and-son relationship between the Messenger and Malcolm
stretched thin and finally snapped; Malcolm was set down from
the ministry late in 1963, officially because he had cheered the
assassination of John F. Kennedy as a case of "the chickens coming home to roost," actually because he had begun trying to secure his own threatened position by spreading tales about

Muhammad's indulgent private life. Malcolm's keen and free-running intelligence had always been a subversive force in the Nation and had been driving him toward the exit for years before even he realized it. Still, when he made his break in March 1964, it was an act of temple politics more than a breach of faith; his stated purpose was to go right on preaching Muhammad's apocalyptic gospels on his own.

His resolve did not last out the single year left to him—or even the first spring of his freedom. He took tutorials in orthodox Islam and in April made his *hajj* to Mecca—a transforming exposure to the company of white Muslims, whose existence he had known about but denied, and to a leveling spiritual brotherhood with them, which he had never before imagined possible. The pilgrimage, he said, "broadened my scope probably more in twelve days than my previous experience during my thirty-nine years on this earth"—deepened his faith, ventilated his politics, and reduced the American white man in his sight from the devil to a fallible human enemy. His development thereafter was an explosive rush from the certitudes of the Black Muslims through a conventional streetcorner black nationalism to a world view of more subtle weave—a shifting and uncompleted blend of orthodox Islam, African socialism, Third World anticolonialism, and that doctrine of racial solidarity known later as Black Power. His destination was no clearer to him then than to us now, in the tangle of contending words and ideas he left us; he was still searching America and Africa for it when he died.

Malcolm was a casualty of our bloodied 1960s, assassinated by black men at a rally of his fledgling Organization of Afro-American Unity in uptown Manhattan in February 1965. Three Black Muslims were arrested, tried and convicted of his murder, and sentenced to life in prison. A considerable body of folklore and published speculation has it that the real culprit was the state—that, whether Muslims pulled the triggers, the assassination was fomented by the Central Intelligence Agency or the Federal Bureau of Investigation and at least passively abetted by the New York City police. My own detailed examination of the evidence does not support this view. There are persuasive grounds for belief that two of the three men imprisoned for killing Malcolm were in fact innocent; there is equally suggestive evidence that the agencies of our justice foresaw an attempt on Malcolm's life and kept a distance long and disinterested enough to let it happen. But the record taken objectively and whole points to the conclusion that the police *theory* of the case was correct—that Malcolm's death was plotted and executed by Muslims in revenge for his blasphemies against Muhammad and that the real miscarriage of justice is that the wrong Muslims were imprisoned for it.

Malcolm could fairly be judged a failure by the conventional measures of leadership; he left behind no concrete program for the deliverance of black Americans, no disciplined following to carry on for him, no organization sturdy enough to survive his death. It does not diminish him at all to say that none of these was his particular gift. He belongs instead to what the political scientist Charles Hamilton has identified as the tradition of spokesmanship in the black struggle; he was an artist of the spoken word, and his contributions cannot be adequately judged by the normal standards of success or failure, as King's could, or Roy Wilkins's, or Whitney Young's. Malcolm, as the movement strategist Bayard Rustin told me in an interview,

> has to be seen over and above the pull and tug of struggle for concrete objectives. King had to be measured by his victories. But what King did, what the NAACP did, what the March on Washington did, what Whitney Young did, what Roy Wilkins did, all that was for the benefit of the Southern Negro. There were no obtainable, immediate results for the Northern ghettoized black, whose housing is getting worse; who is unable to find work; whose schools are deteriorating; who sees constantly more rats and roaches and more garbage in the streets. He, because he is human, must find victory somewhere, and he finds his victory within. He needed Malcolm, who brought him an internal victory, precisely because the external victory was beyond his reach. What can bring satisfaction is the feeling that he is black, he is a man, he is internally free. King had to win victories in the real world. Malcolm's were the kind you can create yourself.

Malcolm's victories, that is, were private victories; and yet they were no less consequential for having been won in the soul instead of in that world of legislation and negotiation and compromise—the world of affairs—that most of us think of as real. He was a force for the liberation of black people, both by the example of his triumph over the degradation of his own young manhood and by the furious war he waged on the myths, manners, and polite hypocrisies of race in America. That he contributed to the education of some few whites in the process was a fact largely lost to him—the explosion of interest in Malcolm began after his death and the publication of his *Autobiography*—and was of secondary concern to him in any case. What interested Malcolm first was the decolonization of the black mind—the wakening of a proud, bold, demanding new consciousness of color and everything color means in white America.

Malcolm pursued this end with utter recklessness of the settled rules of debate and of his own reputation. His genius was attack, for which he offered no apology beyond the argument that a program was pointless until the slumbering black masses were wakened to their need for one. Within range of a camera or a microphone, his marvelous private civility gave way to a wintry public wrath and occasionally to the kind of thoughtless cruelty that moved him to cheer earthquakes and plane crashes—anything that caused white men pain or grief. "This is the thing— whatever I say, I'm justified," he told the black journalist Claude Lewis late in his life. "If I say that Negroes should get out here right tomorrow and go to war, I'm justified." His objectives, when he excoriated the white devils or called for the formation of an American Mau Mau, were precisely to frighten whites and embolden blacks.

He was always challenging the white man, always debunking the white man [the sociologist C. Eric Lincoln said in an interview]. I don't think he was ever under any illusion that a powerless black minority could mount a physical challenge to a powerful white majority and survive. But they could mount a psychological challenge, and if they were persistent, they might at least produce some erosion in the attitudes and the strategies by which the white man has always protected himself and his interests. His challenge was to prove that you are as great as you say you are, that you are as moral as you say you are, that you are as kind as you say you are, that you are as loving as you say you are, that you are as altruistic as you say you are, that you are as *superior* as you say you are.

Malcolm saw his life as combat and words as his weapon. It has been said of him that he had no other strategy—that he stood talking on the sidelines through the most momentous years in our race relations since the Civil War. He was denouncing intermarriage on a radio talk show the night James Meredith and five thousand soldiers "integrated" the University of Mississippi in 1962; he watched the police dogs and fire hoses of Birmingham on television in New York in 1963; he was off in Cairo pursuing a dream alliance with black Africa when the first of the big-city ghetto insurrections exploded out of the alleys of Harlem in 1964. He was always somewhere else, it was said, with a lavaliere microphone or a little knot of reporters, hooting, heckling, scolding, accusing, but never participating.

All of this was true, and probably beside the point. If Malcolm lived at the margins of our national life, he was rarely out of sight. He was a dark presence, angry, cynical, implacable; a man whose goodwill or forgiveness or even pity we could neither earn nor buy. He meant to haunt us—to play on our fears, quicken our guilts, and deflate our dreams that everything was getting better —and he did. "America's problem is *us*," he said in a speech in 1963. Others had been telling us that politely for years, and since his death a blue-ribbon presidential commission on the ghetto riots has subscribed to his once heretical view that we are a society decisively shaped by our racism. The difference was that most of the others held out the hope that matters could be put right with enough conscience, will, and money. Malcolm did not.

He did not even accept that America *had* a conscience; he offered as proof the tragic past of the blacks beginning the day the first trader took the first slave out of Africa. He therefore did not accept the formulation that there is an American dilemma—a constant tension between the ideals of the American creed and the realities of caste and color. Our creed and our Constitution were never meant to include black people, Malcolm told us, and if we argued that the sins of the past ought not to be visited on us, he replied: "Your father isn't here to pay his debts. My father isn't here to collect. But I'm here to collect, and you're here to pay."

Malcolm may never have hated all white people with that uncritical religious passion he brought to his ministry in the Nation of Islam; in his last months he renounced Muhammad's teachings as a racist "straitjacket" and apologized to black America for having repeated them. He absolved white Americans in that period from the blanket judgment that they were all devils and announced that he would thereafter hold them accountable only for their behavior, not for their color or their genes. But he never altered the fundamental terms of his indictment: that American whites collectively were the enemy of American blacks collectively until their actions proved them otherwise. "I'm not blanketly condemning all whites," he told a Harlem rally in the days after his pilgrimage to Mecca accomplished his personal emancipation from hatred. "All of them don't oppress. All of them aren't in a position to. But most of them are, and most of them do."

Even at his most feral in the Black Muslim years, hate was less visceral than a point of principle for Malcolm. He saw rage as a potential liberating force for the retrieval of blacks from what he perceived as the worst crime whites had done them: teaching them to hate themselves. Malcolm himself had been dragged low by self-hatred; had pimped and hustled and sniffed cocaine and had finally done time; had pegged his pants, processed his hair, and pursued white women in what he imagined then to be an accurate imitation of the master class. He understood self-hatred, that is, because he had been there and seen it. "We hated our head, we hated the shape of our nose—we wanted one of the long, *dog*-like noses, you know," he said in a speech in 1964. "Yeah. We hated the color of our skin. We hated the blood of Africa that was in our veins. And in hating our features and our skin and our blood, why, we had to end up hating ourselves."

Malcolm achieved his own liberation and invited black Americans to follow him by creating a new life whole out of the ashes of his past and theirs. He became in his own eyes neither a Negro nor an American but a spiritual refugee, an African Muslim in forced exile from the mother country. "I'm not going to sit at your table and watch you eat, with nothing on my plate, and call myself a diner," he said in a speech in 1964. He was appalled by the degradations of ghetto life and, even more, by the acquiescence of black men and women in them. The original sin in his eyes was the white man's, for having severed the blacks from their past and reduced them to property, but he insisted that the responsibility for their salvation was their own. To Malcolm, this meant getting up out of the mud—out from under the charity as well as the tyranny of white America. It meant renouncing integration, which was only a further denial of the worth of black people, and nonviolence, which was only a newer, subtler form of humiliation before the slavemaster. It meant embracing the African past, till then a source of shame; it meant identifying not with the white majority in America and the West but with the dark majority of the world. It meant the discovery of what Eric Lincoln has termed "a negotiable identity" as black men and women, deserving of the world's respect and their own.

And it meant standing up to "the man." One of the worst humiliations of all, in Malcolm's eyes, was that paralytic silence, that head-bobbing surrender, that seemed to him to afflict so many blacks in the presence of whites. The ghetto had been cursing whitey for years in its own back streets, but seldom to his face; so seldom, indeed, that a black man who did so seemed to whites presumptively insane—a *crazy nigger*—and so was accorded a kind of gingerly safe-conduct against reprisal. Malcolm was the crazy nigger gone public; he undertook to carry Harlem's fury downtown, to tell white people to their faces, in their own mass media, what ordinary blacks had been saying about them backstairs for all those years. He did not "teach" hate, or need to; he exploited a vein of hate that was there already and to which few black Americans were totally immune. He saw himself as waging war—a war of words whose objective was to outrage an enemy to whom black people could not otherwise cause pain.

He could be quite conscienceless doing battle; he believed (and once defended in a debate at Oxford) the Goldwater homily that moderation in the pursuit of justice is no virtue, and, because he believed it, he quite literally did not care what he said. Once, in a debate in New York in 1962, Rustin accused him of engaging in emotionalism, to which Malcolm hotly replied:

When a man is hanging on a tree and he cries out, should he cry out unemotionally? When a man is sitting on a hot stove and he tells you how it feels to be there, is he supposed to speak without emotion? This is what you tell black people in this country when they begin to cry out against the injustices that they're suffering. As long as they describe these injustices in a way that makes you believe you have another hundred years to rectify the situation, then you don't call that emotion. But when a man is on a hot stove, he says, "I'm coming up. I'm getting up. Violently or nonviolently doesn't even enter into the picture—I'm coming up, do you understand?"

By the measure of a society that meters applause, Malcolm nearly always won these encounters, partly because he ignored the niceties and partly because he preempted a kind of moral high ground for himself. To respond that he overstated the indictment was to quibble with details; the condition of the blacks in America was proof enough for him of his basic claims. To oppose him by arguing the necessity of programs and alliances with whites was to throw in with the enemy, since programs and alliances implied the goodwill or at least the tractability of the enemy. And to contend that there had after all been some progress was to deny the continuing pain of the great masses of blacks. "You don't stick a knife in a man's back nine inches and then pull it out six inches and say you're making progress," Malcolm said on a radio talk show in 1963. "It's dangerous to even make the white man *think* we're making progress while the knife is still in our backs, or while the wound is still there, or while even the intention that he had is still there."

Malcolm's war challenged the leaders and the orthodoxies of the civil rights movement in the midst of its glory days, and he paid for it; the cost was a kind of quarantine that lifted only with his death. Alive, he made the leaders of the movement uncomfortable, like an unquiet conscience or an unhappy memory. They thought him a genuine danger to the cause of racial comity; they resented his running attacks on them; they envied his easy access to radio and television; they were embarrassed by his claim to the allegiance of a ghetto lumpenproletariat they had talked about but had never reached. So Malcolm found himself isolated from the front-line struggle, even after he had broken with Elijah Muhammad and wanted to join it. He was isolated from respect as well; the movement—even the radical movement—kept him in a kind of moral Coventry and saw him not as a comrade-in-arms but as a hobgoblin to be held up to whites for a certain scare effect. Malcolm at once acquiesced in this role and was wounded by it. He hungered for legitimacy, for a place among the recognized black leadership; he found himself obliged instead to play bogeyman—to make King's life easier by playing on white America's fantasies of a bloody black revenge. "I don't know why they hate me," he told the actor Ossie Davis, a friend with mainstream connections. "I raise hell in the back yard and they run out front and 'the man' puts money in their hands."

King's celebrity particularly pained him. It has been argued since their deaths that the two men had been moving inexorably together in what might have been a single, irresistible mass movement against racism, poverty, and the war in Vietnam—that they may even have been assassinated to keep their alliance from happening. The dream is beguiling but finally unpersuasive. Malcolm and King were not so much Manichaean opposites as halves in a yin-yang duality deep in the black soul. But there was too much unhappy history between the two men, too many irreconcilable differences of politics, principle, and style. King's moral authority was that he asked black people to transcend their humanity; Malcolm proposed that they embrace it—that they reserve their love for one another and address white people as people have always addressed their enemies. King's politics were insistently multiracial, Malcolm's insistently black; King's means were nonviolent, which Malcolm considered beggarly; King's ends were assimilationist, which Malcolm derided as a fantasy for all but a token few "acceptable" middle-class blacks. The distance between them was the distance between utility and morality; between the street and the seminary; between the American reality and the American dream. When Harlem honored King on his receipt of the Nobel Peace Prize late in 1964, Malcolm and a few followers watched in moody silence from a back row. "He got the peace prize, we got the problem," he told Claude Lewis a few days later. "I don't want the white man giving me medals. If I'm following a general and he's leading me into battle, and the enemy tends to give him rewards, or awards, I get suspicious of him. Especially if he gets a peace award before the war is over."

Malcolm was wounded as well by his outlaw reputation in the press, particularly after he left the Nation of Islam with its iron anti-white certitudes and entered on the extraordinary personal transformations of the last months of his life. He hoped in that period to come into "a new regard by the public," he wrote in the *Autobiography,* but it eluded him during his lifetime; he remained, in print and on camera, a cartoon Black Muslim inciting an otherwise pacific black underclass to insurrection. Malcolm came to understand that he shared the blame for this with the media— that he had been perhaps too willing to pay the price for their attention, which was to say something outrageous. His image, he told a newspaper interviewer in his last days, "was created by them and by me. . . . They were looking for sensationalism, for something that would sell papers, and I gave it to them."

Malcolm gave it to them with a prolixity that troubled his friends, armed his enemies, and deepened his isolation from that respect he sought—gave it to them because there was so little else within his power to give. He had been our Frantz Fanon; the natives in America have neither the numbers nor the guns to do to whites that gratifying violence perceived by Fanon at the heart of the Algerian terror, but at least for a time in the 1960s they could make white people jump when they said *boo!* and that was something. Malcolm discovered this early—discovered, that is, how close the specter of the black revenge lies to the surface of the white American consciousness—and, having discovered it, he could rarely resist its pleasures.

Only in his last months did Malcolm understand the damaging degree to which he was imprisoned by the common expectations of the media and the ghetto that he would scandalize whites—and by his own unfailingly willing response. At the press conference at which he formally declared his independence of Elijah Muhammad in March 1964, he argued that black people ought to get guns and organize to use them in their own defense wherever the government failed in its duty to protect them. It was not an unreasonable position, given the run of unpunished and unrequited acts of violence against blacks in the South and the then rather distant interest of the federal government in protecting them; it was, moreover, only one of several themes Malcolm struck in announcing his breakaway. But, precisely as he anticipated, it dominated the evening newscasts and the morning headlines. "I bet they pass a bill to outlaw the sale of rifles," he told me with visible enjoyment that afternoon, "and it won't be filibustered

either." The problem, as he learned later, was that his talk of guns
—and the attendant suggestion of violence—took on an inflated
priority that he was stuck with and obliged to defend for the rest
of his life. Sometimes, seen through the filter of our mass media,
he seemed to stand for nothing else.

His dalliance with the politics of armed struggle never pro-
gressed beyond rhetoric; the only weapon he was carrying at the
moment of his death was a tear-gas pen. But he understood the
uses of verbal violence as an outlet for black America's helpless
fury and as an instrument of assault on white America's unbudg-
ing resistance. "You have to walk in with a hand grenade and tell
the man, 'Listen, you give us what we've got coming or nobody is
going to get anything,'" he said at a Harlem rally in July 1964.
"Then he might listen to you. But if you go in there polite and
acting responsible and sane, why, you're wasting your time, you
have to be *in*sane." He spoke regularly of riot and revolution and
of the necessity for "reciprocal bloodshed" as against the one-way
flow then running in the South. "I am the man you think you are,"
he announced to white people; he meant that he would respond
as rudely and as dangerously as individuals historically have to the
systematic ruin of one's people.

Malcolm's objective in these flights of rhetoric was the liberation of the *invisible man* from his invisibility—from that vast physical and psychological distance white middle-class society has
placed between itself and the ghetto poor. It was a favorite formulation of his—a statement of his own past as busboy, boot-
black, and hustler—that the servant sees the master, but the master does not see the servant. The serving class, he told a
newspaper interviewer in early 1965, had to change that—had to
"make them see that we are the enemy. That the black man is a
greater threat to this country than Vietnam or Berlin. So let them
turn the money for defense in our direction and either destroy us
or cure the conditions that brought our people to this point." He
saw no way to make white power move except violence—or, as he
pointedly added, "a real threat of it." Yet even then the violence
in his rhetoric had less to do with guns than with manhood. "I
don't believe we're going to overcome [by] singing," he said at a
Harlem rally late in 1964. "If you're going to get yourself a .45
and start singing 'We Shall Overcome,' I'm with you." Malcolm

himself kept the only guns he owned at home, for the protection of his family; he talked about .45s because he wanted black and white Americans alike to understand that the .45 may be the last resort of people for whom there is no other redress.

Malcolm saw no possibility of redress whatever in the alternative posed by King and the mainstream movement—nonviolent actions whose unspoken objective was precisely to provoke white violence against unresisting black demonstrators. He saw nonviolence as degrading and beggarly—the rough equivalent, as he once said, of the sheep reminding the wolf that it was time for dinner. He contended that whites themselves had never practiced "this little passive resistance or wait-until-you-change-your-mind-and-then-let-me-up philosophy" but had conjured it up to unman the blacks when they began getting restless. "When the Japanese attacked Pearl Harbor," Malcolm told me in an interview in 1962, "Uncle Sam didn't say, 'Forget Pearl Harbor.' No—he said, '*Remember* Pearl Harbor.' Uncle Sam said, 'Praise the Lord and pass the ammunition.'"

Malcolm accordingly derided the notion that the movement of the 1960s could accurately be called a revolution. In his "Message to the Grassroots," recorded in 1963 and perhaps his single most influential public utterance, he reminded his black audience that *all* revolutions—the American, the French, the Russian, the Chinese, the Mau Mau—have spilled blood. There "was no love lost, was no compromise, was no negotiation. I'm telling you, you don't know what a revolution is, because when you find out what it is, you'll get back in the alley. You'll get out of the way. . . . Only kind of revolution that is nonviolent is the Negro revolution. The only revolution based on loving your enemy is the Negro revolution. The only revolution in which the goal is a desegregated lunch counter, a desegregated theater, a desegregated park, and a desegregated toilet. You can sit down next to white folks—on the toilet." No, he went on, revolution was bloody and destructive, not polite and nonviolent and psalm-singing, and not trusting in the conscience of its enemy. What the mainstream leadership called a revolution, Malcolm said, was more nearly like a shot of Novocain at the dentist's: "You sit there and 'cause you got all that Novocain in your jaw, you suffer—peacefully." He chuckled.

"Blood runnin' all down your jaw and you don't know what's happening, 'cause someone has taught you to suffer—peacefully."

For most of his public life, Malcolm's alternative to nonviolence was not violence but abstention. He was, for his dozen years in the service of the Nation of Islam, a doomsday fundamentalist; he taught and by every evidence believed that the time of the white devil was at hand and that Allah would shortly visit a terrible vengeance on him. Malcolm's increasing worldliness drew him to the edges of the struggle and to a kind of itchy restiveness to make himself and the Muslims part of it. "The Messenger [Muhammad] has seen God," he told Lomax during his last days as a Black Muslim. "He was with Allah and was given divine patience to deal with the devil. He is willing to wait for Allah to deal with this devil. Well, sir, the rest of us Black Muslims have not seen God, we don't have this gift of divine patience with the devil. The younger Black Muslims want to see some action."

The action they were taught to await was the apocalypse—the descent from space of a Mother Plane piloted by Allah; the release in turn of fifteen hundred "baby planes," each armed with high explosives and piloted by a black man so devoted to revenge that he had never smiled; a firestorm that would set the atmosphere ablaze for 310 years and destroy white life forever. The vision permitted the faithful a certain vicarious pleasure in natural and man-made catastrophes, which were taken to be harbingers of Allah's wrath; once, chafing under Muhammad's restraints, Malcolm announced the crash of a jetload of whites as "a very beautiful thing that has happened. . . . We call on our God and He gets rid of 120 of them at one whop." Otherwise, he lived with a policy of abstention so strict that Muhammad's Muslims were discouraged even from voting. It was a measure of the schizoid tensions this caused him that he could not join the great civil rights March on Washington of summer 1963 and yet could not stay away; he stood at the edge of the event, a bitter black chorus of one deriding it as a circus and a picnic—and acknowledging by his presence that it was locus of black America's heart and soul for a day.

The tug of the struggle drew Malcolm away from Muhammad, dangerously so, for his faith, and so did his discovery that the man he had revered for a decade as the Last Messenger of Allah had turned his pool of nubile young secretaries into a private harem. The erosion of his belief in Muhammad's moral authority quickened the secularization of his ministry even before he left the fold —turned his devotions to the Messenger into mechanical asides in a politics moving toward black nationalism and straining for action. "The Black Muslim movement has nothing within its mechanism that's designed to deal with things on this earth right now," he told Claude Lewis long after his departure. "Most of the Black Muslim movement's objectives are similar to those of the church, the only difference being that the church says you're going to die and go to the Promised Land, and in the Black Muslims I was taught that we get to the Promised Land when God comes and takes us there. Now, I believe in the Promised Land, and I believe in God. But I believe that we should be doing something toward trying to get to it right now. And if God wants to get into the act, good. But if He's not ready yet, we at least won't be sitting around here waiting."

Once on his own, Malcolm spent what little time was left him trying to create a new fighting faith on the wreckage of the old. He began by founding his own Muslim Mosque, Inc., and pledging his continuing allegiance to the gospels according to Muhammad, partly out of belief, partly out of obligation to the Old Muslims who followed him out of the Nation; he continued briefly to preach that whites were devils, that coexistence was impossible, and that the only course of deliverance for blacks was to separate to the African motherland or to a partitioned section of the United States. But his pilgrimage to Mecca and his electrifying exposure to the color-blind democracy of the *hajj* transformed his politics as certainly and as radically as his theology. He did not fall in love with white people, as some black cynics imagined then and some white liberals imagine now; he argued, on the contrary, that the racial climate in the United States remained poisoned against black people—irremediably poisoned, short of the mass conversion of white America to Islam. All he conceded was the humanity of white people—an admission that seemed, to him and to us, to be revolutionary.

Malcolm's ideological development thereafter was free-running, improvisational, and incomplete. Admirers of every tendency from integrationist to nationalist to revolutionary socialist

recognized passages of their own beliefs in his speeches and laid
posthumous claim to possession of the True Malcolm. Their contention, as his friend and lawyer Percy Sutton observed to me, was
rather like the ancient fable of the blind men and the elephant:
"One feels the ear, one feels the trunk, one feels the tail and so
on, and each of them thinks he can describe the whole animal."
The truth, as Malcolm himself kept telling us, was that he did not
know where he was going or what he wanted to be, except *flexible*.
He thought of himself as a teacher, a minister, a Muslim, an
African, an internationalist, and in the most general terms a revolutionary—and, before any of these things, as black. The details
were vague and fluid, subject to change *extempore* from speech to
speech or talk show to talk show. He was searching (some said
groping) for his bearings; in the meantime, he said straight out,
he would ride with the wind, changing his mind and his course as
circumstance changed around him. Where was he headed? "I
have no idea. I can capsulize how I feel—I'm for the freedom of
the twenty-two million Afro-Americans by any means necessary.
By any means necessary. I'm for a society in which our people are
recognized and respected as human beings, and I believe that we
have the right to resort to *any means necessary* to bring that about.
So when you ask me where I'm headed, what can I say? I'm
headed in any direction that will bring us some immediate results.
Isn't anything wrong with that."

By any means necessary: the words of Malcolm were program
enough, slogan enough, ideology enough. They carried a little
edge of menace, which troubled him not at all; they gave him
enormous political maneuvering room, which pleased him greatly.
He had trusted in fixed answers for most of his adult life and now
saw that they had betrayed him. He said, "I'm not dogmatic about
anything any more."

What ideology and program he had in his last months took
form out of the slow agglomeration of all those words he spilled
forth so extravagantly. On two long journeys to the Middle East
and Africa and in his regular rounds at the United Nations, he
made it his first priority to "internationalize" the struggle—to
form an alliance of interest and soul between black Americans
and the nonwhite world and to bring the United States to book
before the United Nations for its racist crimes. His international

politics ebbed and flowed between pan-Africanism—the unity of black people everywhere around their color and common origin in Africa—and a wider identification with the entire Third World from Cuba to Vietnam against the colonialist and capitalist white West. Which label more nearly fit him was not nearly so important as his underlying therapeutic purpose—making black and white Americans alike see themselves on a larger stage, where the old majority-minority arithmetic was reversed and the future, if not the present, belonged to the dark peoples. Late in his life, the Student Nonviolent Coordinating Committee brought a group of teenagers from McComb, Mississippi, to see Malcolm in Harlem —black children for whom even Jackson was a great and distant place—and Malcolm spent an afternoon telling them that there were men of power who looked like them and cared about them in Dar-es-Salaam and Accra and Conakry. "It is important," he told them, "for you to know that when you're in Mississippi, you're not alone."

The formal objective of Malcolm's diplomacy—his effort to bring a human rights case against America in the United Nations —was doomed by the realities of international politics and the dependence of the Third World on American foreign aid. Malcolm was brilliantly received on his travels down the corridors of African power; he met with heads of state, addressed the Ghanaian parliament, and was admitted with semi-official status to the second summit conference of the Organization of African Unity in Cairo—an occasion for which the certified representatives of the U.S. Department of State were largely outsiders looking in. "Our problems are your problems," Malcolm wrote in an impassioned memorandum to the conferees. ". . . We pray that our African brothers have not freed themselves of European colonialism only to be overcome and held in check now by American dollarism. Don't let American racism be 'legalized' by American dollarism." His lobbying was rewarded by the conference with a resolution—a rather guarded affair, praising the United States on the one hand for having passed the Civil Rights Act of 1964, worrying on the other about the continuing evidence of racial oppression, and concluding with the wish that Washington intensify its efforts against color discrimination. The sentiments were disappointingly tame for Malcolm and were substantially identical in thought and tone to a resolution passed without his help at the first all-African summit the year before. What was extraordinary was that he got anything at all; the reach and restraining power of American dollars were even more formidable than he had imagined, and the hedged little bill of reproof from the Africans was the only tangible victory his diplomacy ever won.

A strand of leftist rhetoric crept into Malcolm's public vocabulary in his last days, inspired by his encounters with African socialism and encouraged by Trotskyist and Maoist admirers back home. He continued to see color as central but not necessarily the single motivating force in his world; he began arguing that nonwhite people around the globe had not only their nonwhiteness in common but their exploitation by the West. Occasionally he identified capitalism straight out as an enemy—"You show me a capitalist, I'll show you a bloodsucker," he said—and socialism as the almost universal system among the new Third World nations coming into independence. "Instead of you running downtown picketing city hall," he told a Harlem audience, "you should stop and find out what they do over there to solve their problems. This is why the man doesn't want you and me to look beyond Harlem or beyond the shores of America . . . I mean, what they use to solve their problems is not capitalism."

But the politics of the Left has never sold well in the ghetto; Malcolm's public flirtation with its ideas and its vocabulary was an affair largely conducted downtown, not in Harlem, and it disappeared almost without a trace from his last interviews and speeches. He seemed then to be moving away from Marx and back to Allah—to the mosque as his real base of operations. Friends concluded that he was withdrawing from a system of thought and a society of people that had grown claustrophobic for him—a straitjacket as constricting as the one he had only just shucked off. "He had been moving with a number of people who thought they could use him," one close associate told me. "They didn't think Malcolm was as bright as he was. At the end, he was looking at where he would be the leader and where he would be the victim. . . . He wanted to detach from the Left and reassert himself as a Muslim. He wanted to really compete with Elijah Muhammad. He wanted to be his own man." Old friends who had always regretted his new comrades encouraged this trend—told him that he could use the pulpit as an instrument for social change, just as King had, and that he would be free to create whatever political theology he wanted. These friends believed, with some evidence, that they were winning; Malcolm in his last days had been certified in Cairo as a Sunni Muslim minister, had brought home an African imam as his spiritual adviser, had laid in a supply of orthodox Islamic literature, and was actively shopping for a mosque the day he died.

The shape that ministry might have taken is rather more difficult to define. Its value was precisely that it would have permitted him to say whatever he wanted and so would have suited his real genius. Malcolm was never as much a politician as a moral commentator on politics, and the Sunni mosque he sought would have given him an unencumbered pulpit of his own for the first time— a theater in which to assert his claim to recognition as an authentic man of God *and* as a legitimate political leader.

That recognition reached him only posthumously. Malcolm was perceived in his lifetime as a demonic presence at the edges of our field of sight—an angel of darkness contending with the angels of light for possession of the black soul. It was King who occupied center stage then and eclipsed everyone else in polls of black and white public opinion. Malcolm's day came later, out of the ruin of the riots and the desperation they revealed in the black casbahs of the urban North. T-shirts bearing his likeness appeared in the streets of Watts while the ashes of the rioting there in 1965 were still warm. King could not even go there; he attempted one peacemaking speech near the end of the uprising, was heckled mercilessly, and shortly thereafter left town. The streets were Malcolm's; he had lived there; he belonged. The destruction of the rioting would have appalled him, not because it was illegitimate in his eyes but because it wasted black lives and spoiled neighborhoods where black people lived. But he once guessed that if he had been home during the Harlem insurrection of 1964, he would have died fighting. It was the established leaders who referred to the street people as "they." To Malcolm, there was no such distance; they were always "you and me."

His vision of events was street vision, cynical and mocking, sometimes even cruel, and it held him back from participation in the movement even when he began gingerly to seek it. He helped

energize the established leaders, helped force them into a quick-
ening militancy, but he wounded them, too. "With Malcolm,"
Wilkins once told me, "the only way you could judge things was
whether you did the thing that was *manly,* no matter if it was
suicidal or not. A prosecutor like Malcolm has to be able to put
himself in the shoes of people who did the best they could under
the circumstances." Malcolm had no such gift of toleration. For
all his sense of history, he felt no empathy for the heroes and
heroines of that long middle passage in the black American past
when the National Association for the Advancement of Colored
People and the Urban League were all there was and you peti-
tioned and sued and even swallowed your pride and begged at the
back door if you had to. Malcolm assumed that what was middle
class was venal and that what was polite was cowardly. The mainstream leaders neither forgot nor forgave what he said about
them; even the younger radicals rather wished, nearly to the end
of Malcolm's life, that he would go away. The movement people
reciprocated insult for insult, but their answer to him finally was
that *they* had the bodies and the motion and the pulse of the
times; *they* were out in the rush of history, where the real battles
were fought and the real risks run, and he was not.

The older leaders never quit believing that. But the radical
young did cool off; they went into the 1960s as King's children
and came out Malcolm's. The process of disenchantment was a
broken one, not a revelation but a series of painful recognitions.
It came out of too many beatings and nights in jail and too many
funerals; out of the gathering suspicion that the federal government saw the events of the day not as a moral struggle but as a
contention of interests to be balanced; out of the political, social,
and sexual tensions between the northern white youngsters who
summered in the movement and the southern black youngsters
who would still be there when the whites went home; out of the
great compromise at the Democratic national convention in 1964,
at which the higher necessity of electing Lyndon Johnson took
precedence over the claims to justice of the disfranchised blacks
of Mississippi; out of the creeping paralysis of the old liberal
audience when the struggle moved North and got abrasive and
when ghettos started burning down; out of the discovery that integration was a delusive hope for the black poor, since they did not

have the money to be mobile, and, anyway, the liberals talking integration were not talking about integration with *them*.

Only then did Malcolm's path and that of the radical movement intersect, and with his death and the publication of the *Autobiography*, a process something like beatification began. He left his heirs little that was tangible beyond a legacy of words—his speeches became gospels of the new movement along with Fanon, and, later, Eldridge Cleaver—and an uncompleted set of priorities. It was the stresses that endured—the beauty, and the worth, of blackness; the racism endemic in American society; the legitimacy of defending oneself by any means, including violence; the irrelevance of integration for the black poor and the self-loathing implied in begging for it; the futility of appeals to conscience in the conscienceless; the necessity of connecting with Africa and with the African past; the central importance of confronting power with power, not supplication; the recognition that the separation of the races was not a program but a fact and that blacks ought therefore to control the life and politics of the black community. Malcolm otherwise left no strategy or platform for change; he was to have announced his program for the redemption of the blacks at his last rally, but the committee composing it for him brought it in late and heavy with the commonplaces of black nationalism, and he felt it was unready for publication. His bequest instead was a style of thought; it came back to us beginning in the summer of 1966 codified under a new name—Black Power—and the sayings of Minister Malcolm became the orthodoxies of a black generation.

He was most important as a prophetic figure in our race relations. He could be, as prophets often are, unreasonable; he could stretch, color, heighten, rearrange, distort, and grossly oversimplify the truth; he could contradict himself from speech to speech, or sentence to sentence. Garvey anticipated some of his vision, and Muhammad taught him a lot of it. But Malcolm transmuted the message and combined it with his intuitive genius for modern communications, and it was he in catalytic chemistry with his time who really began the difficult passage from Negro to black consciousness. Semantics was rather a vice of Malcolm's; he placed enormous importance, probably too much, on terminology, as though by redrawing the map one could alter the territory. He argued that the name "Negro" was itself a prison—that it disconnected black people from their land and their history and turned them into denatured, deracinated objects rather than men and women. He advanced this view when it was still a conscious political act to call oneself black—an affirmation of a word and a color that had been matters of shame in the past.

The central object of Malcolm's public life was to reverse that —to reveal to black people their worth as men and women and their competence to find their own way. The point was self-esteem, an assertion of size and place and what King called *somebodyness;* everything else in his politics and his theology was an elaboration of this inner purpose. The success or failure of his particular enterprises—his inability to organize the unorganized, or cobble up a platform, or bring America to justice before the nations of the world—was almost beside the point. He was dealing in symbolic action—attempting the liberation of black people by altering the terms in which they thought and the scale by which they measured themselves.

Malcolm's gift finally was not policy but polemic; he said things that black people had been afraid to say or even to think for years; he forced us to respond to him—forced whites to examine their consciences and blacks to confront their color. The beginning of his appeal for blacks was that he dared identify whites as the devil, and the continuing source of his authority was that he never quit thinking of them in the large as the enemy. Where King appealed to the higher instincts of black people, Malcolm addressed their viscera; he asked them not to sublimate their resentments but to recognize and express them, to turn their hatreds outward against their oppressors instead of inward against themselves. "He was a kind of alter ego for people who were too vulnerable and too insecure to say what they really felt regarding our situation in America," Eric Lincoln said in an interview. "He was trying to strip the white man of his mystique, and that made him a demagogue for most white people."

It made Malcolm an authentic folk hero for blacks, and it was they to whom he primarily addressed himself. His supreme gift to them was that he loved them, that he believed in their possibilities and tried to make them believe, too. His real legacy was his example, his bearing, his affirmation of blackness—his understanding that one is paralyzed for just as long as one believes one cannot move.

His collateral purpose was to educate whites as well—to expose them to the depths of black grievance against them. His message was that whites could neither define nor control black leadership by inviting those who most closely resembled them to the White House; that the goal of integration was a delusion when the sprawl of suburbia testified to the distance even liberal whites wanted to put between themselves and ordinary blacks; that the requirement that blacks address their demands to whites nonviolently was incongruent with our own violent history, from Lexington and Concord to Seoul and Saigon; that the ruin white America had visited on the blacks was about to be returned, out of the explosive anger of the inner cities; that in the back alleys of white consciousness, there were black people who hated whites in direct proportion as whites despised them, and who would rejoice in their deaths; that, for men and women so desperate, parades and pageants and marches on Washington were not an adequate surrogate experience. Whites called him irresponsible for saying so; Malcolm left us the burnt-out ruins of Watts and Newark and Detroit as his evidence. We protested that we were making progress; he responded by quoting what Patrice Lumumba had told the king of Belgium—*we can never forget these scars.*

The sad last irony for Malcolm was that his own martyrdom was a part of the price he had to pay for the legitimacy he had always wanted. The assassination and the *Autobiography* were bracketing events in a year that transformed our understanding of race in America by revealing the explosive furies just beneath the skin—the furies Malcolm had warned us so prophetically against. It was the winter of his death; the spring of the last of the great civil rights parades, from Selma to Montgomery, and the last of the great civil rights victories, the Voting Rights Act of 1965; the summer of the riot in Watts and the attending first signs of the collapse of the ad hoc American majority for racial justice. When Malcolm's memoirs were published that autumn, America was only just getting ready to listen to him, without the intervening scare image that he and the media had created together.

The celebration of Malcolm followed, with a fervor and an ecumenism that would have astonished him. It was an epiphany of his passage from manhood to myth that Amiri Baraka, then still LeRoi Jones, sent Whitney Young a greeting card bearing Malcolm's likeness one Christmas season; the card was meant as a token of unity, which Malcolm would have approved, but the fact that a nationalist like Baraka chose his image and an assimilationist like Young showed it around with pleasure suggested how little was left of Malcolm except his blackness and his sentimentalized legend. The process was carried out by blacks of every tendency—by those who had loved him and those who had been terrified by him; by nationalists and integrationists; by black Marxists and black capitalists; by scholars and street-gang children with nothing but the dimmest sense that Malcolm had been the *baddest;* even, *mirabile dictu,* by white people. Schoolboys from Harlem to Watts wore buttons proclaiming Malcolm OUR SHINING BLACK PRINCE. Black students put on festivals on his birthday. A publicly funded college in Chicago was named after him; so were a Democratic club in Harlem and a black enlisted men's association in the military. The Nebraska Historical Society authorized a marker near his birthplace in Omaha. A black woman officeholder in Washington waved away the Bible at her swearing-in and substituted a copy of the *Autobiography.* Two plays, a movie, a book of poems, and even a ballet were done about him. His memoir and his speeches sold in the hundreds of thousands and were required reading at dozens of universities.

The consecration in the end nearly drained Malcolm's public life of real meaning; his gifts and flaws, his public passion and his private ironies, were smoothed flat and stylized, like the holy men burning coolly in a Byzantine icon. By the mid-1970s, with the death of Muhammad and the gentling succession of his son Wallace to the leadership of the old Lost-Found Nation, even the Muslim mosque in Harlem was named for him; a temple that had once been a center of revanchist incitement against him thus became our most imposing brick-and-mortar monument to his memory. In the streets his memory has receded into a kind of gauzy half-light. A black psychologist mentioned Malcolm's name to a class of teen-aged street youngsters in Harlem and got only the dimmest show of recognition; he displayed Malcolm's photograph, narrow-tied and Ivy-tailored, and was asked, "Why the dude dress so funny?" But the young blacks in that classroom, who were in diapers when Malcolm died, were raised by parents who knew who Malcolm was and were touched by him. Malcolm survives to the extent that they see themselves as he saw them: as men and women of worth, beauty, and untested possibility in white America.

Alex Haley Remembers
by Alex Haley

Destiny has made of Malcolm X a legend, symbol, martyr, saint, hero, prince and inspiration. Alex Haley knew the man. Over a two-year period, from 1963 to 1965, Haley conducted the fifty interviews with Malcolm that produced both The Autobiography of Malcolm X *and a close, warm, trusting friendship between the two collaborators. In this remembrance published in* Essence *magazine in November 1983, nearly two decades after Malcolm's death, Haley recalls the man he knew—the family man as well as the public man— and honors the trust of his friend.*

Time passes so swiftly, but I'm still astounded that it really is eighteen years since that Sunday in February 1965: Malcolm X, then thirty-nine years old and known as El Hajj Malik El-Shabazz, had begun to speak in Harlem's Audubon Ballroom when suddenly gunfire erupted and he fell bleeding from multiple wounds. He was rushed to the hospital, where surgeons tried desperately to save him by opening his chest for direct manual heart massage—but soon a hospital spokesperson or somebody told the press and the swelling, weeping, almost mutinous crowd that had kept vigil, "The gentleman you know as Malcolm X is dead." Through the two years before then, I'd been privileged that Malcolm had given me about fifty lengthy and probing interviews to use as the basis of a book chronicling his life. Now and then he would comment that he wouldn't live to see the book published— and he was right.

During 1960, *Reader's Digest* had commissioned me to write an article about the ten hotly controversial Black Muslims. I first met Malcolm when he was their chief spokesperson. The next year I interviewed him for *Playboy*. The article offered a glimpse of a precocious child growing up in a small Michigan town through the Depression years who then became a teenage hustler in a Boston ghetto, moved on to Harlem and heavier crimes, was eventually arrested and convicted and served over six years in a penitentiary. By the time of his release he was an impassioned convert to the Nation of Islam, of which he ultimately became its most publicized minister and national spokesperson. A book publisher wanted me to obtain Malcolm X's full life story, and finally Malcolm agreed, while cautioning me sternly, "A writer is what I want, not an interpreter." I was elated to try my first book with a subject so obviously exciting.

Usually two nights a week, sometimes three, Malcolm would park his blue Oldsmobile somewhere near my Greenwich Village apartment. It was probably bugged by the FBI, and always Malcolm would snap, "One, two, three—testing!" when he first came in. Next he'd telephone his wife, Betty Shabazz, tell her where he was and jot down messages she gave him. Then, rather than take a seat, for the first half hour, at least, he preferred pacing the room like some caged tiger, talking nonstop about the Nation of Islam and its leader in Chicago, Elijah Muhammad. Whenever I'd gently remind him that the subject of the book was him, Malcolm's hackles would rise. One wintry midnight, however, in sheer frustration I blurted, "Mr. Malcolm, could you tell me something about your mother?" He turned, his pacing slowed, and I'll never forget the look on his face—even his voice sounded different. "It's funny you ask me that . . . I can remember her dresses, they were all faded out and gray. I remember how she bent over the stove, trying to stretch what little we had. . . ."

It was near dawn when Malcolm left for home, having spilled from his memory most of what I'd later use in the first chapter of *The Autobiography of Malcolm X,* appropriately titled "Nightmare." It tells the story of the small boy, Malcolm Little, one of eight children watching their mother's struggles to keep the family intact after the brutal, racially motivated murder of their father, a militantly outspoken Baptist minister and supporter of Marcus Garvey. After that session Malcolm never hesitated to relate any aspect of his later life in the most detail his memory could muster. And I find myself now experiencing a diversity of emotions as I recall random memories of that truly singular and very special human being.

I think my most indelible memory is of how ably he maintained his characteristic manner of controlled calm, when actually he lived amid a veritable cauldron of private and public pressures. Easily the source of most intense pressure was his role as the Nation of Islam's most public figure, while in fact he had been made virtually a pariah within the organization's top hierarchy. This status was due to, as Malcolm put it, "jealousies caused by others' refusal to accept that, when I did my appointed job as the Nation's spokesman, inevitably publicity would focus on me. I think Mr. Muhammad understood that, until others poisoned his mind against me." Nearly a year of our frequent interviewing had passed before he astonished me with a hint of that later public revelation.

Nonetheless, he carried on as "spokesman," maintaining such a grueling public-speaking schedule throughout the United States that some weeks he caught airplanes like taxis. And his blue Oldsmobile stayed on the go when he was in New York. There, particularly, he often faced hostile media people, and this helped him hone his verbal agility into practically an art form.

Malcolm was a master at deftly goading white verbal opponents into such a fury that they could only sputter almost incoherently. "The more the white man yelps, the more I know I have struck a nerve," Malcolm said. A hundred times, if once, I watched his face suddenly crease into a foxlike grin as an angry opponent struggled to retain composure, and then Malcolm would fire verbal missiles anew. He would turn a radio or television program to his advantage in a way he credited to the boxing ring's great Sugar Ray Robinson, who would dramatize a round's last thirty seconds. Similarly Malcolm would eye the big studio clock, and at the instant it showed thirty seconds to go, he'd pounce in and close the show with his own verbal barrage.

Malcolm was at his most merciless with any black opponent who he believed dared to publicly defend whites. His worst victim, probably, was a famed Harvard University associate professor (who was also a Ph.D.), in their widely publicized debate. The professor had been continually attacking Malcolm as a "divisive demagogue" and a "reverse racist" when Malcolm, in the debate's closing seconds, fired back, "Do you know what white racists call black Ph.D.'s?: 'Nigger!' "

But there could also be quite another side of Malcolm X. I just have to laugh, recalling one night during our interviews when he was reminiscing about his finesse as a dancer. Springing up suddenly, with one hand grabbing a radiator pipe to represent a girl, he wildly lindy-hopped for maybe a full minute before suddenly stopping. He sat down, clearly embarrassed, and was practically surly for the rest of that session.

And I remember Malcolm one time laughing so raucously that he could hardly tell me the details of how he had once been menaced in his prison cell by an armed guard and how he had struck instant terror into the man. Abruptly jerking him so close that their noses touched, Malcolm had hissed, "You put a finger on me, I'll start a rumor you're really black, just passing for white!"

And I remember a late afternoon when we happened to be interviewing in a Philadelphia hotel room. A pretty lady volunteer telephoned, then visited, bringing only half of some important typing she was doing for Malcolm and saying that he should pick up the rest at her apartment later. It was obvious to us both: she had eyes for Malcolm. He fretted and stewed and finally asked me to take a taxi and make the pickup. When I returned to my room, the phone was ringing, with Malcolm demanding, "What else did you do, because anything you did wrong was in my name." I told him that as mad as that woman had been when I turned up, there was no way anybody could have damaged his name with her.

"I must be purer than Caesar's wife," Malcolm would often say, hypersensitive that any hint of wrongdoing could so easily become gossip capable of damaging his public image and credibility. And that public presence was indeed so awesome that wherever Malcolm appeared, it was rather like witnessing a force in motion. I saw the man's impact on people many different times and ways. On one afternoon when we were driving in Harlem, Malcolm suddenly jammed on the brakes and sprang from the car. Running across the street, to the sidewalk, Malcolm crouched like an avenger over three young black men whom he'd seen shooting dice near the entrance to the Schomburg Collection of Negro

Literature and History, as it was then called. "Beyond those doors is the world's greatest collection of books about black people!" he raged at the young gamblers. "Other people are in there studying your people while you're outside shooting craps!" The three practically slinked away before Malcolm's wrath. He used to exclaim, "Man, lots of times I just wish I could start back in school, from about the sixth grade. Man, I'd be the last one out of that library every night!"

Although Malcolm X was acutely aware of the physical risks he steadily faced, he was determined not to let the danger muzzle his voice or inhibit his activities. He felt that his greatest safety lay in really trusting only a few people—and those few only to certain degrees. The late author Louis Lomax and I used to laugh about how we didn't discover until much later that once Malcolm had visited and given each of us interviews in different rooms in the same hotel, with never a mention to either about the other, although he knew well that Lomax and I were good friends. When Malcolm and I began the book project, he told me candidly, "I want you to know I trust you twenty-five percent." (Much later I felt great personal gratification when he upped the trust to seventy percent.) Now or then during our interviews he'd mention some people who seemed to me quite close to him—adding a startlingly low trust percentage.

Squarely atop Malcolm's trust list was his wife, Betty Shabazz, of whom he said, "She's the only person I'd trust with my life. That means I trust her more than I do myself." He felt genuine admiration for her, even awe, along with a deep sense of guilt that, while he was so often away from home, she somehow managed to be simultaneously a homemaker, a mother of three—then four—little girls, as well as his busy secretary and telephone answering service. He made it practically a fetish never to stop without immediately telephoning his Betty, saying candidly, "If my work won't let me be there, at least she can always know where I am."

I'm fascinated by the similarities between Malcolm X and Dr. Martin Luther King, Jr., that I observed. For instance, neither could have been much less concerned about acquiring material possessions, and both were obsessed with their work but felt guilty about being away from their families.

Vividly I remember Dr. King recalling among his hardest moments the feeling of mingled anger and shame he had when he and Mrs. King had to explain to their small daughter, Yolanda, that a radio ad for an event she wanted to attend was not meant for their race. Equally vividly I remember Malcolm's sadness one night when he had overlooked buying a present for his daughter, Attallah, for her fourth birthday—and how he beamed when I surprised him with my intended gift, a black walking doll, and insisted that it be his gift instead.

The two men, who pursued their widely variant philosophies (toward the same goal, I believe), met only once, briefly, with photographers recording their smiles and handshake during the 1963 March on Washington—and I smile, remembering the keen private concern each had for the other's opinion of him. I was in the midst of interviewing Malcolm for the book when I traveled to Atlanta to interview Dr. King for *Playboy* magazine. His ever pressured schedule meant I had to make several visits. Dr. King would always let maybe an hour pass before he'd casually ask, "By the way, what's Brother Malcolm saying about me these days?" I'd give some discreetly vague response, and then back in New York, I'd hear from Malcolm, "All right, tell me what he said about me!" to which I'd also give a vague reply. I'm convinced that privately the two men felt mutual admiration and respect. And I've surely no question that they would be pleased to no end to know that their daughters, Yolanda and Attallah, today are friends who work closely together in a theater group.

Attallah is the oldest of the quartet of daughters Malcolm and Betty had by late January 1965, and Malcolm, proud as a peacock that his Betty was yet again pregnant, yet again exulted, "That's that boy!"—one he wished for. But then, as fate chose to play its hand, seven months after Malcolm's interment in the Ferncliff Cemetery in Hartsdale, New York, the widowed Betty Shabazz bore twin girls—whom she named Malaak and Malikah.

The young widow was caught up in a situation that bore graphic similarity to Malcolm's mother's circumstances some thirty years earlier. With six small children—and with her dynamic, outspoken controversial husband brutally murdered—Betty Shabazz, a trained nurse, set out to train and provide for those children in the very best way she could. Attallah, who was then six, remembers, "Our mother kept our home strictly private, and she kept a very low profile, which immensely helped us. We knew she was grieving and that she was working very hard—we were just too little to realize how much of either."

Actress Ruby Dee, with colleagues and friends, raised funds to aid in the down payment on a home for Betty and the children in Mount Vernon, New York. (Later, when my book *Roots* made it possible, I signed over to Betty Shabazz my half of the royalties on the *Autobiography*.) Betty and Malcolm had been determined that the girls receive an excellent education, so Betty worked to increase her own earning power by enrolling at the University of Massachusetts at Amherst, to which she commuted. She won her Ph.D. with honors and later joined the faculty of Medgar Evers College of the City of the University of New York, where today she is director of institutional advancement. Through eighteen years of scrimping, sacrificing, counseling and mothering, she has raised the six daughters to be active young women, who are now pursuing a wide variety of careers.

Of the twins, aged seventeen, Malaak is a college biochemistry major, while Malikah studies architecture. At another college, an apartment is shared by Gamilah, nineteen, studying theater arts, and Ilyasah, twenty-one, majoring in biology. Qubilah, twenty-two, has lived in Paris for four years, studying and working as a journalist. And Attallah, twenty-four, does two hundred-odd theatrical performances annually with her and Yolanda King's group, Nucleus, as well as consultant work in hair care and makeup and clothes designing for private clients.

Of the daughters only Attallah has any memory of her famed father. "Ilyasah can't remember how, when our father telephoned our mother to say he was coming home, she'd always go and sit by the door to wait," says Attallah. "And then he'd put all four of us up on his two big knees and just talk and talk to us and laugh a lot. I remember just his presence was so very calming for us kids."

Malcolm X started me writing books, for which I am most grateful, and from the early days of working with him, I have tried to approach his degree of self-discipline. Looking back, I feel that

Malcolm eminently succeeded in achieving a private goal that he once expressed to me: he believed that somehow, every day, he must demonstrate that only a defiant courage could break the fetters still impeding his beloved black people.

Who Were the Killers?
by Maria Laurino

Political assassinations spawn conspiracy theories. The three most common theories to evolve since the death in 1965 of Malcolm X connect his assassination either to the Black Muslims in the Nation of Islam, to the CIA, or to the FBI and the New York City Police Department. In the following piece, which appeared originally in the Village Voice *on February 26, 1985, Maria Laurino, then a staff writer for the paper, investigates these three theories and raises again the unsettling—and unanswered—questions posed by the assassination of Malcolm X.*

That Sunday, February 21, 1965, when Malcolm X went to address a rally at Harlem's Audubon Ballroom, he knew he would soon die. He had telephoned Alex Haley the day before, his voice shaken, saying that he was looking for a new home for his family since his house had been firebombed the week before. In the preceding months, Malcolm had become violently ill in Cairo and believed that American agents had tried to poison him. His split with the Honorable Elijah Muhammad created a hatred among members of the Nation of Islam who had tried to attack him in Los Angeles and Chicago just weeks before. He was surrounded by hostile forces. Malcolm X entered the Audubon on Sunday afternoon and greeted the crowd with his customary *"Assalaam alaikum,"* when a disturbance erupted in the back of the hall. His attention diverted, Malcolm was killed by a shotgun fifteen feet away.

Twenty years later—with three Muslim men serving jail sentences of twenty-five years to life for killing Malcolm X—many questions raised during the trial have still never been answered.

Three schools of thought about his assassination have developed
since then. The simplest theory is that the Muslims were solely
responsible for his death. Malcolm knew he had to leave the Nation of Islam after he learned that his revered leader, Elijah
Muhammad, had fathered illegitimate children—a violation of
Muslim law—and after he had been silenced by Muhammad for a
comment he made about JFK's assassination. Some of his fellow
Muslims, calling him a traitor, turned against him and wanted him
dead.

A second theory put forth is that the CIA played an active role
in Malcolm's death. In the months before he was killed, Malcolm
had become a major international figure. The CIA and the State
Department were following him throughout his travels in Africa,
and proponents of this theory argue that the government saw
Malcolm X's growing popularity abroad as a clear threat to
American interests. And he was organizing to get a resolution
adopted at the United Nations condemning the U.S. for human
rights violations. On February 9, Malcolm was mysteriously
barred by the French government from entering their country.
According to this view of the events, while the Muslims may have
pulled the trigger, the CIA was behind the murder.

Others who have studied the assassination argue that the FBI
and the New York City police were involved. Clearly, the FBI was
following Malcolm—he had tape-recorded conversations with
FBI agents who had come to his home. The agents tried to pay off
Malcolm in return for the names of the Nation of Islam's members. The Church Commission's Select Committee to Study Government Operations contains references to the FBI tapping his
phone. The New York City police's Bureau of Special Services
(BOSS) had been investigating Malcolm and they had every reason to know his life was in danger. Yet the police failed to provide
adequate protection in the last months of his life.

Malcolm X, in his last conversation with Haley, said that he
believed the forces who were trying to kill him were more powerful than the Nation of Islam. Malcolm originally believed his
house was firebombed by Muslims. Later he modified this position, telling Haley, "But, you know, I'm going to tell you something, brother—the more I keep thinking about this thing . . .
I'm not all that sure it's the Muslims. I know what they can do,

and what they can't, and they can't do some of the stuff recently going on. . . ."

"I don't believe the Nation of Islam alone could have pulled off the assassination that day," Paul Lee, a Malcolm X scholar who has spent the past nine years researching his life, told the *Voice*. Lee says that since Malcolm X had chosen to bar the press from the rally that day, reporters and cameramen were waiting outside the Audubon. The assassins, he believes, had assurances not to worry about the police or the press. "Right now we can draw some general conclusions. . . . Malcolm was a threat to the state of New York and this country. I think the Nation of Islam was used as a tool."

During the last weeks of Malcolm X's life, the Muslims tried to attack him on four separate occasions. But these incidents, which took place in New York, Los Angeles, and Chicago, received virtually no press attention and no arrests were made. The Sunday that he was killed there were only two plainclothesmen in a room next to the ballroom where Malcolm addressed the crowd. The rest of the unit was waiting at the nearest public building, Columbia Presbyterian Medical Center.

The police say that they had offered Malcolm increased protection that week, but he had refused it. This account, however, differs from the stories of Malcolm's associates, who said he had complained of the insufficient security. Lee charges that the police should be convicted "not of benign, but criminal neglect. They peeled away [security] at the time that it should have been most visible."

Talmadge Hayer, also known as Thomas Hagan, was the only one of the three convicted men who was caught by the crowd that day. The initial accounts of the murder in the daily papers said that the police had caught two suspects. George Breitman wrote in *The Assassination of Malcolm X* that the press reported that Hayer and another man were seized outside the Audubon. Hayer was taken to Bellevue prison ward and the other suspect was brought to police headquarters. But the second editions of both the *Herald Tribune* and *The New York Times* dropped the accounts of the second person. The *Tribune* headline read, "Police Rescue One Suspect." Breitman asserts that the second suspect might have been a police agent who was driven away from the scene.

Peter Goldman, a *Newsweek* senior editor and author of *The Death and Life of Malcolm X* rejects the conspiracy theories about Malcolm's death. Goldman says that the police found only one suspect—Hayer—but in the confusion of the events it was reported as two people. "It is a trait of conspiratorialists to doubt everything about the establishment press except its mistakes," asserts Goldman.

In 1979, nearly fifteen years after the assassination, however, Goldman did modify his position that "there was substantial evidence against all three men," and questions if two of the convicted men are innocent. Significant evidence has been put forth that the other two accused men—Thomas 15X Johnson (now known as Khalil Islam) and Norman 3X Butler (Muhammad Abdul Aziz) were not at the Audubon the day of the murder. Hayer admitted during the trial that he shot Malcolm X, but testified that Butler and Johnson were not a part of the murder plan. (Both Johnson and Butler were well-known New York Muslims and those familiar with Malcolm have asserted that neither would have been able to enter the Audubon without having been immediately stopped.) Since Hayer would not say who his accomplices were, the prosecution maintained that he merely tried to get Johnson and Butler off the hook.

But in 1977 Hayer gave attorney William Kunstler detailed descriptions of the four men who he says were part of the scheme, and carefully explained the assassination plot. According to Hayer, the men were Muslims from the Nation of Islam Mosque No. 25 in Newark, New Jersey. Kunstler maintains that Hayer's description of one of the assailants matches an FBI report he obtained: "A member of the NOI (Nation of Islam) from Paterson, New Jersey [who was a member of the Newark mosque], sitting in the last seat on the right side, facing the stage who is believed . . . to be one of the assassins."

Kunstler's argument gained national attention when Mike Wallace reported in a 1981 *60 Minutes* that Butler and Johnson may have been falsely accused of Malcolm X's murder. Wallace interviewed Benjamin Goodman, an assistant of Malcolm who introduced him to the audience that afternoon. Goodman (now known as Benjamin Karim) says that he knew Butler and Thomas and they were not there that day. Goodman had originally testified before the grand jury, but neither the defense nor prosecution called him as a witness during the trial. Wallace also found another witness who now says he lied when he told the jury that he saw Butler and Johnson at the Audubon.

Years later it was discovered that Gene Roberts, who was in the Audubon when Malcolm was shot, was then an undercover cop for BOSS. Roberts was photographed giving Malcolm mouth-to-mouth resuscitation, but he never testified during the trial. When Roberts testified at the Panther 21 trial in 1970 it was revealed that he had infiltrated the Black Panthers in the late sixties, and he was identified as the same person in the assassination photo.

The Manhattan DA's office has filed motions that Hayer's confession is similar to his original testimony and Judge Harold Rothwax has refused to reopen the case based on the evidence he's received. Kunstler, who files for executive clemency for these men at this time every year, has submitted this information to the Congressional Black Caucus. But he explains that Malcolm X's wife, Betty Shabazz, does not want the case reopened, and the Caucus has respected her wishes. Shabazz told the *Voice* that she would not comment on the assassination.

Hayer (now known as Mujabid Abdul Halim) had originally asked Kunstler to represent him in 1965, but the attorney said he refused because of his respect for Malcolm X. But when Hayer invited him to prison and spoke about the innocence of the other men, Kunstler decided to take the case. Kunstler says that he doesn't believe the FBI was directly involved, "But they created the atmosphere where it could occur." He accuses the FBI of discrediting the Nation of Islam and creating hatred between the followers of Elijah Muhammad and Malcolm X. "In their minds they were doing a service. I know that's what motivated Hayer."

To talk against Elijah Muhammad was to talk against God, and Malcolm, in the eyes of the Nation of Islam, committed a heresy. One of the most scathing attacks against Malcolm was led by Louis Farrakhan (known at the time as Minister Louis X): "Only those who wish to be led to hell, or their doom, will follow Malcolm. The die is set, and Malcolm shall not escape, especially after such evil, foolish talk about his benefactor (Elijah Muhammad) in trying to rob him of the divine glory which Allah has bestowed upon him. Such a man as Malcolm is worthy of death. . . ."

Vicious death wishes such as Farrakhan's strengthen, to Paul Lee, the theory that the FBI and the police neglected to adequately protect Malcolm. "I find it impossible to believe that a death threat that broad didn't pass by an FBI agent."

Peter Bailey, president of the New York Association of Black Journalists, who was a member of Malcolm's Organization of Afro-American Unity, and who sat in the Audubon the day that Malcolm was shot, says that one cannot separate Malcolm's growing international importance and his death. "There was tremendous coverage about him in African newspapers." Bailey believes there is a pattern between Malcolm being barred from France, the fire that destroyed his home, and the assassination—three events that took place in just two weeks. It was the influence of an organization "higher than the New York City police" says Bailey.

In Peter Goldman's detailed work about Malcolm's death he argues that Malcolm's violent illness in Cairo was probably food poisoning; the French government refused him for French-African, not French-American reasons; and his proposed resolution before the UN was not a major threat to this country. J. Edgar Hoover, according to Goldman, was more interested in Martin Luther King, Jr., than Malcolm X. Lastly, Goldman maintains the New York City police knew that Malcolm wouldn't want them too close to his rally, so it was logical to deploy only two men in the room next to where Malcolm was to speak.

Yet such neat solutions do not address the government's fear of Malcolm and black nationalism, the state's unwillingness to reopen the case despite the fact that two innocent men may be in jail, and the seeming indifference toward protecting an American citizen whose life was in imminent danger. In an examination of the assassination on Gil Noble's *Like It Is* program in 1981, he stated that the cruelest irony of his death was "that Malcolm was murdered by members of his own race, the very people he was fighting for . . ." But twenty years later, the unanswered questions about the assassination and the obvious police neglect that transpired in the Harlem ballroom that afternoon, leave an unsettling feeling about the forces which gave such certainty to Malcolm's prophecy of his own death.

Malcolm and Martin
by *James Baldwin*

A distance separates the Northern ghetto from the Southern parish, and the city street is not a seminary. Likewise, militant self-defense stands no closer to passive resistance than do hard facts to the glory of a dream. In his brief but dynamic career Malcolm X, proud and filled with rage, shared little with the peacemaking Martin Luther King, Jr. Or so it would appear: "By the time each met his death," James Baldwin argues, "there was practically no difference between them." In this essay, which was first printed by Esquire *magazine in April 1972, foremost American author James Baldwin embraces the fateful experience of both Malcolm and Martin—however divergent their paths, ambitions, stances, strategy—to illuminate the condition of being black in America.*

Since Martin's death, in Memphis, and that tremendous day in Atlanta, something has altered in me, something has gone away. Perhaps even more than the death itself, the manner of his death has forced me into a judgment concerning human life and human beings which I have always been reluctant to make—indeed, I can see that a great deal of what the knowledgeable would call my lifestyle is dictated by this reluctance. Incontestably, alas, most people are not, in action, worth very much; and yet every human being is an unprecedented miracle. One tries to treat them as the miracles they are, while trying to protect oneself against the disasters they've become. This is not very different from the act of faith demanded by all those marches and petitions while Martin was still alive. One could scarcely be deluded by Americans anymore, one scarcely dared expect anything from the great, vast, blank generality; and yet one was compelled to demand of Americans—and for their sakes, after all—a generosity, a clarity, and a nobility which they did not dream of demanding of themselves. Part of the error was irreducible, in that the marchers and petitioners were forced to suppose the existence of an entity which, when the chips were down, could not be located—i.e., there *are* no American people yet. Perhaps, however, the moral of the story (and the hope of the world) lies in what one demands, not of others, but of oneself. However that may be, the failure and the betrayal are in the record book forever, and sum up and condemn, forever, those descendants of a barbarous Europe who arbitrarily and arrogantly reserve the right to call themselves Americans.

The mind is a strange and terrible vehicle, moving according to rigorous rules of its own; and my own mind, after I had left Atlanta, began to move backward in time, to places, people, and events I thought I had forgotten. Sorrow drove it there, I think, sorrow, and a certain kind of bewilderment, triggered, perhaps, by something which happened to me in connection with Martin's funeral.

When Martin was murdered, I was based in Hollywood, working—working, in fact, on the screen version of *The Autobiography of Malcolm X*. This was a difficult assignment, since I had known Malcolm, after all, crossed swords with him, worked with him, and held him in that great esteem which is not easily distinguishable, if it is distinguishable at all, from love. (The Hollywood gig did not work out because I did not wish to be a party to a second assassination: but we will return to Hollywood, presently.)

Very shortly before his death, I had to appear with Martin at Carnegie Hall, in New York. Having been on the Coast so long, I had nothing suitable to wear for my Carnegie Hall gig, and so I rushed out, got a dark suit, got it fitted, and made my appearance. Something like two weeks later, I wore this same suit to Martin's funeral; returned to Hollywood; presently, had to come East again, on business. I ran into Leonard Lyons one night, and I told him that I would never be able to wear that suit again. Leonard put this in his column. I went back to Hollywood.

Weeks later, either because of a civil rights obligation, or because of Columbia Pictures, I was back in New York. On my desk in New York were various messages—and it must be said that my sister, Gloria, who worked for me then, is extremely selective, not to say brutal, about the messages she leaves on my desk. I don't see, simply, most of the messages I get. I couldn't conceivably live with them. No one could—as Gloria knows. However, my best friend, black, when I had been in junior high school, when I was twelve or thirteen, had been calling and calling and calling. The guilt of the survivor is a real guilt—as I was now to discover. In a way that I may never be able to make real for my countrymen, or myself, the fact that I had "made it"; that is, had been seen on television, and at Sardi's, could (presumably!) sign a check anywhere in the world, could, in short, for the length of an entrance, a dinner, or a drink, intimidate headwaiters by the use of a name which had not been mine when I was born and which love had compelled me to make my own, meant that I had betrayed the people who had produced me. Nothing could be more unutterably paradoxical: to have thrown in your lap what you never dreamed of getting, and, in sober, bitter truth, could never have dreamed of having, and that at the price of an assumed betrayal of your brothers and your sisters! One is always disproving the accusation in action as futile as it is inevitable.

I had not seen this friend—who could scarcely, any longer, be called a friend—in many years. I was brighter, or more driven than he—not my fault!—and, though neither of us knew it then, our friendship really ended during my ministry and was deader than my hope of heaven by the time I left the pulpit, the church, and home. Hindsight indicates, obviously, that this particular rupture, which was, of necessity, exceedingly brutal and which involved, after all, the deliberate repudiation of everything and everyone that had given me an identity until that moment, must have left some scars. The current of my life meant that I did not see this person very often, but I was always terribly guilty when I did. I was guilty because I had nothing to say to him, and at one time I had told him everything, or nearly everything. I was guilty because he was just another post-office worker, and we had dreamed such tremendous futures for ourselves. I was guilty because he and his family had been very nice to me during an awful time in my life and now none of that meant anything to me. I was guilty because I knew, at the bottom of my heart, that I judged this unremarkable colored man very harshly, far more harshly than I would have done if he were white, and I knew this to be unjust as well as sinister. I was furious because he thought my life was easy and I thought my life was hard, and I yet had to see that by his lights, certainly, and by any ordinary yardstick, my life was enviable compared to his. And if, as I kept saying, it was not my fault, it was not *his* fault, either.

You can certainly see why I tended to avoid my old school chum. But I called him, of course. I thought that he probably needed money, because that was the only thing, by now, that I could possibly hope to give him. But, no. He, or his wife, or a relative, had read the Leonard Lyons column and knew that I had a suit I wasn't wearing, and—as he remembered in one way and I in quite another—he was just my size.

Now, for me, that suit was drenched in the blood of all the crimes of my country. If I had said to Leonard, somewhat melo-dramatically, no doubt, that I could never wear it again, I was, just the same, being honest. I simply could not put it on, or look at it, without thinking of Martin, and Martin's end, of what he had meant to me, and to so many. I could not put it on without a bleak, pale, cold wonder about the future. I could not, in short, live with it, it was too heavy a garment. Yet—it was only a suit, worn, at most, three times. It was not a very expensive suit, but it was still more expensive than any my friend could buy. He could not afford to have suits in his closet which he didn't wear, he couldn't afford to throw suits away—he couldn't, in short, afford my elegant despair. Martin was dead, but *he* was living, he needed a suit, and—I was just his size. He invited me for dinner that evening, and I said that I would bring him the suit.

The American situation being what it is, and American taxi driv-ers being what they mostly are, I have, in effect, been forbidden to expose myself to the quite tremendous hazards of getting a cab to stop for me in New York, and have been forced to hire cars. Naturally, the car which picked me up on that particular guilty evening was a Cadillac limousine about seventy-three blocks long, and, naturally, the chauffeur was white. Neither did he want to drive a black man through Harlem to the Bronx, but American democracy has always been at the mercy of the dollar: the chauf-feur may not have liked the gig, but he certainly wasn't about to lose the bread. Here we were, then, this terrified white man and myself, trapped in this leviathan, eyed bitterly, as it passed, by a totally hostile population. But it was not the chauffeur which the population looked on with such wry contempt: I held the suit over my arm, and was tempted to wave it: *I'm only taking a suit to a friend!*

I knew how they felt about black men in limousines—unless they were popular idols—and I couldn't blame them, and I knew that I could never explain. We found the house, and, with the suit over my arm, I mounted the familiar stairs.

I was no longer the person my friend and his family had known and loved—I was a stranger now, and keenly aware of it, and trying hard to act, as it were, normally. But nothing *can* be normal in such a situation. They *had* known me, and they *had* loved me; but now they couldn't be blamed for feeling, *He thinks he's too good for us now.* I certainly didn't feel that, but I had no conceivable relationship to them anymore—that shy, popeyed thirteen-year-old my friend's mother had scolded and loved was no more. *I* was not the same, but *they* were, as though they had been trapped, preserved, in that moment in time. They seemed scarcely to have grown any older, my friend and his mother, and they greeted me as they had greeted me years ago, though I was now well past forty and felt every hour of it. My friend and I remained alike only in that neither of us had gained any weight. His face was as boyish as ever, and his voice; only a touch of gray in his hair proved that we were no longer at P.S. 139. And my life came with me into their small, dark, unspeakably respectable, incredibly hard-won rooms like the roar of champagne and the odor of brimstone. They still believed in the Lord, but I had quarreled with Him, and offended Him, and walked out of His house. They didn't smoke, but they knew (from seeing me on television) that I did, and they had placed about the room, in deference to me, those hideous little ashtrays which can hold exactly one cigarette butt. And there was a bottle of whiskey, too, and they asked me if I wanted steak or chicken; for, in my travels, I might have learned not to like fried chicken anymore. I said, much relieved to be able to tell the truth, that I preferred chicken. I gave my friend the suit.

My friend's stepdaughter is young, considers herself a militant, and we had a brief argument concerning Bill Styron's *Nat Turner,* which I suggested that she read before condemning. This rather shocked the child, whose militancy, like that of many, tends to be a matter of indigestible fury and slogans and quotations. It rather checked the company, which had not imagined that I and a black militant could possibly disagree about anything. But what was most striking about our brief exchange was that it obliquely revealed how little the girl respected her stepfather. She appeared not to respect him at all. This was not revealed by anything she said to him, but by the fact that she said nothing to him. She barely looked at him. He didn't count.

I always think that this is a terrible thing to happen to a man, especially in his own house, and I am always terribly humiliated for the man to whom it happens. Then, of course, you get angry at the man for allowing it to happen.

And *how* had it happened? He had never been the brightest boy in the world, nobody is, but he had been energetic, active, funny; wrestling, playing handball, cheerfully submitting to being tyrannized by me, even to the extent of kneeling before the altar and having his soul saved—my insistence had accomplished that. I looked at him and remembered his sweating and beautiful face that night as he wrestled on the church floor and we prayed him through. I remembered his older brother, who had died in Sicily, in battle for the free world—he had barely had time to see Sicily before he died and had assuredly never seen the free world. I remembered the day he came to see me to tell me that his sister, who had been very ill, had died. We sat on the steps of the tenement, he was looking down as he told me, one finger making a circle on the step, and his tears splashed on the wood. We were children then, his sister had not been much older, and he was the youngest and now the only boy. But this was not *how* it had happened, although I thought I could see, watching his widowed mother's still very handsome face watching him, how her human need might have held and trapped and frozen him. She had been sewing in the garment center all the years I knew them, rushing home to get supper on the table before her husband got home from *his* job; at night, and on Sundays, he was a deacon; and God knows, or should, where his energy came from. When I began working for the garment center, I used to see her, from time to time, rushing to catch the bus, in a crowd of black and Puerto Rican ladies.

And, yes, we had all loved each other then and I had had great respect for my friend, who was handsomer than I, and more athletic, and more popular, and who beat me in every game I was foolish enough to play with him. I had gone my way and life had accomplished its inexorable mathematic—and what in the world was I by now but an aging, lonely, sexually dubious, politically outrageous, unspeakably erratic freak? His old friend. And what was *he* now? He worked for the post office and was building a house next door to his mother, in, I think, Long Island. They too, then, had made it. But what I could not understand was how nothing seemed to have touched this man. We are living through what our church described as "these last and evil days," through wars and rumors of wars, to say the least. He could, for example, have known something about the anti-poverty program if only because his wife was more or less involved in it. He should have known something about the then raging school battle, if only because his stepdaughter was a student; and she, whether or not she had thought her position through, was certainly involved. She may have hoped, at one time anyway, for his clarity and his help. But, no. He seemed as little touched by the cataclysm in his house and all around him as he was by the mail he handled every day. I found this unbelievable, and, given my temperament and our old connection, maddening. We got into a battle about the war in Vietnam. I probably really should not have allowed this to happen, but it was partly the stepdaughter's prodding. And I was astounded that my friend would defend this particular racist folly. What for? For his job at the post office? And the answer came back at once, alas—yes. For his job at the post office. I told him that Americans had no business at all in Vietnam, and that black people certainly had no business there, aiding the slavemaster to enslave yet more millions of dark people, and also identifying themselves with the white American crimes: we, the blacks, are going to need our allies, for the Americans, odd as it may sound at the moment, will presently have none. It wasn't, I said, hard to understand why a black boy, standing, futureless, on the corner, would decide to join the Army, nor was it hard to decipher the slavemaster's reasons for hoping that he wouldn't live to come home, with a gun; but it wasn't necessary, after all, to defend it: to defend, that is, one's murder and one's murderers. "Wait a minute," he said, "let me stand up and tell you what I think we're trying to do there." *"We?"* I cried. "What motherf——ing *we?* You stand up, motherf——er, and I'll kick you in the ass!"

He looked at me. His mother conveyed—but the good Lord knows I had hurt her—that she didn't want that language in her house, and that I had never talked that way before. And I love the lady. I had meant no disrespect. I stared at my friend, my old friend, and felt millions of people staring at us both. I tried to make a kind of joke out of it all. But it was too late. The way they looked at me proved that I had tipped my hand. And *this* hurt *me.* They should have known me better, or at least enough to have known that I meant what I said. But the general reaction to famous people who hold difficult opinions is that they can't really mean it. It's considered, generally, to be merely an astute way of attracting public attention, a way of making oneself interesting: one marches in Montgomery, for example, merely (in my own case) to sell one's books. Well. There is nothing, then, to be said. There went the friendly fried chicken dinner. There went the loving past. I watched the mother watching me, wondering what had happened to her beloved Jimmy, and giving me up: her sourest suspicions confirmed. In great weariness I poured myself yet another stiff drink, by now definitively condemned, and lit another cigarette, they watching me all the while for symptoms of cancer, and with a precipice at my feet.

For that bloody suit was *their* suit, after all, it had been bought *for* them, it had even been bought *by* them: *they* had created Martin, he had not created them, and the blood in which the fabric of that suit was stiffening was theirs. The distance between us, and I had never thought of this before, was that they did not know this, and I now dared to realize that I loved them more than they loved me. And I do not mean that my love was greater: Who dares judge the inexpressible expense another pays for his life? Who knows how much one is loved, by whom, or what that love may be called on to do? No, the way the cards had fallen meant that I had to face more about them than they could know about me, knew their rent, whereas they did not know mine, and was condemned to make them uncomfortable. For, on the other hand,

they certainly wanted that freedom which they thought was mine
—that frightening limousine, for example, or the power to give
away a suit, or my increasingly terrifying transatlantic journeys.
How can one say that freedom is taken, not given, and that no
one is free until all are free? and that the price is high.

My friend tried on the suit, a perfect fit, and they all admired
him in it, and I went home.

Alex Haley edited *The Autobiography of Malcolm X*. Months before the foregoing, in New York, he and Elia Kazan and I had
agreed to do it as a play—and I still wish we had. We were
vaguely aware that Hollywood was nibbling for the book, but, as
Hollywood is always nibbling, it occurred to no one, certainly not
to me, to take these nibbles seriously. It simply was not a subject
which Hollywood could manage, and I didn't see any point in
talking to them about it. But the book was sold to an independent
producer, who would produce it for Columbia Pictures. By this
time, I was in London; and I was also on the spot. For, while I
didn't believe Hollywood could do it, I didn't quite see, since they
declared themselves sincerely and seriously willing to attempt it,
how I could duck the challenge. What it came to, in fact, was an
enormous question: to what extent was I prepared again to gam-
ble on the good faith of my countrymen?

In that time, now so incredibly far behind us, when the Black
Muslims meant to the American people exactly what the Black
Panthers mean today, and when they were described in exactly
the same terms by that high priest, J. Edgar Hoover, and when
many of us believed or made ourselves believe that the American
state still contained within itself the power of self-confrontation,
the power to change itself in the direction of honor and knowledge and freedom, or, as Malcolm put it, "to atone," I first met
Malcolm X. Perhaps it says a great deal about the black American
experience, both negatively and positively, that so many should
have believed so hard, so long, and paid such a price for believing:
but what this betrayed belief says about white Americans is very
accurately and abjectly summed up by the present, so-called
"Nixon Administration."

I had heard a great deal about Malcolm, as had everyone else,
and I was a little afraid of him, as was everyone else, and I was

further handicapped by having been out of the country for so long. When I returned to America, I went South, and thus, imperceptibly, found myself mainly on the road. I saw Malcolm before I met him. I had just returned from someplace like Savannah, I was giving a lecture somewhere in New York, and Malcolm was sitting in the first or second row of the hall, bending forward at such an angle that his long arms nearly caressed the ankles of his long legs, staring up at me. I very nearly panicked. I knew Malcolm only by legend, and this legend, since I was a Harlem street boy, I was sufficiently astute to distrust. I distrusted the legend because we, in Harlem, have been betrayed so often. Malcolm might be the torch white people claimed he was—though, in general, white America's evaluations of these matters would be laughable and even pathetic did not these evaluations have such wicked results —or he might be the hustler I remembered from my pavements. On the other hand, Malcolm had no reason to trust me, either— and so I stumbled through my lecture, with Malcolm never taking his eyes from my face.

It must be remembered that in those great days I was considered to be an "integrationist"—this was never quite my own idea of myself—and Malcolm was considered to be a "racist in reverse." This formulation, in terms of power—and power is the arena in which racism is acted out—means absolutely nothing: it may even be described as a cowardly formulation. The powerless, by definition, can never be "racists," for they can never make the world pay for what they feel or fear except by the suicidal endeavor which makes of them fanatics or revolutionaries, or both; whereas, those in power can be urbane and charming and invite you to those houses which they know you will never own. The powerless must do their own dirty work. The powerful have it done for them.

Anyway: somewhat later, I was the host, or moderator, for a radio program starring Malcolm X and a sit-in student from the Deep South. I was the moderator because both the radio station and I were afraid that Malcolm would simply eat the boy alive. I didn't want to be there, but there was no way out of it. I had come prepared to throw various campstools under the child, should he seem wobbly; to throw out the lifeline whenever Malcolm should seem to be carrying the child beyond his depth. Never has a moderator been less needed. Malcolm understood that child, and talked to him as though he were talking to a younger brother, and with that same watchful attention. What most struck me was that he was not at all trying to proselytize the child: he was trying to make him think. He was trying to do for the child what he supposed, for too long a time, that the Honorable Elijah had done for him. But I did not think of that until much later. I will never forget Malcolm and that child facing each other, and Malcolm's extraordinary gentleness. And that's the truth about Malcolm: he was one of the gentlest people I have ever met. And I am sure that the child remembers him that way. That boy, by the way, battling so valiantly for civil rights, might have been, for all I can swear to, Stokely Carmichael or Huey Newton or Bobby Seale or Rap Brown or one of my nephews. That's how long or how short —*oh, pioneers!*—the apprehension of betrayal takes: "If you are an American citizen," Malcolm asked the boy, "why have you got to fight for your rights as a citizen? To be a citizen means that you have the rights of a citizen. If you haven't got the rights of a citizen, then you're not a citizen." "It's not as simple as that," the boy said. "Why not?" asked Malcolm.

I was in some way in those years, without entirely realizing it, the Great Black Hope of the Great White Father. I was *not* a racist—so I thought; Malcolm *was* a racist, so *he* thought. In fact, we were simply trapped in the same situation, as poor Martin was later to discover (who, in those days, did not talk to Malcolm and was a little nervous with me). As the G.B.H. of the G.W.F., anyway, I appeared on a television program, along with Malcolm and several other hopes, including Mr. George S. Schuyler.* It was pretty awful. If I had ever hoped to become a racist, Mr. Schuyler dashed my hopes forever, then and there. I can scarcely discuss this program except to say that Malcolm and I very quickly dismissed Mr. Schuyler and virtually everyone else and, as old street rats and the heirs of Baptist ministers, played the program off each other.

Nothing could have been more familiar to me than Malcolm's style in debate. I had heard it all my life. It was vehemently non-

* Black writer George S. Schuyler (1895-1977) in his later years became an arch-conservative satirist of civil rights leaders and the movement.

stop and Malcolm was young and looked younger; this caused his opponents to suppose that Malcolm was reckless. Nothing could have been less reckless, more calculated, even to those loopholes he so often left dangling. These were not loopholes at all, but hangman's knots, as whoever rushed for the loophole immediately discovered. Whenever this happened, the strangling interlocutor invariably looked to me, as being the more "reasonable," to say something which would loosen the knot. Mr. Schuyler often *did* say something, but it was always the wrong thing, giving Malcolm yet another opportunity. All I could do was elaborate on some of Malcolm's points, or modify, or emphasize, or seem to try to clarify, but there was no way I could disagree with him. The others were discussing the past or the future, or a country which may once have existed, or one which may yet be brought into existence—Malcolm was speaking of the bitter and unanswerable present. And it was too important that this be heard for anyone to attempt to soften it. It was important, of course, for white people to hear it, if they were still able to hear; but it was of the utmost importance for black people to hear it, for the sake of their morale. It was important for them to know that there was someone like them in public life, telling the truth about their condition. Malcolm considered himself to be the spiritual property of the people who produced him. He did not consider himself to be their savior, he was far too modest for that, and gave that role to another; but he considered himself to be their servant and, in order not to betray that trust, he was willing to die, and died. Malcolm was not a racist, not even when he thought he was. His intelligence was more complex than that; furthermore, if he had been a racist, not many in this racist country would have considered him dangerous. He would have sounded familiar and even comforting, his familiar rage confirming the reality of white power, and sensuously inflaming a bizarre species of guilty eroticism without which, I am beginning to believe, most white Americans of the more or less liberal persuasion cannot draw a single breath. What made him unfamiliar and dangerous was not his hatred for white people but his love for blacks, his apprehension of the horror of the black condition and the reasons for it, and his determination so to work on their hearts and minds that they would be enabled to see their condition and change it themselves.

For this, after all, not only were no white people needed; they posed, *en bloc,* the very greatest obstacle to black self-knowledge and had to be considered a menace. But white people have played so dominant a role in the world's history for so long that such an attitude toward them constitutes the most disagreeable of novelties; and it may be added that, though they have never learned how to live with the darker brother, they do not look forward to having to learn how to live without him. Malcolm, finally, was a genuine revolutionary, a virile impulse long since fled from the American way of life—in himself, indeed, he was a kind of revolution, both in the sense of a return to a former principle and in the sense of an upheaval. It is pointless to speculate on his probable fate had he been legally white. Given the white man's options, it is probably just as well for all of us that he was legally black. In some church someday, so far unimagined and unimaginable, he will be hailed as a saint. Of course this day waits on the workings of the temporal power which Malcolm understood, at last, so well. Rome, for example, has desanctified some saints and invented, if one dares to use so utilitarian a word in relation to so divine an activity, others, and the Pope has been to Africa, driven there no doubt, however belatedly, by his concern for the souls of black folk: who dares imagine the future of such a litany as *black like me!* Malcolm, anyway, had this much in common with all real saints and prophets, he had the power, if not to drive the money changers from the temple, to tell the world what they were doing there.

For reasons I will never understand, on the day I realized that a play based on *The Autobiography* was not going to be done, that sooner or later I would have to say yes or no to the idea of doing a movie, I flew to Geneva. I will never know why I flew to Geneva, which is far from being my favorite town. I will never know how it is that I arrived there with no toilet articles whatever, no toothbrush, no toothpaste, no razor, no hairbrush, no comb, and virtually no clothes. Furthermore, I have a brother-in-law and a sister-in-law living in Geneva of whom I'm very fond and it didn't even occur to me that they were there. All that I seem to have brought with me is *The Autobiography.* And I sat in the hotel bedroom all the weekend long, with the blinds drawn, reading and rereading—or, rather, endlessly traversing—the great jungle of Malcolm's book.

The problems involved in a cinematic translation were clearly going to be formidable, and wisdom very strongly urged that I have nothing to do with it. It could not possibly bring me anything but grief. I still would have much preferred to have done it as a play, but that possibility was gone. I had grave doubts and fears about Hollywood. I had been there before, and I had not liked it. The idea of Hollywood doing a truthful job on Malcolm could not but seem preposterous. And yet—I didn't want to spend the rest of my life thinking: *It could have been done if you hadn't been chicken.* I felt that Malcolm would never have forgiven me for that. He had trusted me in life and I believed he trusted me in death, and that trust, as far as I was concerned, was my obligation.

From Geneva I eventually went to London, to join my brother and sister. It was from London that I wired Kazan to say that the play was off, and I was doing the movie. This was only to take K. off the hook, for I wired no one else, had made no agreement to do the movie, and was very troubled and uncertain in my own mind.

Every new environment, particularly if one knows that one must make the effort to accustom oneself to working in it, risks being more than a little traumatic. One finds oneself nervously examining one's new surroundings, searching for the terms of the adjustment; therefore, in the beginning, I made a somewhat too conscious effort to be pleased by Hollywood. There was the sky, after all, which New Yorkers seldom see, and there was space, which New Yorkers have forgotten, there was the mighty and dramatic Pacific, there were the hills. Some very valuable and attractive people had lived and functioned here for years, I reminded myself, and there was really no reason why I could not—so I insisted to myself. I had a few friends and acquaintances here already, scattered from Watts to Baldwin Hills to Mulholland Drive, and I was sure they'd be happy if I decided to stay. If I were going to be in Hollywood for months, there was no point in raising the odds against me by hating it, or despising it; besides, such an attitude seemed too obvious a defense against my fear of it. As hotels go, the Beverly Hills is more congenial than most, and certainly everyone there was very nice to me. And so I tried—too hard—to look about me with wonder, and be pleased. But I was already in trouble, and the odds against the venture were very long odds indeed.

I was actually in the Beverly Hills until more permanent lodging could be found. This was not easy, since it involved finding someone to take care of me—to keep house, cook, and drive. *I* was no help, since I was still, at the beginning of 1968, committed to various fund-raising functions in the East. Part of the irreducible conflict which was to drive both Columbia Pictures and myself up the wall was already implicit during those early days at the Beverly Hills Hotel. The conflict was simply between my life as a writer and my life as—not spokesman exactly, but public witness to the situation of black people. I had to play both roles: there was nothing anyone, including myself, could do about it. This was an unprecedented situation for Columbia, which, after all, had me under exclusive contract and didn't really like my dashing off, making public appearances. It was an unprecedented situation for me, too, since I had never before been under exclusive contract, and had always juggled my conflicting schedules as best I could. I had lived with my two roles for a long time, and had even, insofar as this is ever true, begun to get used to them—I accepted, anyway, that the dichotomy wasn't likely to end soon. But it didn't make the Hollywood scene any easier. It wasn't a matter of wiping the slate clean of existing commitments and then vanishing behind the typewriter, nor was it even a matter of keeping outside commitments to a minimum, though I tried: events were moving much faster than that, creating perpetual crises and making ever new demands. Columbia couldn't but be concerned about the time and energy I expended on matters remote from the scenario. On the other hand, I couldn't really regret it, since it seemed to me that in this perpetual and bitter ferment I was learning something which kept me in touch with reality and would deepen the truth of the scenario.

But I anticipate. People have their environments: the Beverly Hills Hotel was not mine. For no reason that I could easily name, its space, its opulence, its shapelessness depressed and frightened me. The people in the bar, the lounge, the halls, the walks, the swimming pool, the shops, seemed as rootless as I, seemed unreal. In spite—perhaps because of—all my efforts to feel relaxed and free and at home (for America *is* my home!), I began to feel unreal—almost as though I were playing an unworthy part in a cheap, unworthy drama. I, who have spent half my life in hotels, sometimes woke up in the middle of the night, terrified, wondering where I was. But, though I scarcely realized it and might even have been ashamed to admit it to myself, I think that this had partly to do with the fact that I was the only dark person in the hotel. I must stress that in no way whatever did anyone in the hotel ever make me feel this, nor, indeed, did I ever consciously feel it—it's only now, in looking back, that I suspect that it had to be partly that. My presence in the hotel was absolutely unquestioned, even by people who did not know who I was, or who thought I was Sammy Davis. It was simply taken for granted that I would not have been in the hotel if I had not belonged there. This, irrationally enough, got to me—*did* I belong there? In any case, thousands of black people, miles away, did *not* belong there, though some of them sometimes came to visit me there. (People had to come and get me or come to visit me, because I do not drive.) The drive from Beverly Hills to Watts and back again is a long and loaded drive—I sometimes felt as though my body were being stretched across those miles. I don't think I felt anything so trivial as guilt, guilt at what appeared to be my comparative good fortune, I knew more about comparative fortunes than that, but I felt a stunning helplessness. These two worlds would never meet, and that fact prefigured disaster for my countrymen and me. It caused me to look about me with an intensity of wonder which had no pleasure in it.

It began to be very clear that I was never really going to get any work done in the Beverly Hills—my suite was one of the busiest in that busy hotel—and so the producer found a cook-chauffeur, and bundled me south to Palm Springs. There, in that millionaire's graveyard, I actually began to work. Truman Capote was there one weekend, thank heaven, and we had a few drinks together, but he then, very sensibly, left. I took it as long as I could, the sunshine as bland as milk and honey, the eerie streets paved with gold, the thunderous silence of wealth, and then I went north again, to a house in Benedict Canyon.

* * *

There is a day in Palm Springs, shortly before I left there, that I will remember forever, a bright day. Billy Dee Williams had come to town, and he was staying at the house; and a lot of the day had been spent with a very bright, young lady reporter, who was interviewing me about the film version of Malcolm. I felt very confident that day—I was never to feel so confident again—and I talked very freely to the reporter. (Too freely, the producer was to tell me later.) I had decided to lay my cards on the table and to state, as clearly as I could, what I felt the movie was about, and how I intended to handle it. I thought that this might make things simpler later on, but I was wrong about that. The studio and I were at loggerheads, really, from the moment I stepped off the plane. Anyway, I had opted for candor, or a reasonable facsimile of same, and sounded as though I were in charge of the film, as, indeed, by my lights, for that moment, certainly, I had to be. I was really in a difficult position because both by temperament and experience I tend to work alone, and I dread making announcements concerning my work. But I was in a very public position, and I thought that I had better make my own announcements, rather than have them made for me. The studio, on the other hand, did not want me making announcements of any kind at all. So there we were, and this particular tension, since it got to the bloody heart of the matter—the question of by whose vision, precisely, this film was to be controlled—was not to be resolved until I finally threw up my hands and walked away.

I very much wanted Billy Dee for Malcolm, and since no one else had any other ideas, I didn't see why this couldn't work out. In brutal Hollywood terms, Poitier is the only really big, black, box-office star, and this fact gave me, as I considered it, a free hand. To tell the bitter truth, from the very first days we discussed it, I had never had any intention of allowing the Columbia brass to cast this part: I was determined to take my name off the production if I were overruled. Call this bone-headed stupidity, or insufferable arrogance or what you will—I had made my decision, and once I had made it nothing could make me waver, and nothing could make me alter it. If there were errors in my concept of the film, and if I made errors on the way to and in the execution, well, then, I would have to pay for my errors. But one can learn from one's errors. What one cannot survive is allowing other people to make your errors for you, discarding your own vision, in which at least you believe, for someone else's vision, in which you do *not* believe.

Anyway, all that shit had yet to hit the fan. This day, the girl and Billy and I had a few drinks by the swimming pool. The man, Walter, was about to begin preparing supper. The girl got up to leave and we walked her to her car and came back to the swimming pool, jubilant.

The phone had been brought out to the pool, and now it rang. Billy was on the other side of the pool, doing what I took to be African improvisations to the sound of Aretha Franklin. And I picked up the phone.

It was David Moses. It took a while before the sound of his voice—I don't mean the *sound* of his voice, something *in* his voice—got through to me.

He said, "Jimmy? Martin's just been shot," and I don't think I said anything, or felt anything. I'm not sure I knew who *Martin* was. Yet, though I know—or I think—the record player was still playing, silence fell. David said, "He's not dead yet"—*then* I knew who Martin was—"but it's a head wound—so—"

I don't remember what I said; obviously I must have said something. Billy and Walter were watching me. I told them what David had said.

I hardly remember the rest of that evening at all, it's retired into some deep cavern in my mind. We must have turned on the television set if we had one, I don't remember. But we must have had one. I remember weeping, briefly, more in helpless rage than in sorrow, and Billy trying to comfort me. But I really don't remember that evening at all. Later, Walter told me that a car had prowled around the house all night.

I went to Atlanta alone, I do not remember why. I wore the suit I had bought for my Carnegie Hall appearance with Martin. I seem to have had the foresight to have reserved a hotel room, for I vaguely remember stopping in the hotel and talking to two or three preacher-type-looking men, and we started off in the direction of the church. We had not got far before it became very clear that we would never get anywhere near it. We went in this direction and then in that direction, but the press of people choked us off. I began to wish that I had not come incognito and alone, for now that I was in Atlanta I wanted to get inside the church. I lost my companions, and sort of squeezed my way, inch by inch, closer to the church. But directly between me and the church there was an impassable wall of people. Squeezing my way up to this point, I had considered myself lucky to be small; but now my size worked against me for, though there were people on the church steps who knew me, whom I knew, they could not possibly see me, and I could not shout. I squeezed a few more inches, and asked a very big man ahead of me please to let me through. He moved and said, "Yeah. Let me see you get through this big Cadillac." It was true—there it was, smack in front of me, big as a house. I saw Jim Brown at a distance, but he didn't see me. I leaned up on the car, making frantic signals, and finally someone on the church steps did see me and came to the car and sort of lifted me over. I talked to Jim Brown for a minute, and then somebody led me into the church and I sat down.

The church was packed, of course, incredibly so. Far in the front, I saw Harry Belafonte sitting next to Coretta King. Ralph David Abernathy sat in the pulpit. I remembered him from years ago, sitting in his shirt-sleeves in the house in Montgomery, big, black, and cheerful, pouring some cool, soft drink, and, later, getting me settled in a nearby hotel. In the pew directly before me sat Marlon Brando, Sammy Davis, Eartha Kitt—covered in black, looking like a lost, ten-year-old girl—and Sidney Poitier, in the same pew, or nearby. Marlon saw me, and nodded. The atmosphere was black, with a tension indescribable—as though something, perhaps the heavens, perhaps the earth, might crack. Everyone sat very still.

The actual service sort of washed over me, in waves. It wasn't that it seemed unreal; it was the most real church service I've ever sat through in my life, or ever hope to sit through; but I have a childhood hangover thing about not weeping in public, and I was concentrating on holding myself together. I did not want to weep for Martin, tears seemed futile. But I may also have been afraid, and I could not have been the only one, that if I began to weep I would not be able to stop. There was more than enough to weep for, if one was to weep—so many of us, cut down, so soon. Medgar, Malcolm, Martin: and their widows, and their children.

Reverend Ralph David Abernathy asked a certain sister to sing a
song which Martin had loved—"Once more," said Ralph David,
"for Martin and for me," and he sat down.

The long, dark sister, whose name I do not remember, rose,
very beautiful in her robes, and in her covered grief, and began to
sing. It was a song I knew: *My Father Watches Over Me.* The song
rang out as it might have over dark fields, long ago, she was
singing of a covenant a people had made, long ago, with life, and
with that larger life which ends in revelation and which moves in
love.

He guides the eagle through the pathless air.

She stood there, and she sang it. How she bore it, I do not
know, I think I have never seen a face quite like that face that
afternoon. She was singing it for Martin, and for us.

And surely He
Remembers me,
My heav'nly Father watches over me.

At last, we were standing, and filing out, to walk behind Martin
home. I found myself between Marlon and Sammy.

I had not been aware of the people when I had been pressing
past them to get to the church. But, now, as we came out, and I
looked up the road, I saw them. They were all along the road, on
either side, they were on all the roofs, on either side. Every inch
of ground, as far as the eye could see, was black with black people, and they stood in silence. It was the silence that undid me. I
started to cry, and I stumbled, and Sammy grabbed my arm. We
started to walk.

I don't think that any black person can speak of Malcolm and
Martin without wishing that they were here. It is not possible for
me to speak of them without a sense of loss and grief and rage;
and with the sense, furthermore, of having been forced to un-
dergo an unforgivable indignity, both personal and vast. Our children need them, which is, indeed, the reason that they are not
here: and now we, the blacks, must make certain that our children
never forget them. For the American republic has always done
everything in its power to destroy our children's heroes, with the
clear (and sometimes clearly stated) intention of destroying our
children's hope. This endeavor has doomed the American nation:
mark my words.

Malcolm and Martin, beginning at what seemed to be very different points—for brevity's sake, we can say North and South, though, for Malcolm, South was south of the Canadian border—and espousing, or representing, very different philosophies, found that their common situation (south of the border!) so thoroughly devastated what had seemed to be mutually exclusive points of view that, by the time each met his death there was practically no difference between them. Before either had had time to think their new positions through, or, indeed, to do more than articulate them, they were murdered. Of the two, Malcolm moved swiftest (and was dead soonest), but the fates of both men were radically altered (I would say, frankly, sealed) the moment they attempted to release the black American struggle from the domestic context and relate it to the struggles of the poor and the nonwhite all over the world.

To hold this view, it is not necessary to see C.I.A. infiltrators in, or under, every black or dissenting bed: one need merely consider what the successful promulgation of this point of view would mean for American authority in the world. Slaveholders do not allow their slaves to compare notes: American slavery, until this hour, prevents any meaningful dialogue between the poor white and the black, in order to prevent the poor white from recognizing that he, too, is a slave. The contempt with which American leaders treat American blacks is very obvious; what is not so obvious is that they treat the bulk of the American people with the very same contempt. But it will be sub-zero weather in a very distant August when the American people find the guts to recognize this fact. They will recognize it only when they have exhausted every conceivable means of avoiding it.

In the meantime, in brutal fact, all of the institutions of this nation, from the schools to the courts to the unions to the prisons, and not forgetting the police, are in the hands of that white majority which has been promising for generations to ameliorate the black condition. And many white Americans would *like* to change the black condition, if they could see their way clear to do so, through the unutterable accumulation of neglect, sorrow, rage, despair, and continuing, overriding, totally unjustifiable death: the smoke over Attica recalls the bombs of Birmingham and the

liberal Mr. Rockefeller reveals himself as being even more despi-
cable than his openly illiberal confreres farther down.

But it is not important, however irresistible, to accuse Mr.
Rockefeller of anything. He is just another good American; one
of the best. It is unlikely that *any* Western people, and certainly
not the Americans, have the moral resources needed to accomplish the deep and mighty transformation which is all that can
save them. Such a transformation involves unimaginable damage
to the American ego; would reduce all the American religious
ceremonies, including the Fourth of July and Thanksgiving, to the
hypocritically bloody observances many of us have always known
them to be; and would shed too unsparing a light on the actual
dimensions and objectives of the American character. White
Americans do not want to know what many nonwhites know too
well, e.g., that "foreign aid" in the "underdeveloped" countries
and "anti-poverty" programs in the ghetto are simply a slightly
more sophisticated version of the British policy of Divide and
Rule, are, in short, simply another means of keeping a people in
subjection.

Since the American people cannot, even if they wished to,
bring about black liberation, and since black people want their
children to live, it is very clear that we must take our children out
of the hands of this so-called majority and find some way to expose this majority as the minority which it actually is in the world.
For this we will need, and we well get, the help of the suffering
world which is prevented only by the labyrinthine stratagems of
power from adding its testimony to ours.

No one pretends that this will be easy, and I myself do not
expect to live to see this day accomplished. What both Martin and
Malcolm began to see was that the nature of the American hoax
had to be revealed—not only to save black people but in order to
change the world in which everyone, after all, has a right to live.
One may say that the articulation of this necessity was the Word's
first necessary step on its journey toward being made flesh.

And no doubt my proposition, at this hour, sounds exactly that
mystical. If I were a white American, I would bear in mind that
mysteries are called mysteries because we recognize in them a
truth which we can barely face, or articulate. I would bear in mind
that an army is no match for a ferment, and that power, however

great that power may consider itself to be, gives way, and has always been forced to give way, before the onslaught of human necessity: human necessity being the fuel of history.

If my proposition sounds mystical, white people have only to consider the black people, my ancestors, whose strength and love have brought black people to this present, crucial place. If I still thought, as I did when Martin and Malcolm were still alive, that the generality of white Americans were able to hear and to learn and begin to change, I would counsel them, as vividly as I could, to attempt, now, to minimize the bill which is absolutely certain to be presented to their children. I would say: if those blacks, your slaves, my ancestors, could bring us out of nothing, from such a long way off, then, if I were you, I would pause a long while before deciding to use what you think of as your power. For we, the blacks, have not found possible what you found necessary: we have not denied our ancestors who trust us, now, to redeem their pain.

Well. Baby, that's it. I *could* say, and they would both understand me: Don't you think Bessie is proud of Aretha?

Or: Do you think that Americans can translate this sentence both out of and into the original? *My soul is a witness for my Lord.*

INDEX